The Development of a Child Psychiatric Treatment Program

The Development of a Child Psychiatric Treatment Program

by

Helen K. Grace

A Halsted Press Book

Schenkman Publishing Company

JOHN WILEY AND SONS

New York -- London — Sydney — Toronto

Copyright © 1974 by
Schenkman Publishing Company, Inc.
3 Mt. Auburn Place, Cambridge, Mass. 02138

Distributed solely by Halsted Press, a Division
of John Wiley & Sons, Inc. New York.

Library of Congress Cataloging in Publication Data

Grace, Helen K.
  The development of a child psychiatric treatment
program.

  1. Child mental health services. I. Title.
[DNLM: 1. Child psychiatry. 2. Community mental
health services. 3. Organization and administration.
WS350 G729d 1974]
RJ111.G7   362.7'8'2   74-8752
ISBN 0-470-32084-2

Printed in the U.S.A.

ACKNOWLEDGEMENTS

This book began as part of doctoral research at Northwestern University. I am appreciative of the support and inspiration of my thesis committee: Professors Howard S. Becker, Remi Clignet and Bernard Beck. I am especially grateful to Howard S. Becker for his repeated review and critique of the manuscript and his consistent support, encouragement, and help in transforming random observations of psychiatric organizations into an organizing framework.

My thanks also to Dr. Melvin Sabshin, Chairman of the Department of Psychiatry at the University of Illinois and Dr. Bernard Rubin of Northwestern Medical School, Department of Psychiatry, psychiatrists who encouraged me to raise critical questions about psychiatric care systems.

Professor Rue Bucher initially encouraged me to analyze carefully the intricacy of the relationships between those who work in psychiatric settings and through the years has been a friend and needed critic.

Rubye Hill carefully typed the final manuscript.

The research that made possible the writing of this book was funded by U.S. PHS, Bureau of Health Manpower, Fellowship Number F4-NU-27, 128-02.

DEDICATION

To Elliott, for his consistent support, for reading and re-reading the manuscript, and for providing much needed insights into the dilemmas surrounding those who work with children who present problems within our society.

TABLE OF CONTENTS

DIAGRAMS

TABLES

Part I
The Backdrop

Chapter I

The Development of Psychiatric Organization: A Theoretical Perspective

How do organizations develop? In our organizational society each individual plays out his life enmeshed in numerous organizational networks. In some instances, the individual is a working member of an organization, while he relies upon others for the provision of needed goods and services. Entangled in this morass of institutionalism the individual rarely questions the effectiveness of these organizational systems. Organizations proliferate and feed upon each other as epiphytes obliterating any understanding of the organization's original reason for being.

Psychiatric treatment programs are illustrative of this problem; they build upon one another and are manned by professionals indoctrinated by a specific system of thought. Any originality of purpose in this type of organization is quickly obliterated, and, on observation, they all appear to be the same. While their avowed goals may appear to be different, the patient experience and the activities of the psychiatric professionals are remarkably standardized.[1]

Further, organizations are generally assumed to arise out of a societal need for the goods and services they provide. [Based on this assumption, psychiatric treatment programs supposedly originate in response to a societal need for services for emotionally disturbed individuals. The questions of what constitutes mental illness and, secondarily, what is the nature of programs designed for treatment are not raised. Mental illness is accepted as a given verity and the belief that psychiatric hospitals treat this particular type of disease is maintained. Theoreticians, instead of questioning these basic assumptions, develop elaborate constructs as to the causality of mental disturbance, on the one hand, and modes of treatment, on the other. Researchers, calling upon these theoretical models, report that a percentage of specified populations enter psychiatric hospitals and are therefore presumed to be mentally ill. Extensive histories are taken on those identified as psychiatric patients to validate the theoretical constructs with no question as to

[1] For a comparative view see Corrine Huessler, "The Gilded Asylum," in Glenn Jacobs (ed.), *Participant Observation*, (New York: George Braziller), 1970, pp. 92–121 and Erving Goffman, *Asylums*, (New York: Doubleday Anchor), 1961.

3

whether the same etiological factors identified with a "sick" population might be found in comparable histories taken from a "normal" population. Effectiveness of treatment is measured by discharge and recidivism rates and the apparent ability of the patient to "fit into society" with little consideration for the individual and his needs.]

Because of the unique position of the medical profession in our society, and psychiatry as one part of that profession, the consumer of psychiatric services does not have the opportunity to question the efficacy of these services. For example, a parent whose child does not learn in the school system may readily ask the school for an explanation. In contrast, if a parent questions whether a psychiatric organization is helping his child he becomes suspect; the parent, considered to be implicated in his child's problems, is discounted. The questions raised are either ignored or interpreted away. Psychiatric organizations are immunized from the usual types of societal controls. The psychiatric system of thought includes its own defenses against all outside questioning.

This study, which calls into question some of these basic assumptions, traces the development of a psychiatric treatment program for children during its first year of development. [Specifically, this study traces the process whereby initial goals of treating large numbers of poor, inner-city children on a short-term basis are transformed so that at the end of one year only five middle-class children, carefully selected so they will not be troublesome, have been chosen for long-term treatment.] This study raises questions as to the societal functions of such organizations: Do psychiatric treatment programs provide services for children or jobs for psychiatric specialists? Do such organizations treat or merely control deviance? What type of people compose the organization? What are their personal goals and aspirations, and how is the organizational context influential in the attainment or frustration of these goals? Does a newly forming organization respond to the needs of the clientele or does it primarily concern itself with the politics of survival in a pre-existent organizational structure? What is involved in the process of organizational development? These are some of the questions to which this study addresses itself.

A Model of Psychiatric Organizational Development

How do people form organizations? Most explanations advanced stress the rationality of organizational formation. For example, Stinchcombe defines an organization as "a set of stable social relationships deliberately created, with the explicit purpose of continuously accomplishing some specialized goals or purposes."[2] But how are these stable social relationships established, if indeed they are? Who has the power to "deliberately create" them, particularly when the parts composing the organization consist of people? And how are these specialized goals and purposes defined when the product to be produced involves changing human personalities?

Kreisberg, recognizing the complexities inherent in establishment of organizations, states that "at a minimum, organizations consist of people carrying out different activities which are so coordinated and interdependent that the combined activities yield some output."[3] The symbolic interactionists hold that organizations are created through the interaction processes generated amongst the participants. Individuals engage constantly in the process of working out agreements amongst themselves; as an outgrowth of this process rules of their particular game become established. Each individual comes into an organization with a background of experiences. Each has motives and goals he would like to attain within this particular work experience. But the attainment of these personal goals hinges upon abilities to work out agreements with others within the organization.

In addition to the individual perspectives of each member, organizational meanings must be generated. According to Denzin, the participants must find ways to "join lines of action in a consensual and meaningful way. For consensual lines to develop there must exist a common community of symbols."[4] Participants in an organization must work out the rules of the game, ways of communicating with one another through use of common symbols, and mechanisms for coordinating their lines of action. Denzin attributes stability in group structure to the development of these shared meanings:

> Through the process of *self-lodging* humans translate crucial features of their own identity into the selves, memories, and imaginations of other relevant others. . . . By lodging the self in interaction and in the selves of others, a reciprocal bond is formed and the firm foundations for future relationships are established.[5]

2 Arthur Stinchcombe, "Social Structures and Organizations" in James G. March (ed.) *Handbook of Organizations,* (Chicago: Rand McNally), 1965, pg. 142.

3 Louis Kreisberg, "Internal Differentiation and the Establishment of Organizations" in Howard S. Becker, *et al.* (eds.) *Institutions and the Person,* (Chicago: Aldine Press), 1968, pg. 142.

4 Norman Denzin, "Symbolic Interactionism and Ethnomethodology" in Jack D. Douglas, *Understanding Everyday Life,* (Chicago: Aldine Press), 1970, pg. 261.

5 *Ibid.,* pg. 262.

A study of organizations based upon this model focuses upon the ways in which individuals enter the organization, their organizational perspectives, and the way in which they project themselves into the organization. Through this "self-lodging" pattern the initial working agreements are reached.

Individual participants must coordinate their lines of action to achieve certain organizational goals. Kreisberg outlines these basic components:

> People act in organizations to produce goods or services. . . . These producing activities need supporting activities . . . all these activities must be coordinated and the relationship between the organization and the environment mediated. There can be no continuing production unless the output is consumed by someone. . . . Finally to maintain the producing, supporting and coordinating activities, paying or contributing activities are needed.[6]

Applying this to psychiatric organizations, the developmental process necessarily includes solutions to the following set of problems: (1) The nature of the services that this particular organization deems as appropriate must be defined. (2) The production of services, in this case therapy, requires such supports as, for example, space in which therapy is to be conducted, a communication system for maintaining contacts with clients and others implicated in therapeutic work, and a secretarial service for maintaining records of the services provided. (3) The work of therapists requires coordination. In psychiatric organizations this requires supervisors who coordinate therapeutic work as well as psychiatric professionals who serve to socialize novices into the norms and values of the system. (4) The relevant environments that a psychiatric treatment organization must consider are: (a) the psychiatric professional world; (b) the larger bureaucracy of which a psychiatric organization is often a part, and (c) other organizations involved with a similar population of clients, in the case of children schools, courts, etc. (5) The needs of a client population muust be discerned. (6) Finally, to continue its existence, a psychiatric organization must promote an image of producing services that will elicit the needed resources essential to maintain the organization. A study of the development of a psychiatric organization, then, includes descriptions of the ways in which individuals within the organization go about solving these basic organizational problems.

Kreisberg likens the establishment of an organization to:
  a game during which potential players reach an agreement about the

  6 Kreisberg, *op. cit.*, pp. 142-143.

rules by which later games will be played. In reaching the agreement, the players simultaneously assess their own interests and those of other players and the relations between them, the relative costs of various ways of teaming together or not at all, and they weigh what they will give or demand for others playing different roles. Of course, some potential players have access to more resources than do others during the process of reaching an agreement. Once established, the balance of interests and organizational arrangements and the inclusion and exclusion of persons from the reservoirs of potential members constrain future activities of the component categories. Yet the very establishment and operation of the organization also transforms the participants. New interests and relations are established. None of the potential participants foresee all the implications and consequences of the actual organizational operations. As a result, the game of remaking an organization continues as long as the organization exists.[7]

But what are some of the issues underlying the game? A consideration of some of the underlying organizational conflicts is of particular significance in the study of the development of psychiatric treatment organizations.

The Mission of Psychiatric Organizations: A Dilemma

Psychiatric institutions for the treatment of the mentally ill are enigmas in our society. Denoting an organization as designed for "treatment" presupposes an entity "mental illness." Further, such an entity implies causal agents and specific treatment for particular categories of illness. While causality and specificity of disease entities cannot be demonstrated positively, psychiatric professionals define their work as that of treating the mentally ill.[8] Lacking specifics on which to build a treatment model, psychiatric professionals engage in ideological arguments.[9] For example, those holding psychoanalytic views argue that mental illness must be defined in a manner similar to other medical problems and that treatment must be based upon diagnosis and therapeutic intervention on an individual basis. In contrast, those holding sociotherapeutic views maintain that the immediate environmental situations in which the individual lives are problematic and precipitate mental illness. Treatment, in this perspective, consists of manipulation of en-

[7] *Ibid.,* pg. 156.

[8] Charles Perrow in "Hospitals: Technology, Structure and Goals" in James G. March (ed.) *Handbook of Organizations,* (Chicago: Rand McNally), 1965, pp. 10–71 advances the argument that a developed technology is noticeably lacking in psychiatric hospitals.

[9] Anselm Strauss, *et. al. Psychiatric Institutions and Ideologies,* (New York: The Free Press of Glencoe), 1964.

vironmental factors rather than of individuals per se. Psychiatric professionals, lacking agreements on *what* to treat, the individual or the
group,[10] can hardly reach agreements as to the nature of psychiatric
treatment.

A third conflicting view, making note of the discrepancies surrounding
the concept of treatment, advances the idea that psychiatric hospitals
instead serve as custodial institutions to contain and control residual
forms of deviance.[11] Those who occupy psychiatric hospitals are those
labeled by society as deviant. In contrast to prisons, who are similarly
responsible for society's deviants, psychiatric hospitals generally feel
compelled to present an image to the outside world that they are doing
"treatment," while in actuality their prime function is that of custody
and control.

A further complication arises in that psychiatric treatment programs
frequently originate within large-scale governmental agencies. They
are placed on a level with other departments charged with responsibilities for the health and welfare of the poor. Located in such bureaucracies, these programs are subject to controls and standards that may be
in conflict with professional standards. The model of a bureaucracy,
efficiently organized with a hierarchical chain of command, centraliza-
tion of authority, and emphasizing discipline, rationality, technical
knowledge and impersonal procedures, is in conflict with what professionals consider to be treatment; the open-endedness of what constitutes
treatment has more appeal for the "professional."

Professional organizations, as a specialized type of bureaucracy, are
more obviously political arenas with varying factions competing for
position and control.[12] Common factions that develop are those centered around commitment to a profession, as well as to differing ideological preferences. A professional comes into the organization with a

[10] The social group most frequently mentioned in connection with children is
the family. For a view of the family treatment approach see Ivan Boszormeny-
Nagy, "Intensive Family Therapy as Process" in Ivan Boszormeny-Nagy and
James Framo (ed.) *Intensive Family Therapy,* (New York: Harper and Row),
1965.

[11] See Thomas Szasz, *The Myth of Mental Illness,* (New York: Hoeber), 1961,
Thomas J. Scheff, *Being Mentally Ill: A Sociological Theory,* (Chicago: Aldine
Press), 1965, and Howard S. Becker, *Outsiders: Studies in the Sociology of
Deviance,* (New York: The Free Press of Glencoe), 1963 for the development
of this view.

[12] This view of professional organizations is outlined by Rue Bucher and
Joan Stelling in "Characteristics of Professional Organizations" in *Journal of
Health and Social Behavior,* Vol. 10, No. 1, January, 1969, pp. 3–15.

background of professional training and experience unique to his professional group. He must mediate between two competing demands for loyalty; those inherent in the standards and values of his professional group and those involved with the production of work that conforms to the norms of the organization that employs him. Faced with these divergent demands for loyalty, professionals engage in negotiation and bargaining in an attempt to reconcile their differences. The professional, who sees his role as that of a specialized expert with exclusive possession of highly developed skills, tends to reject and resist controls imposed by larger bureaucratic structures.

Considering these conflicting tendencies, it is reasonable to assume that the goal of "custody for deviants" is more compatible within the framework of a governmental bureaucracy. Treatment, as a goal, is more consonant with the orientation held by professionals. Conversely, the attainment of treatment goals within a bureaucratic structure is problematic; psychiatric professionals are not likely to openly promote custodial goals. Table I illustrates these dichotomies.

DIAGRAM I
Compatability of Goals with Types of Organizations

Goals	Type of Organization	
	Professional	Bureaucratic
Treatment	+	—
Custody	—	+

A psychiatric treatment program thus develops in the context of a number of opposing forces. Society expects psychiatric institutions to control and contain deviants; professionals wish to diagnose and treat an ill-defined entity, mental illness, and the larger bureaucracy demands efficiency, order, and control. This study traces the establishment of a treatment program for children that takes into account all of these conflicting tendencies.

Children: A Further Complication

When children are those "treated" or "controlled" the problem becomes even more complex in that children are not considered to be capable of speaking for themselves. Other institutions, such as the family, the school, the church, or the police provide accounts of the child's behavior. A psychiatric treatment program must not only treat the children sent its way by varying institutions, but must define its functions vis-à-vis these other institutions.

A consideration of the way in which a child is defined as trouble-some may serve to clarify further the set of expectations which a psychiatric treatment program for children must take into consideration in the process of development. "Disturbed" children arrive at a treat-ment agency only after they have experienced difficulties in other settings where their behavior has been considered troublesome. The process all too frequently incorporates particular sequences of events.

These troubled children have violated standards that society con-siders indicative of normality. R. D. Laing points out that alienation is the prevailing state in our society today:

> The 'normally' alienated person, by reason of the fact that he acts more or less like everyone else is considered to be sane. Other forms of aliena-tion that are out of step with the prevailing state of alienation are those labelled by the 'normal' majority as bad or mad. . . . Society values its normal man. It educates children to lose themselves, and thus to be normal.[13]

A consideration of what becomes identified as problematic in the context of varying societal institutions will serve to clarify the plight of children in our society. Frequently the child is judged on the basis of his parents' behavior; for example, the child who enters society "ille-gitimately" begins life at a disadvantage. The psychological literature subtly advances a view that for the child to develop "normally" he should have a father, that goes to work every day to support the family, and a mother who stays home to take care of the children. Anything short of this ideal supposedly creates difficulties for the child's emotional development. These values are carried over into treatment programs and incorporated into criteria for admission that specify that eligibility is based upon the child being a member of an intact family. Lacking this, the child, who has had nothing to say about the "intactness" of his family, becomes defined as "untreatable."

Values in American society frequently conflict with the norms of behavior imposed upon our children. We value such ideals as self-direction, independence, creativity, and initiative, yet behavior on the part of the child indicative of these tendencies frequently reaps censure. Aggression, while essential if one is to survive in American society, is not tolerated in children. Although the television media brings to the child's view a world of luxury and material things that are not part of his daily existence, stealing as a means of attainment brings punish-

[13] R. D. Laing, *The Politics of Experience,* (New York: Pantheon Books), 1967, pg. 12.

ment. "Bedwetting" and "firesetting" are behaviors certain to evoke negative responses from parents. "Abnormal" behavior of this type precipitates the process of parents seeking "treatment" as a means of correcting their behavior. Although we verbalize ideals to the contrary, the "normal" child fits passively into the mold imposed upon him; the model child incorporates the middle class values of industry and integrity and views education as a way to get ahead in life.

If the child does not conform to this model, societal institutions attempt to correct him. The school is usually the first agency outside of the family that becomes involved in attempting to correct the child. Aggressive behavior or lack of interest are troublesome to teachers. Instead of questioning the methods of instruction that fail to capture the child's attention, the child frequently becomes identified as a troublemaker. One way of getting rid of troublemakers is via the testing route. If a child's I.Q. falls below a certain level, transfer to an Educable Mentally Handicapped room follows. In the process, the child begins to identify himself as inferior. Instead of altering the behavior, the child may accelerate the aggression as a reaction to being defined subnormal. The next stop is likely to be the Socially Maladjusted Room. By this time the child has probably violated some law and transfer to a correctional school ensues. The clergyman frequently becomes involved to exert his influence upon the child to "repent from his wicked ways." The parole officer similarly becomes involved in attempts to correct the child's behavior. All of these agencies and individuals become involved in the attempts to transform him into a "normal" child; in the process, the child, as an individual, is forgotten. His alienation from society progressively increases. The end result frequently includes referral to a psychiatrist and exclusion from school until "therapy" corrects his behavior. The alienation process becomes complete upon admittance to a treatment program for children.

The problem becomes defined as one of "mental illness." The institutions that have been involved with the child to this point have failed to correct the child's behavior with their methods of handling the problem; he has resisted their efforts to teach, convert or control him. Since their methods have failed, the next alternative attempted becomes that of "restructuring the child's personality" as a way of making him good.

Psychiatric treatment organizations for children become the recipients of these "troublemakers" who have failed to live up to the demands of other societal institutions. The problem becomes compounded in that dramatic change rarely occurs; children are as resistent to treatment as a means of control as they have been to the methods used by other institutions.

A number of unique problems surround the development of a psychiatric treatment program for children. First, they are unable to transform "troublemakers" into "good" children by means of psychiatric treatment, the expectations held for them by other societal institutions. Since they cannot adequately fulfill this function, they must maintain a facade of doing something if they are to continue in existence.

The Use of Power in Organizational Development

Faced with this set of problems how can a psychiatric program develop? The organization must first develop ways of generating sufficient power to allow for success in the competitive bargaining arena of the larger organization. What are the sources from which initial power generates?

Provision of services appropriate to the needs of a client population is a first source of power in a psychiatric organization. But when children compose the client population and "mental health services" constitute the need, even this elemental stage for developing a base of influence becomes problematic.

Contrasting a child psychiatric treatment program with other organizations similarly involved with children such as the schools and the penal system, may serve to clarify this dilemma. School systems, as Bidwell points out, are "social units specifically vested with a service function, in this case the moral and technical socialization of the young. . . . the central goal of any school system is to prepare its students for adult status, by training them in the moral orientations, which adult roles require."[14] Schools clearly provide a service needed by society.

Penal systems similarly are designed in response to specific societal needs. Cressey, in specifying common attitudes toward control of crime outlines the following societal functions:

> First, there is the desire for retribution. . . . Next, there is the desire that suffering be imposed upon criminals as a deterrent to potential criminals. . . . Third . . . there is an obvious desire for protection against the criminal. . . . Finally, there is in our society a desire to reduce crime rates by changing criminals.[15]

Prisons serve multiple functions of protection, punishment, and correction for society.

Treatment programs for children, in contrast perform functions com-

[14] Charles E. Bidwell, "The School as a Formal Organization" in James G. March (ed.) *Handbook of Organizations,* (Chicago: Rand McNally), 1965, pg. 973.

[15] Donald Cressey, "Prison Organizations" in James G. March (ed.) *op. cit.,* pg. 1025.

mon to both school systems and prisons but without societal legitimation. The recommendation for treatment commonly arises when children are resistant to the socialization process, such as that engaged of the school system. On the other hand, when a child steals or engages in some form of antisocial behavior the societal response that would be elicited were he of adult status is not forthcoming. The status of being a child interferes with the attitude of wishing to punish the offender. Psychiatric treatment becomes the modus vivendi between these societal institutions. The expectation held is that psychiatric treatment will remove the obstacles that prevent the socialization process on the one hand, and will control deviant behavior on the other.

The power base underlying psychiatric treatment programs for children arises, then, from the numbers of children who do not fit into other "people-processing" institutions. The need for psychiatric services cannot be substantiated in the same way as can the need for schools, where the need for services are in direct proportion to the number of children of school age. Lacking precise figures on which to base estimates for the need for psychiatric services such programs look to other factors to substantiate the need for their services. They go to the courts, schools, clergy, family service agencies, or other psychiatric facilities for referral estimates. Because of the numbers of children identified as troublesome by other agencies the need for psychiatric services for children is usually substantiated.

Characteristics of a Successful Leader

Having established the need, the second problem is that of recruiting a leader capable of developing an organization. What characterizes a successful manager? Dalton in his studies of industrial organizations, identifies the following characteristics of strong managers:

> the strong have high tolerance for conflict . . . they flee neither necessary conflict nor responsibility for making decisions. They are able to act quickly and effectively and are skilled in turning ambiguous and contrary situations to their needs. By almost imperturbably resolving contrary demands on themselves, they aid superiors as well as subordinates and thus exert influences beyond the limits of their official status. Where the weak look for protection in the letter of the rules, the strong oppose strict interpretation.[16]

[16] Melville Dalton, "Managing the Managers" in Albert H. Rubenstein and Chadwick J. Haberstrom, *Some Theories of Organization,* (Homewood, Ill.: The Dorsey Press), 1960, pg. 136.

A successful leader, then, has the ability to exert influence in a wide range of situations. The leader must be able to extend influence (1) upward in the organizational hierarchy, (2) outward to the significant environmental factors, and (3) downward to those who are workers within the program itself. Establishment of a leadership position, it may be hypothesized, rests upon the ability of a leader to garner sufficient power to influence others to a greater extent than the influences to which he is subject.

Cartwright asserts that the "ability to exert influence arises from the possession and control of valued resources."[17] The resources to be controlled within a psychiatric setting are first money, and secondarily the things which money can buy—space, personnel, furniture, equipment, etc. A successful leader first secures access to the resources of the organization, and, from this power base moves into the bargaining arena of the organization. Instead of forming primary liaisons with psychiatric professionals the wise leader quickly allies himself with business administrators who dispense these valued resources.

A power position, once established, must constantly be renegotiated. Competing for the resources of the organization poses hazards for the leader, in that, as Blau summarizes,

> The achievement of a position of leadership in a group entails a dilemma since it requires that a person command power over others and receive their legitimating approval of this power, but many of the steps necessary to attain dominance tend to antagonize others and evoke their disapproval.[18]

Thus a crucial factor in assuming a power position within an organization is accurately assessing the probabilities of evoking disapproval from significant others and calculating the risks accordingly. Allies must be identified as well as those a leader can afford to antagonize.

Maintenance of a Power Position

Establishment and maintenance of a power position within an organization depends upon access to adequate and accurate information. Receiving adequate information makes it possible to adjust internal organizational goals to the expectations held by others outside the pro-

17 Dorwin Cartwright, "Influence, Leadership, and Control" in James G. March (ed.) *op. cit.,* pg. 5.

18 Peter Blau, *Exchange and Power in Social Life,* (New York: John Wiley & Sons), 1964, pp. 316–317.

gram.[19] Secondarily, channels of communication must be worked out as well as ways of coding and condensing information.[20] Information is a valued resource in power maneuvers within an organization. In bargaining situations information may be introduced to support a position and thereby gain advantage over an antagonist. Information may be withheld in an attempt to control program participants. The person who has access to information from multiple sources has power, provided he knows how to judiciously make use of this information to advance his position.

Not only must control of input from the outside be achieved, but a series of internal managerial problems must be successfully mastered in the development of a psychiatric program. One difficulty in maintaining controls within psychiatric settings arises from the professional status of the work force. Bucher describes the problem they present: "they expect to be accorded the license to determine what should be done, how it should be done, and whether it is being done properly. In other words they believe they have the right to work autonomously."[21] Professionals perceive themselves to be independent of organizational control and thus present a challenge to any administrator within a psychiatric setting.

The types of power available to a leader in a psychiatric organization composed of those oriented to the values of professionalism are limited primarily to referent power, that based upon identification with the leader, or expert power, that based upon the possession of superior knowledge and skill.[22] The acceptance of the leader by followers is crucial in psychiatric organizations. As Etzioni points out:

> For the organization, the single most important bridge to the participants motivational and normative orientations is its ability to provide leadership to the small groups to which they belong. . . . If the participants accept the organizationally provided leader . . . their non-calculative commitment to the organization can be obtained. . . . Socializing organi-

[19] Norbert Weiner, "Cybernetics in History" in Walter Buckley (ed.) *Modern Systems Research for the Behavioral Scientist,* (Chicago: Aldine Press), 1968, pg. 32.

[20] Daniel Katz and Robert Kahn, *The Social Psychology of Organizations,* (New York: John Wiley & Sons), 1966, pp. 227–229.

[21] Rue Bucher, "Power in Medical School" Mayer Zald (ed.) *Power in Organizations,* (Nashville, Tenn.: Vanderbilt University Press), 1970, pg. 14.

[22] John Schopler, "Social Power" in Leonard Berkowitz (ed.) *Advances in Experimental Social Psychology,* Vol. 2, (New York: The Academic Press), 1965, pg. 182.

zations require deep commitment of the lower participants; the changed state of these participants is their 'main product.' This requires subordination of instrumental to expressive leaders.[23]

The dualism inherent in a psychiatric organization demands that a leader be able to function in the instrumental realm if he is to be successful in the intricacies of the bureaucracy. Conversely, in the realm of the internal organization the leader primarily must function in an expressive manner.

One way of managing internal relationships consists of limiting the number of highly trained psychiatric professionals with their external commitments and, instead, recruiting a body of unskilled workers lacking these commitments. The process of training these unskilled workers can then be used as an opportunity for socializing them into a way of consistently doing their work in the organization, i.e. taking psychiatric histories in a way that makes it possible for a psychiatric professional to attach the proper diagnostic category. The non-professional, lacking exposure to any conflicting views, readily incorporates the teaching and becomes a functionary of the organization.

The final factor to be controlled in the development of a psychiatric organization is the client population. Who are the consumers? Choice of an appropriate client population becomes a crucial factor. The program must promote an image that it is accomplishing something. There are two alternative routes open. The first consists of demonstrating the effectiveness of psychiatric treatment in curing mental illness. Since demonstrating success is difficult, a second alternative is usually chosen, choosing a client population deemed untreatable by other societal institutions. By relieving the family or the school of troublesome children no further questions are raised as to the effectiveness of psychiatric care.

This study traces these power maneuvers as a psychiatric treatment program for children develops. The story will be told in four parts. Part I provides the background for the study. Chapter II outlines the research perspective and methodology while also providing relevant historical factors. An overview of the major events occurring within the first year of program development is provided, as well as the cast of characters.

Part II describes the process of emergence of the program from the larger organizational structure. Chapter III provides a description of the Program Director and her entrance into the organization while Chapter IV traces her initial maneuvers in establishing a power position

[23] Amitai Etzioni, "Dual Leadership in Complex Organizations," *American Sociological Review*, Vol. 30, No. 5, October, 1965, pp. 691–695.

within the organizational network. Chapter V describes processes of negotiation and change. Part III concerns itself with the development of program identity. Chapter VI describes the participants, their goals and aspirations. Chapter VII describes the internal managerial ploys used in structuring relationships between participants while Chapter VIII details the process of "Staging the Production." Chapter IX details the training processes, specifically outlining the ways in which non-professionals were instructed to categorize and identify problematic behavior.

Part IV delineates characteristics of the program at the end of the first year of development while Chapter X describes the diagnostic process and the ways in which a client population was identified. Chapter XI reports staffs perceptions of their work contrasted with the characteristics of children actually accepted and rejected by the program. Chapter XII provides a summary and conclusions.

Chapter II

The Research Scene

The Bureaucracy

This psychiatric treatment program for children was developed within a newly built regional state-sponsored mental health center. In the preceding decade many dramatic changes in mental health programming had occurred in this particular state.* Only eight years prior to the initiation of this program, mental health care had been under the sponsorship of a combined governmental agency charged with "public welfare": care for the mentally ill was but a part of a larger concern for the poor and needy. Since that time a separate department had been formed for the "mentally ill." Bond issues had been passed for the building of new mental health facilities, and the over-all administrative structure had been decentralized into regions.

Since the creation of a department specifically concerned with mental health problems, increased money and other resources had been directed toward meeting this social problem. President Kennedy's message to Congress concerning Mental Illness and Mental Retardation added impetus to this movement. The President's speech of February 5, 1963 included the following objectives:

> First we must seek out the causes of mental illness and mental retardation and eradicate them. . . .
> Second, we must strengthen the underlying resources of knowledge and, above all, of skilled manpower which are necessary to sustain our attack on mental disability for many years to come. . . .
> Third, we must strengthen and improve the facilities serving the mentally ill and the mentally retarded. . . . The emphasis should be upon timely and intensive diagnosis, treatment, and training, so that the mentally afflicted can be cured or their functions restored to the extent possible.[1]

Later in the same speech President Kennedy proposed his plan for comprehensive community care:

*This analysis is partially based upon my personal experiences in working as a psychiatric nurse within this department in varying capacities and in a number of institutions during this time span.

1 President John F. Kennedy, Message from the President of the United States Relative to Mental Illness and Mental Retardation, Delivered February 5, 1963, 88th Congress, 1st Session, Document No. 58, pp. 2–3.

> We need a new type of mental health facility, one which will return mental health care to the mainstream of American medicine, and at the same time upgrade mental health services. I recommend therefore that Congress 1) authorize grants to the state for construction of comprehensive community mental health centers . . . 2) authorize short-term project grants for the initial staffing costs of comprehensive mental health centers . . . and 3) facilitate the preparation of community plans for these new facilities as a necessary preliminary to any construction or staffing assistance.[2]

The Regional Mental Health Centers in this state developed to implement these directives.

Prior to the introduction of the new Mental Health Centers, the only institutions in the state Mental Health System were the immense state hospitals. Children were hospitalized, in many instances, on the same units with adults. There was little provision for any specialized care. The situation in this state was similar to conditions reported in a study conducted by the National Institutes of Mental Health in which they estimated that "nearly 1,000,000 children needing treatment did not receive it . . . 27,000 children were under care in state and county mental institutions in 1966."[3] Children for whom there were no services in the community were

> expelled from the community and confined in large state hospitals so understaffed that they have few, if any, professionals trained in child psychiatry and related disciplines. It is not unusual to tour one of these massive warehouses for the mentally ill and come upon a child, aged nine or ten, confined on a ward with 80 or 90 adults.[4]

Following the presidential mandate, the Mental Health Department embarked on a course of dramatically changing their systems of caring for the mentally ill and the mentally retarded; the emphasis was upon transforming care of the mentally ill from mere custodialism to a more therapeutic approach.

Accompanying this movement toward a more therapeutic orientation for the existing institutions was a plan to build a series of new Mental Health Centers. These were to be community based, progressive in orientation, based upon a model of community mental health. The governmental agency responsible for care of the mentally ill began to ad-

2 *Ibid.,* pg. 4-5.

3 Report of the Joint Commission on Mental Health for Children, *Crisis in Child Mental Health: Challenge for the 70's,* (New York: Harper & Row), 1970, pg. 5.

4 *Ibid.,* pg. 5.

ministratively decentralize into eight regional areas. In each of these regions a modern Mental Health Center was built to serve as a center for the administrative management of the Region. In addition to this administrative function these centers were also planned to provide additional mental health services for the area. The responsibilities of the Regional Directors, who were newly appointed and had no prior experience within the state bureaucracy, included responsibility for the administrative control of programs within their region. In addition to those mental health services currently available in the state institutions the Regional Directors were responsible for developing programs to bridge the gaps between current needs and available services. The mental health needs of the people within these regions were to be met by institutions within that geographical area.

The geographical area served by this particular center consisted of one-half of the area of the city, suburban, and rural areas surrounding a large metropolis. The population residing within the area was approximately 3.7 million, representing divergent socio-economic and ethnic groups. There were no existing facilities for care of mentally ill children within the regional boundaries. This was an obvious need that the Regional Director had responsibility for meeting.

The regional structure was superimposed upon an already existing network of mental institutions. Within the region in which this program was developed there were two existing state facilities: a six thousand bed state hospital and a Mental Health Center for six hundred beds that was to serve one specific suburban area within the Region. The Mental Health Center in which this children's program was developed is a two hundred fifty bed structure with facilities for extensive out-patient care in addition to the in-patient potential. Four units within this center were designated for Children's Services. The architectural design specified that two of these units were to be used for residential care while the other two were for day-care, out-patient, recreation, and school activities. The total in-patient capacity was projected to be sixty.

Within this organizational network the Mental Health Center had to compete with the pre-existent institutions for needed resources. Since there had been no children's services in the region, this children's program not only had to plan for children who would become mentally ill, but also for those dispersed throughout the state in other regions. Additionally, in the light of the "community mental health movement" such a program had to be able to predict the types of services that they should plan that would garner the support of those who controlled the resources.

Departments such as Personnel and Budgeting were controlled by long-term state employees who had worked their way upward through the hierarchy. For example, a top level state administrator had begun his career as a psychiatric aide in a state hospital and worked his way to the top echelons of administration. Since all employees were protected by Civil Service they could not be fired and they served out their remaining years until retirement. This administrative structure, top-heavy with administrators oriented to the past, measured program success by numbers of patients discharged, cost of care per patient per day, and similar accounting procedures. Newer programs, such as those directed toward prevention, could not be measured in those terms. Given this structure, a prime consideration in the development of any new program was that of convincing these administrators of the efficacy of a new treatment approach. Since children's services for the mentally ill had never been part of the planning there was no pre-existent criteria other than those developed for adult programs. The children's program was faced with the problem of charting its developmental course within the context of this rigid structure.

The Professional Setting

Prior to the introduction of these changes and the building of the new Mental Health Centers the administration of mental health facilities had been totally in the hands of non-psychiatric doctors. With the program of regionalization, psychiatrists were appointed as Directors both at the state and regional levels. The psychiatrists were super-imposed upon the pre-existing system. The Regional Directors were confronted with the need to simultaneously develop new types of treatment facilities while administratively directing the pre-existent institutions. They inherited employees oriented and embedded in the old "state system."

Psychiatrists recruited into the positions of Regional Directors had limited prior experience in public psychiatry; most of them had been recruited upon completion of educational programs or from private practice. Administratively, the Regional Director in the area in which this Children's Program was developed was responsible for three hospital facilities in addition to developing a comprehensive network of mental health services. Prior to taking this position his only experience was private psychiatric practice with limited contact with hospital psychiatry. Although the Regional Directors had responsibility for mental health services in their areas much of the control of essential resources was retained by central administration. The psychiatrists, while specialists in mental health, were novices in public administration.

A further complication was that even though psychiatrists could be considered specialists in individual psychotherapy they were not experts in treating the masses of people found within the state hospitals. Patients seen in private office practice can hardly be equated to those found in large-scale mental institutions. Psychiatrists, by virtue of their socialization tend toward a psychotherapeutic orientation; ideologically they are committed to a one-to-one relationship to patients.[5] But the one-to-one model has limited application when dealing with thousands of "untreatable" patients. Couple this with the ideological orientation of other mental health workers lower in the status hierarchy and the problem becomes compounded. Psychologists and social workers, lacking the professional status that allows them to engage in private office practice necessarily are more familiar with treatment of patients similar to those found within state hospitals. The Regional Director had the responsibility of providing direction to a staff that was considerably more knowledgeable about management of large numbers of patients.

The psychiatrists were surrounded by career administrators on the one hand, and, on the other by professionals with more relevant experience and training for work with the masses of patients served by the state Mental Health System. Add to this the concept of "community mental health" and all of the elements necessary, to a state of administrative chaos, exist.

Preventive psychiatry was the new vogue. As Caplan defines this field

> 'preventive psychiatry' refers to the body of professional knowledge, both theoretical and practical, which may be utilized to plan and carry out programs for reducing 1) the incidence of mental disorders of all types in the community ("primary prevention"), 2) the duration of a significant number of these disorders that do occur ("secondary prevention"), and 3) the impairment which may result from these disorders ("tertiary prevention").[6]

Community psychiatrists were to be the specialists to plan comprehensive programs ranging all the way from reducing incidence of mental illness through social action in the community to rehabilitation of those impaired and hospitalized for mental illness. While the Regional Directors had been socialized to treat highly selected patients that fall into the middle of this preventive continuum, they were now expected to automatically become instant experts in an expanded field. Expectations for community psychiatrists articulated by Caplan include

[5] Strauss, *et. al., op. cit.,* pg. 137.

[6] Gerald Caplan, *Principles of Preventive Psychiatry,* (New York: Basic Books), 1964.

he must acquire knowledge of a wide range of issues—social, economic, political, administrative— . . . which will enable him to plan and implement programs that focus not only on individual patients but beyond them on community problems of which they are a part.

He must learn to coordinate his activities with those of many other professionals and non-professional workers who are actively involved in dealing with the health, educational, legal, and social aspects of the community problems posed by the mentally ill.

The close working relationships must include collaboration with social scientists, economists, legislators, citizen leaders, and professional workers in the public health, welfare, religious, and educational fields.[7]

The Regional Directors with their limited backgrounds had little experience in public psychiatry. Ideologically, they had been indoctrinated to see one-to-one therapy as the "treatment of choice." Any other approach was an inferior substitute given the predominant value systems in the psychiatric field. Although they were to engage in "preventive psychiatry,"[8] how they were to do this was for them to discern. The psychiatrists, used to seeing patients on a one-to-one basis in office practice now were to come forth onto the community scene; they were expected to "relate" to a multitude of people within the community that they had never encountered before. Simultaneous with their emergence on the community scene, the Regional Directors were expected to administer a multi-million dollar business, often in conflict with administrators who had more extensive knowledge of the system. They were similarly expected to supervise a wide range of other mental health specialists, representing divergent ideological commitments. The Director of Children's Services was directly responsible to the Regional Director; it was within the context of these countervailing forces that this psychiatric treatment program was developed.

Development of the Research Problem

For seven years prior to the initiation of this study I had been employed, on two separate occasions, within this Mental Health Department. First I had been employed within a large state hospital training psychiatric aides. It was there that I first became interested in the problems of large-scale mental institutions. Following completion of a graduate program in psychiatric nursing I again returned to this same mental health system, this time to work in an administrative capacity with a newly appointed Regional Director in the coordination and development

---

[7] *Ibid.,* pp. 16–17.

[8] *Ibid.,* pg. 17.

of programs for his area. The chaotic nature of this experience was the force precipitating my move into the field of sociology.

Throughout the two years experience in the Regional Programs I had observed approximately ten highly qualified psychiatrists recruited from throughout the nation come and go. Psychiatrists were recruited to establish programs in such areas as drug addiction, alcoholism, children and adolescents, geriatrics, and those based upon specific catchment populations. Additionally, two psychiatrists were hired to become superintendents of hospitals within the mental health system. Two highly skilled Hospital Administrators had similarly been recruited for the new Mental Health Center. These were but a few of the qualified professionals who came to establish programs during this time span and left shortly thereafter in complete frustration.

At the end of the first two years of the Regional Program only a few patients were receiving treatment in the new facility; a two and a half million dollar building was virtually empty, except for the large number of psychologists, social workers, and nurses that had been hired by Program Directors who had subsequently resigned. These experiences led me to question what contributed to the failure of so many programs. My personal experience and those of others who were employed at this time raised a number of related concerns. Although little was being done in the area of direct patient care, the large numbers of employees who had been hired were direct patient care staff. Lacking patients to work with, why was everyone seemingly so busy? Was care of patients the "real" work of the organization? If this is not the work of the organization what are alternate functions of psychiatric treatment institutions?

The pattern that emerged from this rapid turnover of Program Directors consisted of the following sequence of events. The Program Director would enter the organization with a flourish; a series of meetings would be arranged with others in associated program areas. For example: a Program Director for Children's Services would meet with his counterparts in other regions, and in associated organizations such as the schools and the legal system. The second step was that of gathering a number of statistics validating the need for his particular type of program. At his stage the Program Director would begin his recruitment of professional staff. This was based upon the assumption that professional staff was extremely scarce and therefore it was necessary to hire any professional at any time even though there was no particular need for them at the moment.

The Program Directors wrote elaborate program proposals outlining an urgent need for services for their particular interest group and the type of services they planned to provide. These plans included detailed projections of the numbers of patients they planned to serve as well as the staff needed to accomplish these goals.

In most cases these steps were accomplished without interference. It was only after the program proposals were submitted that difficulties arose. The Program Directors would be told by the Regional Director that their staffing plans called for too many employees, that they were asking for too much money, or similar complaints. The Program Directors, in most instances, would make revisions in their plans only to encounter further frustrations. The process usually culminated in the resignation of the Program Directors. The usual reason given for their resignations was that they had expected autonomy in establishing their programs but in finding that this was not to be, they made their decisions to leave. They left, either to return to private practice, or to go elsewhere in the hopes of realizing their aspirations. The employees accumulated during these years spent a considerable portion of their time comparing notes and predicting when Program Directors would leave. During this time only one Program Director (a non-psychiatrist) ever developed his program to the operational phase.

Since I was part of the Regional Director's staff my view of the organization was based primarily upon an administrative perspective. Although I frequently talked with staff at all levels of the organization, I did not have detailed knowledge of the dilemmas confronting them. Based on these observations and experiences I wanted to study in a more objective and detailed manner the evolution of a program within this setting. I wanted to view this process as an insider in an attempt to identify factors that contributed to difficulties in establishing a psychiatric treatment program in this setting. With this in mind, I asked the Regional Director for permission to do such a study. This study began with the recruitment of a new Program Director for Children's Services.

Resume of Events

Because of the complexity of the organizational process it is necessary to provide an overview of the events that this study will describe. At the time this study began the state mental health system had been decentralized into Regions for the past four years. Diagram 2 depicts the organizational setting surrounding the program.

DIAGRAM II.   STATE ORGANIZATIONAL STRUCTURE

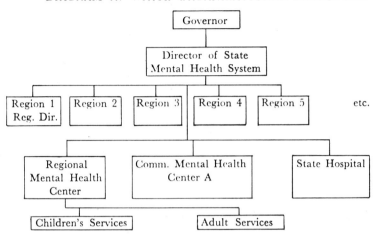

The Regional Director for the area in which the Children's Program was to be established was Dr. Dixon,* a psychiatrist. Since there was no superintendent for the Mental Health Center Dr. Dixon also assumed this responsibility. Although the Mental Health Center had been completed for a full year it was still not operational. Dr. Dixon recruited Mrs. Davis one year after the prior Program Director had resigned. She began her employment in January with the agreement that she would have Children's Services operational within four months. The following sequence of events occurred within the first year and form the framework for this study:

(1) By February 1, Mrs. Davis had written her original program proposals. These initial written documents formed the basis for her negotiations with Dr. Dixon, and through this process alliances were formed not only with Dr. Dixon, but also with the Hospital Administrator and the Personnel Officer.

(2) In March Mrs. Davis moved out of the Administration Building

---

* Names in this study are coded in the following manner:

Directors—names beginning with the letter "D"
Psychiatrists—names beginning with the letter "P" (Dr. P.)
Psychologists—names beginning with the letter "P" (Mr. P.)
Social Workers—names beginning with the letter "S"
Child Care Workers—names beginning with the letter "W"
Child Care Aides—names beginning with the letter "A"
Nurses—names beginning with the letter "N"
Teachers—names beginning with the letter "T"

and into the Children's Units. She succeeded in having an office redesigned for her that had been designated for other purposes. Mrs. Davis inherited three staff members, two psychologists and a Senior Social Worker from the prior Children's program and they formed the core staff.

(3) April. The first opening date passed. By this time a staffing plan had been developed and furniture had been ordered, but no services for children were in evidence. The two psychologists left the program. Mrs. Carroll, a Social Worker Consultant was hired to conduct training seminars, and a few social worker trainees were hired.

(4) May. More beginning social workers, child care aides, and child care workers were hired and the training seminars began. A second opening date passed without any services available except for a telephone Intake service.

(5) June. A major reorganization of the structure of the state mental health system occurred. The geographic catchment areas were redefined and this mental health center was paired with a different state hospital. Dr. Dixon was transferred to another region, and Dr. Daniels, another psychiatrist, became the new Director. Mrs. Davis renegotiated her position within the new structure and in so doing defended her program from intrusions. Dr. Cartwright, a child psychiatrist began to conduct diagnostic seminars, and was used to sanction or validate diagnostic decision-making. A beginning identification of the children to be accepted into the program occurred. A third opening date passed: at this time a few parents were being seen, but mainly as part of the staff educational program. A third psychologist was hired.

(6) July. Miss Travis was hired to be Acting Director of the Day Care Program. She began planning meetings with the staff, primarily Child Care Workers and junior Social Workers who had been hired. Two more projected opening dates passed and a fifth date of August 25th was established. By the end of the month Miss Travis was removed from her position and assigned responsibility for supervision of the teachers and Mrs. Davis again took primary responsibility for the Day Care planning. Diagnostic Interviewing of parents was now ongoing, but the children still had not been evaluated directly by staff. Mr. Camin, a Social Worker with advanced analytic training in the treatment of children was hired to begin to interview the children. His views conflicted with those of Dr. Cartwright.

(7) August. As the August 26th date approached prior criteria that had been outlined as to the type of child to be accepted into the program were redefined. Children were admitted on the basis of the need

to have a client population rather than on any strict diagnostic criterion. Dr. Carey, another Social Worker with experience in running a Day Care Program for children entered the organization. He began conducting seminars directed to the management of Children in the Day Care Unit. On August 26th the Day Care Unit opened with 5 children. The staff at this time consisted of a total of 17: 6 child care workers, 5 social workers, 1 social work supervisor, 1 teacher, 1 teacher supervisor, 1 nurse, 1 psychologist, and Mrs. Davis. This full-time staff was supplemented by 5 consultants.

(8) September. Mr. Camin was encouraged to resign his consultant position because of conflicting views.

(9) October—December. The program continued with the five original children. All of the seminars, (a) Intake training, (b) Diagnostic, (c) Child management, and (d) staff meetings continued. Dedication ceremonies were held in October which provided the public with their first view of the program. The one remaining psychologist left. A Day Care supervisor was hired, Mr. Carey became a full-time staff member, and another Day Care supervisor was hired. By the end of December Mrs. Davis was questioning the competence of these new staff members and was contemplating reorganization. Plans for admitting a few more children were made for January.

Research Methodology

The primary research method used was that of participant observation[9] as an officially designated researcher within the setting. The length of time covered by this study is one year from the time the Program Director was hired. Throughout this time I spent a minimum of three days per week in the setting. Because of my close involvement with the program I became identified, in the eyes of staff, as "one of them." I attended their parties, ate lunch with them, accompanied them to meetings, and in reality shared their lives with them for this period of time.

In addition to field notes, tape-recordings of all formally scheduled meetings were made. The average number of such meetings was three one and a half hour meetings per week. Verbatim transcripts of these meetings were made, and were subsequently analyzed. In addition to the actual transcripts, all staff meetings were attended and on-going records maintained.

9 For the rationale underlying the participant observation approach used in this study see: Howard S. Becker, *Sociological Work,* (Chicago: Aldine Press), 1970, Aaron Cicourel, *Method and Measurement in Sociology,* (The Free Press of Glencoe), 1964, Chap. 2, "Theory and Method in Field Research", pp. 39–72.

A third dimension of the study was tape-recorded interviews of all employees hired into the organization during the time-span of the study. The interviews focused upon information relevant to the background of the individual, socio-economic factors, development of occupational interests, educational background, recruitment into a specific career line, specific factors about this work situation that were appealing, and evaluation of initial experiences within the organization. The average length of these interviews was one hour and the tape recordings were transcribed verbatim.

At the conclusion of the study a questionnaire was administered to all staff employees within the program, with the exception of supervisors. The major purpose of this questionnaire was that of gathering quantifiable data as to the consensus of definitions relevant to the work situation among participants within the organization. These data provided a basis for validating the "structure" that had evolved during the course of this study.

Analysis of Data

The major form of data analysis employed throughout this study includes content analysis of field notes, tape-recorded transcripts of meetings, interview data, and questionnaires. The primary procedure used in analyzing these transcripts and field notes consisted of the establishment of content categories. All data fitting within a particular category was entered on file cards, designating the source and date of the interaction. All material was filed on a time sequence basis as well as according to category. Thus, material could be evaluated not only according to themes but also in developmental sequence.

Interview and questionnaire data were similarly analyzed, the primary difference being that the categories guiding data collection were pre-established.

The pursuit of the defined problem dictated that as wide a range of data as possible be considered. In view of the experiences of other Program Directors I had no assurance that this program would make it. Since there was no predefined organization at the start of the study, it was impossible to predetermine what aspects would become significant in the developmental process. I needed to keep a record of as many factors that might influence the development within the program as possible.

Needless to say, a massive amount of data were accumulated. This analysis captures only the most obvious parts of the process. Further generalization of the findings to other developing organizations or precise formulations of the process must necessarily rest upon subsequent studies of comparative organizations.

Part II

The Emergence of the Children's Program

Chapter III

Paths to Power

The first problem to be solved in establishing an organization consists of generating a need for the product to be produced. Once the consumer is convinced of a need for the product an organization proposes to produce they are apt to lend their support to the establishment of the organization. The next step in the organizational process, once this initial need has been defined and the initial flow of resources has begun, involves the recruitment of a leader that will be able to use these resources in solidifying a power position.

Translating these processes into a child psychiatric treatment program the first step consists of making the public aware of the large number of children who can be classified as "mentally ill" in their midst. Secondarily, the inadequacy of present institutions, such as schools, in meeting the needs of these children must be demonstrated. Once this has been established the logical outgrowth is that there is an overwhelming need for additional and new psychiatric treatment facilities for children. Convinced of the large number of children in need of psychiatric services public support is generally forthcoming.

Once the need has been defined and the initial financial support been allocated the next problem consists of recruiting a psychiatric professional as a leader with the abilities to convince the public, on a continuing basis, that these large numbers of children are being helped and that they are getting adequate return for the resources invested in the establishment of an organization. Success as a leader in this organization was contingent upon management of relationships within the larger organizational environments as well as the internal relationships within the program.

Specifically, the Program Director had to mediate between the demands of the bureaucracy and those of psychiatric professionals and reconcile incongruencies. She had to compete successfully with other Program Directors for resources, including money and personnel, in establishing her program. Additionally, she had to recruit and train a staff capable of producing work that would further the goals of the program. Finally, the Program Director had to find a client population of children to whom services could be administered that would demonstrate the success of the program. These are but a few of the managerial feats the Program Director had to master if she were to experience success. Diagram III depicts the network of relationships the Program Director had to successfully manage.

DIAGRAM III

FIELD OF RELATIONSHIPS SURROUNDING THE PROGRAM DIRECTOR

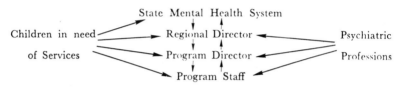

How, faced with these numerous demands, was power generated to consolidate the Program Director's leadership position?

Sources of Power: The Need

The perceived need for this particular type of psychiatric treatment program was generated from several sources. First, in the Region in which this program was located, there were no Children's Services available in any of the pre-existent state facilities. This, despite the fact that this area of the Metropolitan region admitted more children into state hospitals than any other area of the state. These admissions were primarily to two state hospitals in another Region which served the other half of the city. This situation was a constant source of contention between the two Regional Directors; it was repeatedly pointed out that this area was not meeting its responsibilities. The annual admission rate for this area was approximately two hundred and fifty children, with an estimated need for services of varying types for six hundred children.* Thus, one major external factor was the conflict between the two Regional Directors as well as the estimated need for services for children of this area.

A second factor influencing the perceived need for Children's Services arose from the population of the area served. The area which this Region encompasses includes the most impoverished ghetto areas in the

*I do not know the basis of these projections but these were figures commonly cited.

entire state. Poverty, high density housing projects, incomplete family situations, and similar features of life in the ghetto influenced the Regional Director's perceptions of the need for Children's Services. Based on an awareness of these problems, and the knowledge that middle and upper class children could get help from other agencies, the Regional Director wanted to develop a Children's Treatment Program that would particularly relate to the needs of the poorer segments of the population. Because the population of this area was predominantly black, the program was also to be relevant to the needs of this population.

A third major factor making the development of Children's Services a matter of some urgency was the stated philosophy of the Department that outlined their commitments to the needs of the people. An illustration of the philosophical tenor of the time was set forth in documents issued by the Mental Health Department:

> As a result of the $150,000,000 Mental Health Bond issue passed by the citizens . . . funds are available to meet the public demand for better care and treatment for the mentally ill, more hospital beds, and training for the mentally retarded.
> The new centers, located as they are throughout the state, will bring into reality the goal that no citizen . . . will have to travel more than ninety minues by automobile to reach a center where mental health services are provided.
> Our new Zone centers will provide additional beds, thus reducing waiting periods of the past; will encourage early treatment because help is close, and will enable families and friends of patients to keep in touch, always important in times of illness.

Eight years later these Regional centers were still not operational. It was in such a context that the Children's Program was to be developed; a major impetus for the development of this program was the need to demonstrate that the money expended was, in fact, providing services for the people.

Power of the Person:
The Program Director

Successful leadership within this organization rested upon the ability of the Program Director to 1) maneuver and negotiate within the bureaucratic structure, 2) elicit support of the professional child psychiatric community, 3) manage a large number of staff members to do the work of the organization, and 4) maintain clinical skills and demonstrate these capacities within the clinical setting.

Considering the enormity of the task and the overwhelming needs outlined by the Regional Director what type of individual would consider themselves capable of performing these leadership functions? Any analysis of the development of an organization would be incomplete without a consideration of the personal motivations of the individual in the leadership position.

Mrs. Davis had moved from the South to the Metropolitan area following completion of her undergraduate education. Her work career began as a public aid caseworker. While employed as a caseworker she completed Masters' degree preparation in Social Work. Upon completion of her graduate education she was employed in a family service agency where through a period of years she moved to the highest supervisory levels within this organization. Her future aspirations were to become part of a policy-making body, preferably at the national level, concerned with Children's problems. The position as a Program Director within a State system was perceived as a steppingstone to these future aspirations. Success was extremely important to Mrs. Davis.

Mrs. Davis, having worked and lived in a bureaucratic society was well versed in the dynamics of large scale organizations. Initially she perceived her basic problem as that of gaining power. Attainment of a power position rested upon her abilities to convert perceived status deficits into assets. Mrs. Davis embodied three minority positions within society: she was black, female, and a social worker. Her primary problem, as she perceived it, was to turn these handicaps into assets in the competitive organizational arena. Her major preoccupation became that of developing strategies for dealing with the complexities surrounding her; a major commitment was to successfully establish a Children's Program that would provide needed services for those in particular need, poor and black children.

Being black and coming from a southern background made Mrs. Davis sensible to a range of issues which could otherwise have been ignored. Perhaps the best illustration of the imprint of the past upon current patterns of behavior was evidenced by her stories of her grandmother. For example: she related how her grandmother had been criticized for subscribing to the local "white establishment" newspaper in their home town in the South. The neighbors had constantly told her grandmother that this was a waste of money. Her grandmother, stating the reasons for subscribing, taught her "You've got to know what your enemies are saying about you." This became one of Mrs. Davis' guides to successful maneuvering within the organizational arena; one of her first strategies was to sort out an array of potential allies while similarly identifying the "enemy camp."

As part of a minority group, Mrs. Davis also knew that "real power" was not always synonymous with position on an organizational chart. She accurately perceived that those with "actual power" frequently were those low in the status hierarchy of the organization. No staff member was too lowly for her to associate with—the housekeepers, dietary personnel, clerical staff in the business office, and the personnel clerks formed a solid body of allies. Such alliances resulted in the completion of work via informal routes that never would have been managed following more traditional approaches. It was through such alliances that the Program Director gained access to the significant resources within the organization to solidify her power base. It was through such techniques, learned through past experiences, that Mrs. Davis demonstrated proficiency in successfully managing the bureaucracy.

A second factor crucial to the success of the Program was the ability to coalesce staff in a commitment to the goals of the program. Being black was a significant factor in this process. Initially Children's Program staff was all white. Many of the staff members came from suburban middle-class families who had had little contact or experience with black people. Many of these young people were in rebellion against the prejudices and values of their parents. Employment in this situation gave them first-hand experiences in testing out relationships with which they were previously unfamiliar. Their interpretation of initial impressions of Mrs. Davis reflects these views:

> Mr. Andrews: When I talked to her on the phone for the first time, there was a flavor in her speech and in the back of my mind I thought 'Gee Whiz' she's Negro, I bet . . . she was telling me some of the things about her own experiences with her kids, and in my mind I don't see her kids as being Negro so I suppose that maybe I don't see any difference. . . . I firmly believe all people should be treated equal, but in the society that I was brought up in there was a big stigma about this.
> Mr. Anderson: I was interviewed by Mrs. Williams . . . and she didn't tell me the neatest thing, that our director was Negro. This is a multi-problem kind of thing and to have a Negro director is really neat—somebody has a lot of faith in her. And talking to her on the phone is a funny thing—you can't really tell much, and Davis is a common name—it's Irish—but it's neat.

As relationships progressed within the program one of the outstanding characteristics of staff members views was their loyalty and devotion toward Mrs. Davis. Leadership within the program itself could best be described as charismatic. Relationships with staff became similar to those within a family setting; staff on informal occasions referred to Mrs. Davis as "mother" and she in turn called them her "children." Being black was also an asset in the eyes of the Regional Director; he assumed that Mrs. Davis would be effective in developing satisfactory relationships within the black community and would be committed to providing services to black children.

Being a woman similarly became an asset in developing the program. Although Mrs. Davis had no prior experience working directly with children (her experiences had been with families), she had three adolescent sons. Consequently, when theoretical knowledge was sometimes lacking, practical experiences were substituted; management of children within a treatment program was just a larger operation. Being a woman was also helpful in developing working relationships with the staff. Most of the staff originally hired were young, newly married women who were working until they retired into a motherhood role. Mrs. Davis as an elder member of the group provided support and understanding as they talked about their experiences as wives and potential mothers. Treatment of children was but a substitute for rearing children of your own; there was no incompatibility between the work role of a child-care worker and that of a mother, in fact this work served to prepare women for advancement to a maternal role.

In recruiting a Program Director, the Regional Director assumed that a Social Worker would be more knowledgeable about the community than other professionals. Since social workers are not part of the usual medical hierarchy, it was further assumed that a social worker would be more comfortable working outside of a traditional hospital setting than would other psychiatric professionals oriented toward a medical model of treatment. Because of the noticeable lack of success of psychiatrists within the organization, the selection of Mrs. Davis as Program Director, in the Regional Director's mind, was a logical solution.

Although the Regional Director perceived Mrs. Davis' professional background as a Social Worker as an asset, she perceived herself as low in the professional hierarchy. In particular, Mrs. Davis felt that as a social worker diagnostic decisions were not within her realm of competence. This put her in a vulnerable position vis-à-vis the larger professional communities. Her solution to this dilemma was to call upon outside medical consultation. In making this alliance, Mrs. Davis was managing what she considered to be current threats to the establishment of the program. This alliance, while contributing to program survival, had the secondary effect of steering the program in a direction far removed from its original intent, a process that will be documented in the remainder of this study.

In summary, the scene was set. The original power base being the perceived need for services for children, the investment of public monies for community mental health services, and this mental health center's position vis-à-vis other organizations was established. A leader that offered promise of being able to develop services appropriate to these perceived needs had been recruited. Establishment of a treatment program for children was contingent upon using these potentials in generating sufficient power to successfully compete in the larger organizational and political arenas.

Chapter IV

Power Maneuvers

Having developed a public awareness of their need for the goods or services an organization proposes to produce, the leader recruited to deliver the product must make decisions as the most expeditious way of marketing his commodity. Long before a product ever reaches the outside public it must be successfully sold to those who control the internal resources of the organization necessary to the development of the mechanisms essential to the production process, i.e., money and personnel.

Several important steps are basic to successful management of this process. First, a successful manager seeks to promote an image to his superiors that he alone possesses the unique qualifications necessary to the production of the desired goods or services. He cannot allow his superiors any opportunity to question whether someone else might be more qualified or capable to meet their expectations.

Secondly, the successful manager must quickly scan the organizational field for those who control significant resources. Simultaneously, the leader must identify those who are competitors for the same resources and develop bargaining strategies to reciprocate. From an analysis of others within the organization, allies and antagonists are identified.

Thirdly, the wise leader erects boundaries around his area of functioning. Boundaries serve to protect the activity from direct scrutiny of superiors or others within the organization. If "outsiders" cannot directly observe the production process their judgments of the effectiveness of the operation are based solely upon the reports of the production manager and, secondarily, upon the quality of the goods produced.

Translating this into the development of a psychiatric treatment program for children, Mrs. Davis first had to convince Dr. Dixon that she would be able to establish the program envisioned. Significant resources were under the control of non-psychiatric administrators, i.e., the Hospital Administrator was responsible for budgeting and management of the mental health center while the Personnel Officer had responsibilities for recruitment and hiring of staff across program areas. Other program directors, who were the psychiatric professionals in the organization, were vying for the same resources. Mrs. Davis, faced with these problems, had to develop ways of establishing her position within the group. An important stage in the emergence of the Children's Program from the rest of the mental health center involved the engineering of boundaries in that this served to provide necessary distance. Through successful management of these stages Mrs. Davis expanded her power base within the organization.

The Program Proposal

The first action taken by Mrs. Davis was that of immediately outlining her "program." This served to reassure the Regional Director that she was capable of meeting his expectations. Since the Regional Director had publicly committed himself to the provision of services for children within his area, he desperately needed reassurance that at long last a Children's program would be forthcoming.

A program proposal within a psychiatric setting generally includes some description of the extensiveness of a particular problem, the population the program proposes to treat, and the methodologies to be employed. Writing a program proposal within this setting posed numerous problems. Mrs. Davis' management of this dilemma provides the first indications of how she would subsequently maneuver within this setting.

First, Mrs. Davis wished to indicate that she would be able to provide "services for children." But what were the services she would provide? Being a manager in a psychiatric organization differs from a managerial position in a goods-producing organization in that the end product is rarely defined. A factory, for example, has clearly specified end-products; effectiveness can be measured in terms of quantity and quality of the goods produced. In contrast, it may be assumed that psychiatric treatment programs for children are to produce "mentally healthy children." But the conjectural nature of "mental illness" and the questionable effectiveness of treatment makes writing a program proposal for a child psychiatric program at best problematic. How did Mrs. Davis circumvent this problem?

While the psychiatrist who proceeded Mrs. Davis had spent extensive amounts of time meeting with others before committing his ideas to paper, Mrs. Davis proceeded in an entirely different manner. Within the first week of employment a program proposal was written. While the psychiatrist included extensive discussions of theoretical treatment issues, none of this was included in Mrs. Davis' documents. Mrs. Davis, in contrast, demonstrated two things; 1) her commitment to the philosophical ideals inherent in statements made by the Regional Director, and 2) a plan for the rapid processing of large numbers of children through the program.

Comparison of the Regional Director's philosophical statements with the Program Proposal illustrates this matching process. The Regional Director was committed to the development of short-term treatment programs for emotionally disturbed children that emphasized maintaining the child within the family structure. Consequently, his preferences were for Day-care and Out-patient treatment with minimal emphasis on residential care. The overall philosophy for the Mental Health center outlines this view.

> In keeping with this pivotal position (of the mental health center) between distant state facilities and community mental health agencies . . . (this center) dovetails its efforts and programs with the existing network of private organizations, other governmental agencies, and community caregivers whose interest and responsibility parallel or complement that of the staff of the Center.
>
> Priority for services is given to mentally ill and mentally retarded persons in high risk of immediate institutionalization. All age groups will be served. Day-Care, In-Care, and Out-Care Programs are provided to assure that people in trouble are treated with minimal removal from their ordinary ways of life.

Emphasis was to be placed upon coordination of services with other agencies and immediate short-term treatment for those in need.

The initial program proposal advanced by Mrs. Davis illustrates her attempts to demonstrate commitment to the ideals inherent in the Regional Director's statements.

> 1) Day-Care Program: 20 patients, ages 6-13, who are withdrawn and/or psychotic. Excluded from this group will be the autistic and hyper-aggressive group. . . .
>
> 2) In-Patient service consists of 30 beds, 10 of which will be for a mix of mentally retarded with acute emotional problems . . . 20 beds will be available for mentally ill children 6-14 who are (a) psychotic and withdrawn, (b) for unremitting panic states, and (c) who are actually suicidal.
>
> 3) Out-Patient: The main role will be that of consultant to community agencies and to patient families. We will assist in diagnosis, evaluation, and plan appropriate treatment. The latter will be in terms of providing direction to existing programs.

The program proposal affirmed that the services would complement those of other agencies, that both mentally ill and retarded children be served, and those most in need would be provided services.

An accompanying set of rules outlined responsibilities for parents and referring agencies:

> Parents of all patients must be involved.
> Referring agencies must maintain cooperative involvement.
> Staffing will be held on all dispositions.

A further facet of the program proposal concerned logistics:

> Parents will be seen for six to eight sessions.
> Parents will join the child in Day-Care program for 2-3 weeks.
> Child will be admitted to in-patient for 4-6 weeks.
> Child moves back to day-care for 2-3 weeks.
> Parent joins child in day-care for last 4 days.
> Agency referral will be implemented for follow-up out-patient care upon child's release.

The emphasis upon moving the child through the program and the obligations placed upon parents and outside agencies served as affirmation of an emphasis upon short-term treatment. The lack of attention to the way in which treatment was to be affected in this time interval corresponded to organizational statements that advanced philosophy but advanced no plans for how these ideals were to be translated into action. The program proposal outlined above was the only statement of rules or policies that existed, in written form, for the first three months of the program's existence; it was on this basis that the Program Director negotiated with the Regional Director.

The broad philosophical statements relevant to the "mission" of the Regional Center were translated into practical procedures designed to accomplish two goals: 1) to advance an impression that the Children's Program would provide short-term treatment services, and 2) to simultaneously build in a set of safeguards that would protect the program from excessive demands made from the outside. If children did not advance rapidly through the program, blame could be attributed to a lack of cooperation from other agencies or the parents. The child, in this set of statements, becomes an inanimate object to be propelled through the program. No guidelines nor expectations for treatment were included. Mrs. Davis elicited the support of the Regional Director through statements indicating that the program would, in fact, meet his expectations. *How* this was to be accomplished was not specified.

In not talking of treatment, Mrs. Davis successfully avoided potential conflict. It was assumed that although the rationale and methodology underlying treatment was not outlined, Mrs. Davis, as a psychiatric professional, had something in mind. No one could quarrel with the proposal outlined, it was sufficiently vague. To attack the program would be equivalent to criticizing motherhood or God. This proposal did not restrict the program to any course of action. There was no way in which anyone outside of the program could evaluate progress based on this document. If a child did not progress according to the outlined sequence this could be attributed to unforeseen changes occurring within the child, the family, or other agencies. The Program Director avoided any ideological conflict with the Regional Director and thereby protected herself in an area of vulnerability. In this maneuver, Mrs. Davis initially freed herself from the control of Dr. Dixon and advanced an image of her capabilities of establishing a program to meet his expectations.

Allies and Antagonists

After committing herself to the establishment of the program through the writing of the program proposal, Mrs. Davis next faced the problem of devising ways to implement these plans. Implementation of program plans required money and people. Mrs. Davis needed a positive relationship with two departments within the organization: Personnel for the hiring of staff, and Business Administration for supplies and money. Since she was competing with other program directors for these resources she could not risk prematurely antagonizing them. The hazard in testing out power positions with the other Program Directors was the possibility that they might unite against her and thus counteract her effectiveness in the bargaining arena. The choice of an appropriate target issue was crucial.

Mrs. Davis fortunately was confronted with a ready-made issue that facilitated her move into the organization. The opportunity arose around staff members who had been hired by the previous Program Director. In the process of confronting this challenge, Mrs. Davis not only tested her power within the organization, but simultaneously made needed alliances with those who controlled significant resources. In the process she demonstrated abilities in successfully managing problems that had confounded the other Program Directors; she gained their respect through her management of the situation.

A common problem in professional organizations arises around highly trained professionals who do not "fit into" the organization. They frequently possess educational training and experience that surpasses that of their superiors. Perhaps because of this, they feel that they should participate in decision-making and should share in defining programmatic goals. Such psychiatric professionals pose threats to leaders newly recruited into organizations.

A particular case serves to illustrate Mrs. Davis' management of such a problem. Miss Nelson, a nurse holding a Master's degree in child psychiatric nursing with five years experience in a highly specialized prestigious child therapy program, had been hired by the previous Program Director. For a year Miss Nelson had no identified functions within the organization since there was no children's program. Miss Nelson held the highest rank in the nursing hierarchy and finding a place for her was an organizational problem. The difficulties were compounded in that the Program Directors in the mental health center did not perceive Miss Nelson as capable of assuming administrative responsibilities; they repeatedly questioned her "emotional stability."

The magnitude of the problem was heightened by the bureaucratic structure of the mental health system. Although Miss Nelson was perceived to be incompetent to manage administration of nursing services no other nursing administrator could be hired until she was moved into Children's Services.

The solution to the dilemma was to move Miss Nelson into Children's Services, "where she belongs," as quickly as possible once Mrs. Davis had been hired. The first day Mrs. Davis reported for work, she was told that both the Regional Director and his top assistant were busy for the day. Miss Nelson had been assigned responsibility to orient Mrs. Davis to the prior planning of Children's Services. Assigning Miss Nelson to the task of orienting Mrs. Davis was meant to accomplish the purpose of identifying her as "belonging" to Children's Services. This was the precipitant of the situation around which Mrs. Davis tested out her power and position within the organization. The issue was that of determining Mrs. Davis' obligation to honor commitments made by others before her. Inherent in this problem was the question of the limits of Mrs. Davis' authority; did she have the power to decide who she would accept as employees in the program or was she subject to the dictates of higher administrative authorities? There was no way of assuring Miss Nelson's loyalty to Mrs. Davis should she accept her. Miss Nelson had more experience in work with children than did Mrs. Davis; her presence within the program would pose a threat.

Although Mrs. Davis accurately perceived that she was expected to accept Miss Nelson into her program, she did nothing to facilitate this move. Three weeks later Mrs. Davis reported a conversation held with the Assistant Regional Director in which she had been told: "Miss Nelson has been very upset this week, but we are planning to encourage her to take a long vacation and then when she comes back she will report to Children's Services." At the time Mrs. Davis did not question this, but the following day she arranged a meeting with the Regional Director at which time she raised the question of her obligation to Miss Nelson. He responded: "I don't want her either, but that is my problem and you need not be concerned about it—you do not need to take her."

The problem came up in another form the following week when the Assistant Regional Director informed Mrs. Davis that Miss Nelson had been hired into a position that was officially designated by Civil Service as belonging to Children's Services, and therefore she would have to take her. Mrs. Davis again did not immediately respond, but instead obtained the job specifications from the Personnel Officer and determined that this was not so. Mrs. Davis then took steps to permanently solve the problem by removing the Nurse Administrator position from her staffing plans maintaining that her program did not call for that level of nursing skills. In this way she permanently blocked any further attempts to move Miss Nelson into Children's Services. In so doing, Mrs. Davis also blocked the development of plans for organization of nursing services for the remainder of the mental health center, a situation that prevailed throughout the time of the study.

In this process, Mrs. Davis established her independence further by not allowing herself to be manipulated. In the process she learned a number of valuable lessons: 1) that the Regional Director supported her despite the recommendations of his top assistant, 2) that staffing plans could be written as a means of controlling those to be employed within the program, and 3) that the influential and powerful figures in the organization were the Personnel Officer and the Hospital Administrator. This knowledge is summarized by Mrs. Davis:

> Friday (the Regional Director's) office called, and he wanted to see me at 4:00 p.m. (His assistant) had written him a memo about what I had said to her . . . I told him that that was what I had said, that I didn't want her in my program. He promised to take care of it . . . I haven't heard anything more.
>
> I thought the (Regional Director) and (his assistant) got along so well they would communicate back and forth about these things, but I've learned differently.
>
> I made another terrible mistake this week . . . I didn't realize what the Hospital Administrator's position was. I went in there about this and he told me how upset he was about something I had done . . . I didn't realize that he was responsible for everything outside of clinical matters—it would really help if a person were oriented to some of these things—fortunately he's the kind of person he is, and he was able to tell me without letting it drag on and on.

This experience aided Mrs. Davis to assess the balance of power within the organization, it provided an opportunity for testing the solidity of her position, and served to illustrate ways to circumvent pitfalls. Although the development of a staffing plan was incidental to this occurrence, Mrs. Davis learned, through talking with the Personnel Officer, how this could be used to control staff recruited into Children's Services.

In establishing a power position within the organization Mrs. Davis confronted the hazard of encountering conflicts with others similarly vying for position, in this case the Regional Director's Assistant and Miss Nelson. Having ascertained that there was a schism between Dr. Dixon and his top assistant the lines of conflict were drawn. In the process of solving this problem Mrs. Davis established alliances with the Hospital Administrator and the Personnel Officer that greatly facilitated gaining access to resources necessary to subsequent program development. Although she failed to rid the organization of their problems with Miss Nelson, Mrs. Davis' abilities to manage the Assistant Regional Director provided evidence to the other Program Directors of her abilities to maneuver within the organizational arena. Mrs. Davis was thus assured of a power position within this group.

Solidifying the Power Position

Within the first month of employment Mrs. Davis had successfully established herself within the organizational hierarchy. The Regional Director had given his "vote of confidence" by backing her instead of his Assistant. But the gains made in such a setting can never be considered to be permanent. A Program Director could be "winning" one day and out the next. Mrs. Davis now had to develop ways of protecting her position.

A particular hazard was the location of Mrs. Davis' office—next to that of the Regional Director's Assistant. Located in close proximity to someone whom she already had challenged was likely to pose a difficulty in "impression management." The ambiguities surrounding psychiatric treatment coupled with the difficulties of "making it" in the bureaucracy made it essential that the program be protected from direct scrutiny. Mrs. Davis' next maneuver was that of changing the location of her office. Through distancing herself from direct observation, opinions of the program could be formed on the basis of what Mrs. Davis reported; the visibility of the program would be diminished and Mrs. Davis' power would be increased.

The physical space occupied by an individual indicates his status within the pyramidal hierarchy of the organization. Although the Mental Health

Center facility was specifically designed to do away with such differentiations, staff at all levels spent considerable time rearranging the design of the buildings to achieve recognition of their differential positions within the organization.

The Mental Health Center was designed with a central core building designed to house Administrative staff. Surrounding this central building were twelve patient units; four of these units were designed for children. Mrs. Davis' original office assignment was to the Executive Suite in the Administration building. Mrs. Davis decided to move to the Children's Units on the basis of the following considerations: "I need to be close to my staff, and therefore I need an office over in the Children's Units rather than in the Administration building . . . I need to get the feel of the place to plan realistically for the type of program we can have there."

The original plan for the Mental Health Center complex had been heralded as an advance in architectural design for psychiatric hospitals. Numerous innovations in functional design had been made to promote the newest in psychiatric treatment modalities. One of the facets emphasized was the treatment potential of the buildings rather than an emphasis on such things as offices for staff members. The offices that were originally designed were all similar in size with built-in desks as standard equipment. The offices did not reflect a status differentiation among staff members. If Mrs. Davis were to move her office from the Administration building, where there was variation in office size, the offices available to her on the Children's Unit were similar in size to those staff members of a lower rank would also occupy.

In considering this political plight, Mrs. Davis realized that she must first isolate herself from the Administrative structure of the Mental Health Center so that she would have adequate freedom to maneuver. Secondarily, her office should be a visible symbol of her relative position. Based on these considerations, Mrs. Davis concluded that it would be detrimental to use an office similar to those occupied by others employed within the program. The solution advanced was to transform one of the rooms originally designed for a treatment area into office space for Mrs. Davis.

The Regional Director granted Mrs. Davis permission to move into a unit of Children's Services. The next step was that of making necessary adjustments in architecture to provide an office appropriate to her position. A room originally designed for learning activities was chosen. Having made this choice, Mrs. Davis had to convince others to make the necessary modifications. These negotiations were reported by Mrs. Davis:

> It's really funny how status-oriented everybody is around here. What I've been through to get my office. . . . First of all they've been trying to tell me where to put my office. First they said there wasn't a phone hookup where I wanted it. Finally they got out the blueprints and there were phone cables all over the place. . . . Every time I tell someone where I want my office they end up by telling me how bad they've got it. They end up asking me if I know where their office is, and how cramped and crowded they are. (The chief engineer) told me how he was down in the basement all crowded in with his secretary. I was just about ready to give up when Dr. — (consultant) came in the other day. I was so frustrated I was about to cry. He told me I was absolutely right, and that it was a disgrace where they wanted to put me. Finally (the Hospital Administrator) suggested the other room for my office, which is just right. But sometimes you wonder if it is worth the battle.

Repercussions from this move were felt several weeks later when Mrs. Davis reported a statement made by the Regional Director in an executive staff meeting:

> (He) said in the staff meeting that he didn't want any of the staff from the different programs housed on the units—their offices should be in the Administration building. He doesn't want people drilling holes through brick walls to make telephone connections.

Although Mrs. Davis concluded that the Regional Director was referring to her, she did not feel, since it was a public meeting, that it was the place to discuss the problem. Rather, she brought it up in a private conference with him: "It's impossible to run a program if you are not located in the building where the program is housed—especially if it is for children," was Mrs. Davis' position. These series of negotiations and maneuvers further served to solidify the independence of Mrs. Davis' position within the organization, both in relationship to the peer group as well as to those in higher administrative positions. Manipulation of physical space was a vital part of early impression management.

Although the original plans were to admit children three months after Mrs. Davis' arrival, Children's Services had just reached a stage of differentiation from the larger organizational structure. Mrs. Davis' major activities had consisted of political maneuvering within the Mental Health Center structure and little attention had been directed toward the children whom the program was supposed to treat. Mrs. Davis had established her position; the next step was to begin to develop the Program.

Chapter V

Negotiations and Change

Outlining program goals and establishing a power base within an organization does not imply permanence. Indeed, in the constant negotiation and renegotiation which occurs the goals themselves become negotiable items in the bargaining process.

In any organization a subsystem faces at least two options in plotting its own developmental course. First, goals of a subsystem may be formulated to conform to those of the larger organization. In this instance, the leaders of a subsystem devote extensive time and energy discerning the goals of the larger organization and developing strategies of piloting his particular part of the organization in a complementary direction. As organizational goals change, so do those of a subsystem. In other instances, the goals of a subsystem may be in conflict with those of the larger organization. Successful leadership of a subsystem with conflicting goals hinges upon the leader not only being knowledgeable of the goals of the larger organizations but also upon capabilities to develop strategies to accomplish conflicting programmatic goals. For example, the strategies which might be invoked consist of masking the conflict; in this instance, the leader would promote an image of conforming to organizational goals while in actuality propelling his part of the organization in a divergent direction. A second approach consists of developing other alliances outside of the organizational structure that serve to increase the power of a particular subsystem to such an extent that they become more powerful than the parent organization.

The possibilities of conflict between parts of an organizational system are accentuated in psychiatric organizations. In this case, the Children's program with its innovative goals for treatment was located within an organizational context, the state mental health system, with its implicit function of providing custody for those defined as "mentally ill." The professional psychiatric community provided a potentially powerful external alliance that could be used to further conflicting programmatic goals. Further, since the means of accomplishing the goal of treatment are ill-defined the possibilities of masking actual conflicts are multitudinous.

51

Maintenance of a position in conflict with that of the larger organizational system rests upon the ability of a program to garner sufficient power to assure a degree of autonomy. The sources of power available to this particular treatment program consisted of (1) providing a service needed by the larger organization, in this case treatment service for children, (2) developing powerful allies external to the larger organization, (3) developing strategies to cancel out the endeavors of higher administrative authorities to exercise control over the program, and (4) developing an ideological value system that could be advanced to defend the program from outside intrusions.

Internal program development was plotted against an external environment that was constantly changing. While the Program Director initially developed a program proposal directed toward meeting the expectations of the Regional Director for a short-term treatment program for children these plans did not materialize. Although the initial goals were to have the program operant within three months after Mrs. Davis assumed her position, children were not admitted into any phase of the program until the opening of the Day Care unit six months after the original projected starting date. The inability to meet these original goals was partially a result of changes in expectations advanced for this program by the outside organization. Instead of being able to organize around a consistent set of goals and purposes complementary to those of the larger organization, the process became one in which the program organized in a defensive manner to ward off the intrusions from the external world.

The Program Director spent the majority of her time and energy in negotiating within the context of the larger organization, and called upon consultants as a major resource in developing the internal structure of the program. The survival of the program became a major preoccupation, leaving any consideration of what the program was to accomplish as a secondary concern. Impression management, development of alliances, and control of input into the program and output into the larger organization became focal activities.

The New Administration

Mrs. Davis had successfully negotiated and established her position with the Regional Director, but having accomplished this, there were a series of major administrative changes that made it necessary for her again to go through a similar process with a new administrative leader.

While the Metropolitan area in which this Regional center was located was originally divided into two Regions, administrative reorganization merged these areas into one Metropolitan region under one administrative head. Simultaneously, the entire Metropolitan area was divided into three Subdivisions. The psychiatrists who had been Regional Directors were transferred to the Subdivision level and a state hospital Superintendent was promoted to the third sub-director position. They were placed under the administrative control of a Metropolitan area director. The logic underlying this reorganization was that it would yield a coordination of services for the Metropolitan area that previously had not been attainable. However, after only one month, the Metropolitan area director resigned his position. The ensuing or resulting reorganization had the effect of creating new divisions rather than unifying the organization.

Since the transfer of the two Regional Directors to Subdivision positions was considered by most to be a demotion, the psychiatrist transferred to this mental health center, Dr. Daniels, needed to create a positive impression in the eyes of the larger organizational structure. Dr. Daniels entered the organization with a set of statements indicating his orientation toward the community mental health movement and the needs of the "poor," popular causes in the state mental health system. His views are reflected in a "working paper" written two weeks after coming to the mental health center:

> Another step toward community based mental health services will be taken here this week as (we) prepare for full operation of the new System. Designed to deal more effectively with the overwhelming mental health problems of (the Metropolitan area) and nearby communities. Central features of this plan include:
> —bringing mental health services closer to people in need through 'screening, planning, and linking centers' in local communities.
> —equalizing the work load among state hospitals and among mental health centers.
> —pairing mental health centers and state hospitals in partnership for better service.
> —relating specific geographical areas to specific treatment units in the Mental Health facilities.
> —allowing for a unified administration which can deal with city, county, and metropolitan wide agencies.

The ideology advanced by Dr. Daniels was further specified in "Working Paper No. (3)" circulated three weeks later:

> *Most of these people are poor.* In many cases their financial status will be precarious or deteriorating. Many of them will be people without jobs or job skills. . . . Some will be passively dependent upon public welfare . . . Many will be unable to manage money when they get it . . .

these will be people struggling to survive in a hostile jungle full of economic hazards and threats. Their neighborhoods will have high rates of unemployment, crime, and delinquency. Many will come from broken homes, and whether black or white, more often than not headed by a woman deserted by men who have copped out, unable to cope with the strains of family responsibility. . . . Many of our clients will be social isolates . . . all of them will be unhooked, socially . . . These anxious, alienated people need to be linked up, not just to agencies, but to persons and groups.

These initial statements were sufficiently ambiguous and were interpreted by Mrs. Davis as supportive of the type of program she wished to develop.

A common hazard in interpreting such statements is to take them literally without considering that these statements of goals and philosophy are necessarily written to create and promote an impression, rather than to portray reality. The dichotomy between a public statement of purpose and the actual plans Dr. Daniels had in mind for Children's Services is reflected in Mrs. Davis' account of her first private meeting with her new "boss."

The first thing that bothered me was when he told me how great the program was (where he had been).

The first disagreement arose around the use of the word treatment in connection with the in-patient unit—he said that he preferred that I use the word management instead of treatment.

We toured the units and he was extremely negativistic and pessimistic about the suitability of the pavilions for the treatment of children . . . he related his prior experiences where children had been dumped in on them and they proceeded to destroy the building. He said 'Of course you intend to medicate the children and control them in that way' . . . that was one thing that I couldn't accept, so I began to respond with, 'I know I'm not a doctor—' He interrupted and said 'That's right.' But I continued, 'There is one thing that I feel strongly about and that is that medications should not be given unless it is absolutely indicated . . . medication should not be given just to control children.' He made no further comment.

He made it clear that he doesn't want children from the Metropolitan area here—he wants only children from the suburbs—he said that he didn't want this turned into a 'shithouse.'

He asked what I intended to do about autistic children. When I said that I didn't intend to take them into the program, he asked 'What will the public think?' I answered, 'You can attempt to please everybody and please nobody.' He didn't press me any further on the issue.

The battle lines were drawn. The difference between publicly stated philosophy and private policy is apparent: on the one hand the stated philosophy was to "serve poor people," but, on the other, if poor people are admitted to this modern facility they will only wreck it.

Mrs. Davis perceived her new superior to be a "threat" to what she wished to accomplish. From this point, the direction she chose was largely predicated upon opposition to the supposed outside enemy, Dr. Daniels, and the rest of the organization. Evidence of this tendency is shown in Mrs. Davis' account of an Executive staff meeting immediately following the announcement of administrative changes:

> The first thing that happened was that (the former Assistant Regional Director) pointed out that the budget was inadequate to open the remainder of the programs this biennium—in her presentation she completely cut Children's Services out, and this was not mentioned. However, when I brought this to the attention of the group they said that it had been an oversight.

Incidences such as this were interpreted as being an indication that the higher administration was against the development of Children's Services, and the battle became identified as one for survival. The lines are more clearly drawn in an interchange in Executive staff meeting one month later:

> I really blew up in staff meeting today—they were going on and on about the budget for adult services. . . . I raised the question about Children's Services . . . 'You will get what is left over' was the response and the discussion continued. Later I said, 'Now just a minute—I've been sitting here steaming—you said that when you were done with adult services Children's will get what is left over—now what is your intention for Children's Services?' . . . I have been here five months and have received no support . . . They had the nerve to suggest I was upset because I was a woman, and that Prestige and status issues were my concern. . . . I responded, 'I don't care about myself—I care about the program—either the program goes or I tell my staff it isn't going to go'. . . . I need two things—money to hire staff and knowledge that you aren't going to come along in a few months and say I can't do what I am doing.

In these initial encounters with Dr. Daniels there was some indication of attempts to negotiate differences; but as time progressed, there was steady deterioration in these attempts.

Two events served as culminating points in the test of power and the consolidation of the conflict situation. The outcome of these encounters served to solidify Mrs. Davis' power position within the larger organization. The first situation was an attempt on the part of Dr. Daniels to bring a Nursery School Program in from the Mental Health Center where he previously had been in charge; the second was an endeavor to hire a psychiatrist into Children's programs without Mrs. Davis' prior consent. Both maneuvers were an attempt to bring Children's Services under tighter administrative control by Dr. Daniels.

The first incident occurred three months after the administrative re-organization when Mrs. Davis reported that Dr. Daniels had announced in Executive Council that the Nursery School Program was being trans-ferred. This announcement was made without any prior consultation with Mrs. Davis. The previous day Mrs. Davis had been introduced to the Director of this Nursery School Program but without any indication that a decision had been reached to transfer this program into the or-ganization. Mrs. Davis interpreted this move as "undercutting my au-thority, and it is intolerable for me to stay in this position." Her immediate response was to write a letter of resignation. Having written this letter, she decided against submitting it until the following day, and in the interim, a number of events ensued that convinced her not to resign. Mrs. Davis related the following sequence of events:

> I called Dr. Cannon and he advised me not to leave. He said, 'That man is rotten—that's what I told you when he came.' Dr. Cartwright told me to 'stay and fight.'
> The (Personnel Officer) outlined a strategy whereby she might be able to absorb some of the staff from the Nursery School Program into my staffing plan, and thereby place them all under my authority—in the meantime, the (Personnel Officer) is attempting to stop up all of the key slots so that there will be no positions available to use for hiring higher levels of staff.

Subsequent steps taken by Mrs. Davis included contacting the Nursery School Director and attempting to ascertain the exact situation, and, in so doing, clarifying her position as administrative head. Then, a memo-randum to the Director of the Nursery School Program was written in which Mrs. Davis expressed the need to work out a number of details. The need for staff "to work in all areas of Children's Services" rather than in any one specific area, such as the Nursery School Program, were defined as problems.

The implication reiterated throughout the memorandum was that the staff working within the Nursery School Program would be taken into Children's Services on the same basis as any other staff members that might be recruited, and that the Nursery School Program would no longer have a unique identity. The Director of the Nursery School Pro-gram responded by stating that she had no desire to move:

> Dr. Daniels approached me about the move . . . but I have lots of re-sources here and can work things out—it would be personally incon-venient and also my staff needs to stay together because of the specialized nature of the program.

Through such negotiations external to those between Dr. Daniels and Mrs. Davis, the movement of the Nursery School Program into Children's Services was averted.

Another attempt to gain inroads into Children's Services was attempted by Dr. Daniels when he arranged to hire a psychiatrist for Children's Services without first consulting Mrs. Davis. His rationale was that Mrs. Davis as a Social Worker, was not qualified to interview doctors and that since this doctor was not trained in child psychiatry, she would need supervision which could only be provided under the auspices of Dr. Daniels. The psychiatrist, Dr. Peters, was to work in Children's Services only two days per week, and, according to Dr. Daniels, was to participate in establishing In-patient services. Again Mrs. Davis saw this as a threat to her authority. In response, she mobilized her primary consultant, Dr. Cartwright, who raised questions as to the qualifications of the psychiatrist for this position. Again, the attempt on the part of Dr. Daniels to make inroads into Children's Services was blocked, and again Mrs. Davis gained impetus in the struggle for power. Mrs. Davis, in justifying her power maneuvers stated that this was the only means by which she would be able to develop the type of program to which she was committed.

The process of modification and transition of program goals was plotted against a series of negotiations with the external world in which the independence of Mrs. Davis in developing her program was at stake. In these maneuvers for power positions, boundaries were engineered and maintained, the outside intrusions were fended off.

External Alliances

Success in handling conflict situations within the overall organization was based not only upon skill in direct power maneuvers with Dr. Daniels but also was dependent upon a series of outside alliances mobilized as a source of counterpressure. The following three alliances are of particular importance: (1) those with the external psychoanalytic community, (2) those with the state hospital within the region, and (3) those with a Metropolitan council headed by the former Regional Director, which had convened to collaborate in the discussion and planning of services for Children and Adolescents throughout the entire region.

Perhaps the most significant factor that was to shape the ultimate development of the program was the alliances built with the psychoanalytic community, and through this, alliances with the Director of the entire state mental health system. A continually recurring problem in

Mrs. Davis' power negotiations was her status as a social worker as compared to the other psychiatric professionals, particularly the high status psychiatrists. Since the prevailing view still holds that mental disorders constitute an "illness," the primary responsibility for treatment lies within the medical realm. This medical definition places restrictions on the area of functioning of other psychiatric professionals; particularly in the areas of diagnosis and treatment planning. Accordingly, decisions involving selection of patients into the program and plans for treatment necessitated consultation and collaboration with a physician. Unable to recruit a physician as a member of the program staff *per se,* Mrs. Davis had to rely upon the services of a consultant to perform these services.

The consultant hired to function in this capacity, Dr. Cartwright, had, at a prior time and in a different agency, been a supervisor of Mrs. Davis. The contracting by Mrs. Davis for the services of Dr. Cartwright represented a direct reversal of their former relationship of supevisor and supervisee with Mrs. Davis now in the role of supervisor. The awkwardness of this role reversal was further complicated when Dr. Daniels had attempted to hire a psychiatrist into Children's Services without the consent of Mrs. Davis. At this point Mrs. Davis was forced to call upon Dr. Cartwright as her representative from the physician group to review the credentials of the new doctor. Dr. Cartwright negotiated directly with Dr. Daniels in keeping the new physician out of the program. In order to block any further inroads of Dr. Daniels, Mrs. Davis necessarily aligned herself with Dr. Cartwright, although Dr. Cartwright was not a bonafide member of the staff. While this maneuver checkmated Dr. Daniels in such a way that he could not coerce her into following his directives, it also served to place Mrs. Davis in a position of dependency upon Dr. Cartwright.

Given this tenuous relationship to Dr. Daniels in which Mrs. Davis perceived herself as receiving no support for the development of the program and having already tested the power structure via her prior negotiations, her next step became that of building up alliances with alternative resources within the mental health system. Again Dr. Cartwright was consulted and came to the assistance of Mrs. Davis. Within the Metropolitan area in which this program was being developed there is a large and powerful psychoanalytic community; a number of child psychiatrists are a subgroup within this larger community. Dr. Cartwright identified herself with this community and used meetings of the Child Analysts as a forum to advance Mrs. Davis' cause.

At one meeting of the Child Analysts Dr. Cartwright attempted to get an audience for Mrs. Davis to present a report on the progress of the development of services for children. This request was denied because of Mrs. Davis' status as a social worker. Instead, the speaker at this meeting was the Director for the State Mental Health System. The major thrust of his presentation, according to Dr. Cartwright, was to present the on-going progress throughout the entire state in the area of Children's Services. His presentation was greeted by loud and persistent criticism on the part of the analysts. After a lengthy laceration of Children's Services Dr. Cartwright conceded that in general she was in agreement with her colleagues but that in her capacity as a consultant, she had witnessed a number of positive results in one particular program, that of Mrs. Davis. She then proceeded to quote facts and figures provided to her by Mrs. Davis before the meeting. On this note the formal meeting ended. Following the meeting, Dr. Cartwright was approached by the Director who thanked her for the support. Dr. Cartwright in turn used the opportunity to further advance the cause for Mrs. Davis.

Through this contact, Mrs. Davis arena of negotiation was altered and expanded. Subsequently when matters arose that could not be satisfactorily managed through Dr. Daniels Mrs. Davis found a way of directly approaching the state-wide director; in this way she circumvented the administrative hierarchy within the mental health center.

A second type of external alliance was formed with the State Hospital in the area. Prior to the reorganization there had been no other Children's Services available in the entire area, but with the realignment of facilities, the state hospital paired with the Mental Health Center provided a program for Children and Adolescents. This alliance was of particular importance in the face of ideological conflicts.

If this particular Children's program was to be selective in choosing patients "appropriate" to the setting, an alternative program for those deemed "inappropriate" must be provided. The significance of this alliance lay in the fact that it afforded an alternative resource for these children. The original reorganization plan called for each mental health facility to take patients from a specified geographic area. Through a series of conferences with the Director of Children's Services at the state hospital the following points of agreement were reached:

> The mental health center would take all clients from its specified geographic area *provided they were not judged to be long-term treatment cases,* in which case they would be referred to the state hospital.
> The mental health center would take only children *under the age of 16.* All adolescents in need of hospitalization would be sent to the state hospital.
> If the state hospital should evaluate someone from their area as in need of short-term treatment or a day care program they would be referred to the mental health center for those services.

This alliance provided an unprecedented amount of flexibility as well as providing the opportunity for the Children's Program to define the population it wished to serve. It also created a transferral mechanism so that the more difficult treatment cases could be moved to (or shunted off on) the state hospital system. Since very few children were likely to be considered as short-term treatment candidates it was highly unlikely that there would be many referrals from the state hospital to the mental health system.

A third alliance was formed with the Council for Children's and Adolescent Services chaired by the former Regional Director, Dr. Dixon. This council, composed of all heads of Children's programs throughout the Metropolitan area, provided a forum in which they could discuss their common problems and form coalitions. Mrs. Davis was discouraged from attending these meetings by Dr. Daniels who maintained: "they can do nothing—they are only an advisory body." Not heeding his advice, Mrs. Davis became an active member of the Council. The major significance of this alliance was that it allowed other Children's programs throughout the entire Metropolitan area to work out agreements in an informal manner which could bypass the (bureaucracy.) This added to the flexibility and the options open to the Children's program. These meetings provided critical information regarding the need for Children's Services which could bypass the bureaucracy. This added to the flexibility mental health center. This was a place where inferences about "administrative pressures" against Children's Services could be dropped with the assurance that they would fall on sympathetic ears. As this group developed they became further solidified in that they maintained "children's problems are different from adult problems; and therefore require a unique kind of planning and programming." In this way, the Council became a subtle force eliciting support and resisting external pressures which would otherwise attempt to control Children's Services.

The struggle for power and recognition, for successful bargaining and negotiation within the broader organizational context of this program played a large and crucial role in the development of this program. Virtually nothing which took place within the program was independent of a consideration of these external factors. And, although the program did not develop in accordance with the mandates of the external organization, the conflict was a motivating force in determining the ultimate direction and character of the program, its independence from the broader organization.

Part III
Development of Program Identity

Chapter VI

The Players

Who are the people who compose an organization? Any organization needs a wide variety of people with varying skills and personality attributes to produce an end product. For example, in a goods-producing organization there are those who participate in decision making as to the nature of the product to be produced as well as the means of production. There are those who design and create the machinery prerequisite to goods production. The bulk of employees in such organizations man the machines while a portion of this number supervise the operation. Still another segment of the work force participates in marketing the product. The contributions expected from each segment of such an organization are relatively well-defined and each individual has some idea of the nature of his contribution to the total organization.

Psychiatric organizations differ in that there are few clear definitions as to what varying segments of an organization are expected to contribute nor discrete definitions of the work to be performed. The end product to be achieved consists of changing an individual, the "patient." The means of accomplishing this end involves interaction with another individual, the "therapist." Although decision makers may write directives as to the numbers of patients each therapist is to treat and the duration of the treatment process the actual control of the operation resides in the hands of the therapist. Each therapist creates his own treatment devices; his techniques are not open to observation of others and the only accounts given of the treatment process are those offered by the therapist. Measures of efficiency or effectiveness are ill-defined and subject to debate. In short, the components of the production process in psychiatric organizations are ill-defined; the work of each individual within such a setting is largely a matter of personal choice and individual style.

Having established a position within the larger organizational arena, the next problem confronting Mrs. Davis was that of recruiting a staff that would reinforce her position as a leader. Since Mrs. Davis was a social worker, a profession somewhat low in the professional hierarchy,

63

recruitment of a staff was especially problematic. The dilemma confronting Mrs. Davis was this: To legitimate the work of the organization Mrs. Davis needed highly respected professionals as part of the staff, in particular child psychiatrists. Since she was a social worker, the presence of such highly trained specialists would pose a threat to her control of the program. On the other hand, if her staff were composed solely of lesser trained personnel, it would be difficult to maintain an image of providing the most advanced psychiatric treatment methods. A compromise between these alternatives had to be chosen whereby psychiatric professionals were available to the program to promote an image while the working staff was composed of lesser trained personnel.

A psychiatric treatment organization attracts a wide variety of people ranging from the highly trained professionals, such as the child psychiatrists with extensive education and preparation with allegiances to a larger psychiatric community, to unskilled staff whose training is totally within the confines of a particular program. The basis of commitment of these participants range from one rooted in personal advancement in career lines within a profession, such as the psychiatrist who uses the organizational setting as a base for the furtherance of his career, to one grounded in providing a basic, sustenance level of existence, as in the case of the unskilled laborer. Each participant comes from a distinctly individual background with divergent interests and outside commitments, but all interact within the organizational setting to further their own goals and, hopefully, to advance organizational goals. Their life paths, as it were, intersect within the organizational setting, and the fate of the organization to a large measure hinges upon the types of agreements and arrangements that people representing such diversity work out.

In this context, recruiting desirable applicants into the program and subsequently offering them sufficient incentives to assure their continued participation in the work of the organization becomes an organizational problem. Furthermore, a proximate problem is posed when those judged "desirable" are hired, and, once within the organization, prove themselves to be unsatisfactory. The ensuing dilemma becomes one of shunting these "undesirables," into diversionary channels, either within the organization or outside, so that they do not interfere with what becomes defined as the "work of the organization." Some stay and others leave but both categories play a significant role in the patterning that occurs within the organization.

In the case of this program, success within the political arena of the organization was not only contingent upon successful maneuvering and negotiation but was also based upon the program's ability to demonstrate a capacity for independent action. This, in turn, hinged upon the types of employees this program was able to recruit.

Two alternative routes were possible: highly skilled, professionally-trained staff could be recruited and the quality of their credentials used to provide evidence to the external world of the quality of the program, or a primarily unskilled, highly motivated, intelligent, young staff, was the other option. If the latter alternative were chosen, a selected group of professional staff would be necessary for purposes of training. And this was the choice made.

This course was chosen partially by design and partially in accordance with the inherent limitations of the Civil Service service system. More significant, however, was the fact that Mrs. Davis, being engaged in continuous conflict within the larger organization, needed to maintain complete control of her staff. Highly trained professionals, with their external alliances with a professional community and allegiances to values inherent within their group, would pose a threat to such control. This was particularly true of psychiatrists and psychologists who belonged to higher status professional groups. The non-professional workers not only had no qualifying credentials to present to the outside world, but would have only limited contact with others outside of the program hence limiting the possibility of their developing information that might prove detrimental to the program "image." Lacking as yet strong professional commitments, they represented a body of individuals anxious to learn. By entrusting the training of these workers to consultants who were highly trained professionals and yet loyal to the Program Director, the dual problem of maintaining in-group loyalty to the Program Director and impressional management within the larger organization was attacked. Having a group of untrained workers also afforded an excellent opportunity to indoctrinate them, without questioning, into predominant ideological values advanced within the program.

The "Therapists"*

The recruitment of staff into the program followed a developmental sequence. Segmentation of the staff into staff and supervisory levels did not occur until close to the end of the first year's operation. As staff were initially recruited a sorting out process occurred. Some decided to leave the program because it did not meet their expectations. Still others did

*The term "therapist" is used to designate that part of the staff providing direct services to parents or children in contrast to others, such as supervisors and consultants who provided indirect services.

not fulfill expectations held by Mrs. Davis and were shunted into diversionary functions. As the program developed the type of employee appropriate to this particular program became more clearly defined. An analysis of characteristics of those experiencing success within the organization as well as those sorted out lends perspective as to the nature of the program which developed.

Those involved in providing direct services within this Children's program consisted of psychologists, social workers, child care workers, child care aides, nurses, and teachers. Psychologists were the most professionalized participants within the organization. They defined their work as that of doing "therapy," while others tended to view their work as that of "testing." Of the four psychologists employed during the course of the study three were pursuing doctoral degrees. They composed the most highly educated segment of the staff; all left this program within the year.

Professional certification for social workers consists of completion of a Master's degree program and two years' supervision under a certificated social worker. Of the five social workers on whom data are presented, only one social worker, besides the Program Director, met these standards. This certified Social Worker, while technically a supervisor according to job classification, never functioned in that capacity. Three were classified as Social Work Trainees, while the fourth was, according to job classification, a Child Care Worker, but she saw herself as a Social Worker. Only one of this group, Miss Selby, had a Master's degree in social work; all others held Baccalaureate degrees. All were female; Miss Selby was the only single social worker.

Social workers were similar to psychologists in that, lacking the usual qualifications for their positions, they identified themselves with a professional group. A unique feature of such settings as this is that an individual, upon entry into the system, is given a professional label and patterns behavior according to that expected of a particular psychiatric discipline. As long as the individual remains within that system, or one similar to it, this professional identity is not challenged.

Social workers differed from psychologists in that they did not see themselves engaged in "scientific work" but rather in the interpersonal perspective of "working with people." Social workers primarily distinguished themselves from Child Care workers, who had similar qualifications, by emphasizing their role of working with families and doing therapy. Contrastingly, child care workers classified their role as that of "working with children," and were hesitant to designate this as therapy, even though their backgrounds of education were equivalent to those of the untrained social workers. Of this sample of social workers, only Miss Selby, the Social Worker Supervisor inherited by Mrs. Davis, left the organization during the time span of this study. All of the lower ranking social workers remained.

A total of four child care workers were interviewed: three were female and one was male. The primary requirement for this position was a Baccalaureate degree, preferably with a major in some area of liberal arts or social sciences, and successful completion of a Civil Service examination. Child care work does not fall within any single professional category. The binding characteristic holding this group of workers together is their interest in "working with children," and, in seeking employment, the opportunity to do such work took precedence over any professional career interests. This contrasted with the Social Workers whose interest in "social work" as a career line was of more significance than a particular program area.

Child care aides are differentiated from child care workers in that there are no specific educational requirements for the position; training for such work is conducted on the job. Four child care aides were employed during the course of this study; two remained and were functioning on a level equivalent to that of social workers or child care workers, while the other two left after only brief employment within the program.

The two remaining child care aides, Mr. Anderson and Mr. Andrews, were both attending college on a part-time basis and have career aspirations to become, respectively, a psychologist and a psychiatrist. They view their job as a means of subsidizing their income while gaining experience that will prove valuable in the furtherance of professional goals. The most significant aspect about this category of workers was that their self-ascribed status was far more significant in determining the nature of the work they were to do in Children's Programs than was their actual status. Mr. Anderson, like the child care workers, was directly involved in working with children, while Mr. Andrews saw himself as a "therapist" and was actively involved in this role.

In contrast, Mrs. Askew and Mrs. Allen were employed for a brief period of time early in the development of the program. Both were black. Both viewed this job primarily as a means of supplying necessary income and involving a type of work better than the "factory work" they had previously been involved with. Both left after only two weeks of minimal contact with the program; Mrs. Allen decided to work in adult services because "there was something to do there" and Mrs. Askew left employment in the Mental Health Center. Little effort was exerted to encourage them to remain within the program, and observations were made that it was perhaps "premature to hire child care aides" until the program was better established.

Only one nurse and one teacher are included in this study. They represent groups not specifically defined as "mental health specialists." Their experience within the organization illustrates two alternative routes individuals with their respective backgrounds chose in attempting to integrate their peculiar professional training into a treatment program for children. Mrs. Newman assumed the role of a child care worker and only secondarily used her special skills as a nurse and was successfully incorporated into the program. Mrs. Tatum, with defined career goals as a special education teacher, was unsuccessful within this framework and was encouraged to leave.

In summary, the group who were to be the primary participants in the work of the organization were composed mainly of young people with limited experience and varying career orientations. All were white and middle-class, with the exception of two black child care aides who left after only a limited contact with the program. The staff was composed primarily of women with the exception of the psychologists, all of whom left, and some child care workers. The highest attrition rate was in the group who saw themselves as professionals in particular, the psychologists, the social work supervisor, and the special education teacher; and, at the other end of the continuum, the unskilled, black, child care aides. The greatest stability was in the group of participants who had a generalized educational background with no specialized professional education other than that given within the context of the work setting.

Becoming a Therapist

How does an individual become a therapist? At some point in time an individual develops an image of what he/she wishes to become. For some a career identity develops early in life and provides the basis for structuring subsequent activities. For others, the development of particular career interests arise through associating with teachers or friends; with others, experience that causes an individual to perceive himself as "good" in some particular field of work acts as a precipitant. The participants in this particular program initially entered career lines in the psychiatric field by a variety of routes.

All the psychologists came from working class families, and all had worked to support themselves while acquiring an education. All were male. None held doctoral degrees, although one was enrolled in such a program at the time he became employed within the setting while another was attempting to gain entrance to such a program. The third had not yet acquired a Master's degree and revealed no aspirations to further his education.

Experiences in educational settings influenced psychologists in their career choices:

> Mr. Paulson: In high school I was sort of steered in the direction of philosophy. . . . I started reading things like Sartre and Camus . . . and then my French teacher said that for some of the underpinnings it would be good to read psychology—and then I went to college and it was high temperature chemical engineering . . . and then I just got discontented with it and went into psychology—I was thinking of something close to it like Industrial Psychology—I was thinking about Personnel work—so I figured I could get there by Psychology just as well—so I switched and it worked.
>
> Mr. Peters: I was interested in becoming an English teacher originally— I wanted very much to work with adolescents—for some reason I had the ability to work with kids—and apparently the desire to work with kids overroad the interest in English, because I later transferred and changed to social work . . . and then I became interested in psychology.

The two psychologists aspiring to a doctoral degree stressed the scientific aspects of the field as most appealing to them:

> Mr. Paulson: First of all it's a science—it really hits all aspects of human existence in depth and comprehensiveness and scope—you really get on top of the things that are happening—it makes you better able to deal particularly with the mental health field.

Mr. Packard stressed the research aspects of the psychologists role as most appealing to him, while Mr. Peters, with the most limited educational background, focussed upon "doing therapy" as his particular area of interest.

Social work, in contrast to psychology, was viewed as a way of doing something "practical." All social workers were female. Social work was viewed as an occupation compatible with their perceptions of appropriate work for women in our society.

The socio-economic profile of the parents was as follows: of the fathers, one was in a professional category, two in semi-professional occupations, and two were laborers; of the mothers, two had at one time been employed in clerical positions, but all, at the time of study, were unemployed housewives.

The process of recruitment into the profession was an outgrowth of experiences in college. All had majored in Sociology and looked upon Social Work as an outgrowth of this background.

Mrs. Shane: The introductory (Sociology) course was taught by a real neat guy and I got interested in that . . . and when I got finished with college it (being a social worker) was the only thing that I was equipped to do.

Mrs. Samter: . . . if I had known what I was doing I would have majored in psychology . . . that would have given me a better background for working with people. Sociology gives you a good background, but it doesn't give you any of the specifics. The courses that gave me a good background were the psychology courses.

Mrs. Sanders: My degree is a B.S. in correctional work. It was a sociology degree . . . and then I took minor work in anthropology and psychology. . . . I was interested in some kind of social work—some type of helping profession—something concrete. Sociology was so vague there wasn't much that you could do with it—. . . . So if you wanted to do something concrete, corrections seemed to be the thing to do. I'm not the type to be a teacher—I want to get out and do something.

All had majored in sociology in college, and all expressed a desire to be involved in what they characterized as the "real" world, implying a desire to help people in a direct way. Entry into social work to them was a compromise between their educational background, which they saw as abstract, and a concrete world of real problems and real people.

Child care workers, in contrast to psychologists and social workers, developed a desire to "work with children" in the context of earlier familial experiences. Occupational backgrounds of the fathers of these workers included two professionals (college professors), a small business owner, and a semi-skilled tradesman. Again, none of their mothers were currently employed, although two had worked for a short time as secretaries. Two female child care workers were married while the other two were single.

One of the major defining characteristics of this group, as contrasted to others, was the emphasis, rooted in their family origins, on the achievement of independence. Although the child care workers were from divergent socio-economic backgrounds, this tendency was evident in their interviews. This press toward independence perhaps motivated them to seek jobs outside of the usual professional categories; they were willing to chance pursuing non-traditional types of work. This desire for independence is expressed in interview data first from the college professors' daughters:

Miss Wilson: I never thought about going to college—it wasn't really a question of would I go, but where and what would I major in. I never considered not going . . . my father has always talked to me about how great it would be for me to be a teacher, and he wanted me to be a kindergarten teacher, but I never wanted to teach; I always had it in

the back of my mind that I wanted to work with children in some way.
Mrs. Williams: It was never questioned that we would go to college—
it was just what college are you going to. . . . I had a couple of summer
jobs working in southern rural areas—working with people who definitely
weren't too well off financially. . . . Two summers I worked in a community in Pennsylvania where the coal mining had gone out, . . . we
set up a day camp to help the children—to try to give them a better
outlook on life and to help them realize that there are better things than
what they are experiencing and maybe they could help influence their
parents.

Although expressed differently and stimulated by different environmental
pressures, Mrs. Wakefield and Mr. Waters revealed similar tendencies:

Mrs. Wakefield: I am especially getting into a bind with my parents—
they have thought that they have educated their children so that they
would get nice, good, jobs— . . . but they tend to forget that with it
comes a tremendous responsibility and increasing demands upon you as a
person to increase your education, and to keep up with what is going
on, and you get to a point in your life where you can't go back and keep
up with their ideals, and their ideas about what goes on in society—
they are on a different level, and once you get on a certain level, you
can't go back.
Mr. Waters: When I became 16 an unfortunate situation put me as head
of the family— . . . I actually supported the family while going to
college full time and working full time.

All child care workers majored in sociology while in college. The reasons for this choice were expressed in terms of "interest in people" rather
than in "things".

Mrs. Williams: Originally I thought that I wanted to go into social
work. Sociology seemed like a natural background, and the anthropology
(minor field) was what I was really most interested in . . . most of the
sociology courses dealt with research and methods rather than applied
sociology . . . but in anthropology we were studying the actual situations. . . . I've always thought that I wanted to work with people.
Miss Wilson: I thought about going into medical technology—I always
have liked science—but then I changed my major to sociology in the
middle of my junior year . . . I wanted to work with people rather
than be isolated.

Their interests and commitments to working with children grew out
of early experiences in which these individuals perceived themselves as
"good at working with children."

Mrs. Williams: I had experiences in working with children in my
summer jobs through the church . . . and when I came out of school I
wanted to work for awhile. But all the jobs that I was hearing about at
that time involved sitting at a desk writing reports for all of the people

> with Master's degrees. And then I began thinking that social work
> wasn't what I wanted because I wanted to be out working with people—
> I wanted to work with children . . . and then there was an ad in the
> paper wanting activity therapists for (a retarded children's hospital).
> Miss Wilson: I had two little cousins who were adopted, and I always
> thought that it would be interesting to work on adoption cases . . . and
> I worked for two years as a volunteer in a Children's Home.
> Mrs. Wakefield: I decided to take some Civil Service tests for the state,
> and I took one for Child Care Worker, which at the time didn't mean
> that much to me—I got a notice of a position available at the Pediatric
> Institute and they had a child care position open for a residential center
> for emotionally disturbed children— . . . I decided to try it . . . partly
> because I was desperate for a job at that point, and it seemed closer to
> what I was interested in than anything before.
> Mr. Waters: I told Mrs. Davis when I came here when she asked me
> what I wanted to do—I have come in through the back door—you have
> a service that I would like to work on because I like to work with kids—
> in some direct way—to assist them and help them with their problems,
> whatever they may be.

All of the child care workers had strongly developed interests in "working with children."

The "therapists" come from a diversity of experiential backgrounds.
The psychologists were upwardly mobile and saw this experience as but
one step on their career ladder. Female social workers, in contrast, viewed
this experience as complementary to their other roles as women in the
larger society. Child care workers had developed an early and enduring
wish to "work with children" and work in this program was a realiza-
tion of these aspirations. The Children's program provided the place
where the life paths of these individuals intersected.

Entrance into the Children's Program

Having made initial career choices in the direction of becoming psychiatric workers what precipitated the movement of these individuals into
this particular Children's program?

Three of the four psychologists employed within the program had had
prior experience in other areas of the mental health center. They described these experiences and the factors precipitating their move:

> Mr. Packard: I had been involved in research in the beginning. . . . The
> research involved a mass screening of children in an elementary school
> . . . we were interested in the detection of early indications of mental
> illness . . . the analysis is still ongoing, but the study itself is actually
> completed.
> Mr. Paulson: I was originally interviewed at a professional meeting by
> (a psychologist) from here, and he was just tremendous. . . . I came to

work here in the Out-Patient Department. . . . It was pretty crappy. (The psychiatrist) wanted me to maintain strictly testing . . . I got patients from some of the other staff in Intake . . . and then all of a sudden there wasn't a service anymore . . . and then since most of my experience had been with Children and Adolescents it was suggested that I come here.

Recruitment into the Children's program was a matter of expediency for Mr. Paulson and Mr. Packard upon the phasing out of their areas of employment. They viewed their present jobs as temporary fillers until such time as opportunities for other jobs that had more to offer in terms of professional interests and career advancement presented themselves. Thus, they were quickly disillusioned and dissatisfied with their experiences in Children's Services. Mr. Packard expressed this in relation to his first experience within the program:

Mr. Packard: (Mrs. Davis) didn't tell me how I was to function. . . . And then on my first day on the job I had three women telling me when I should test and who I should test . . . which is something that I had never had before . . . and that made me mad. . . . Mrs. Davis hadn't said anything about testing—and this was not part of the bargain, so to speak. And all of a sudden these people are bossing me around— telling me when to test, and how I should use my time. Frankly it perturbed me.

Mr. Peters, in contrast, expressed initial enthusiasm about the program in general and his contact with Mrs. Davis in particular:

First of all I was impressed by Mrs. Davis and her ideas—some of the ideas, for example, of assigning workers to work through all areas of the program and having the worker adapt rather than the child . . . . I like some of her ideas about taking children from the inner city.

The three psychologists inherited by Mrs. Davis quickly left the program while the fourth was recruited from outside. All viewed the program with a degree of skepticism.

Social work, to the untrained worker, was something that you "learn on the job." Upon graduation from college all took social work positions in a variety of agencies and reported their problems in coping with totally new situations:

Mrs. Sanders: I wanted a job in (my home town) when I graduated and the corrections jobs were all filled . . . Mental Hygiene had openings —I went to where they (a hospital) were just introducing Social Workers into the program without Master's degrees. . . . One of the problems that I had was that I didn't know about interviewing—I knew what I wanted to do—but there were probably some techniques that I didn't know . . . I was assigned to cases when I first started with no experience whatsoever . . . I would ask my supervisor how to deal with a problem situation. . . . Like what is the best way to lead into something—what is the most tactful way for me to get the responses, and she would sort of tell me . . . Of course it comes by trial and error, and you don't want to mess a family up when you don't know what you are doing . . . you get a vague feeling for the parent and you figure out how you are to approach them—just a feeling tone, that was the hardest thing—to know how to say something that could be so important to a family—and I felt so insecure in the whole thing.

Mrs. Simpson: When I came here I went to work in one of the Mental Health Centers. I was interested in working with the retarded or the southern white migrants and I did neither, working for them . . . they put me in what they called a Social Service Worker slot, but they didn't know what I was to do—it was a job with a salary and I did pretty much what I wanted to do—but I didn't know anything about the city and I was pretty lost. I did a lot of community work—and then I did Intake and some work with children and adults—but it was very helter-skelter, and I had no supervisor and I received no training.

Mrs. Samter: After college we came here and I went to work at ——— State Hospital. I went to work on an adult female ward . . . there was a lot to do and conditions were so poor that anything you did gave you a sense of satisfaction. . . . Practically, I think, I learned a lot there about being a social worker. . . . When I first came there I didn't know how to relate to them, and was even afraid to say something like 'Where did you come from?' because I was afraid that anything I might say would upset them. . . . after awhile I felt that I had gotten used to it, and that was one of the reasons I left, because I felt that I was getting as institutionalized as anyone else.

Mrs. Shane: I first went to work for a child abuse center—cases were referred there by hospitals and doctors when they suspected child abuse, and we carried parents in treatment—we were mainly set up as a diagnostic unit—they were analytically oriented and I learned a lot—at first it was really great because we had good supervision—and then the whole place changed.

Socialization into the social work profession occurred within the context of "on the job" experiences; they were ambivalent about additional educational experiences within this setting. On the one hand they recognized a need for continued learning and supervision, but on the other they felt the seminars conducted jointly for them and the Child Care staff were too unsophisticated. This image of themselves as "quasi-professionals" may be contrasted with Miss Selby's definition of her role as primarily one of teaching and supervising junior staff members. Her view of social workers with graduate training included the idea that they were still unprepared: "Social workers when they come out of school are not considered finished products . . . the system is usually that you have a supervisor until you are ready to supervise others." With this backlog of experience and with this concept of the Social Worker as a professional, Miss Selby had considerable difficulty adjusting to her position within the Children's program. Ultimately she left to join another state program which afforded her an opportunity to work with "colleagues having similar backgrounds and training—these workers are not equipped to handle the work they are assigned."

Social workers were recruited into the Children's program at a time when other avenues of employment appeared to have reached a "dead end." Miss Selby and Mrs. Simpson had been employed in other areas of the Mental Health Center. Mrs. Shane and Mrs. Samter had been employed in other agencies within the Mental Health network, and Mrs. Sanders was newly married and had come from another state where she had worked in a Department of Mental Hygiene facility. They had been referred to this particular program either by friends who worked within the Mental Health Center or by the central office of the Mental Health Department. Factors that they cited as influential in affecting their choice of accepting a job in this program centered around their perceptions of the situation—that they would be able to do the type of work they were interested in, and their favorable impression of Mrs. Davis.

> Miss Selby: We talked about using a short-term hospitalization, and then moving the child to day care and into the community. . . . I think she expects me to help her in the evolvement of the program. . . . I think the plan is an excellent one—if I have any reservations they are definitely related to my experience—where I think there are few children that can make a change in this time.
> Mrs. Shane: One of the people from my unit was out here, and I decided that I had to get out of that agency . . . . I was very impressed with Mrs. Davis. She seemed like a real dynamic person who had a lot to offer and someone I could work with.
> Mrs. Samter: I get the feeling here that there is more of an emphasis on quality than quantity. . . . Here you can look at who possibly can be help and concentrate on helping those few, rather than having to deal with so many, and this I agree with.
> Mrs. Sanders: She said they were just in the planning stages and it wasn't all clear cut—that there would be both mentally ill and retarded children and that there would be a team approach—that we would be working a lot with families, and this is approximately the same thing I was doing before.

This program, to the social worker, offered the possibility of continuing in a chosen professional line, and, in this way, advance a career that had been initiated in a somewhat haphazard manner.

Three of the four child care workers had prior work experience with children following college and before being employed in this program.

Mrs. Wakefield and Mrs. Williams worked in Children's programs in the Mental Health System while Mr. Waters had worked one year as an elementary school teacher. Prior experiences served as a baseline in projecting their expectations for the future within this Children's program. Mrs. Wakefield, who had been employed in a program for emotionally disturbed children described her experiences:

> When I went in there I wasn't prepared for what was coming . . . . there was always a lack of proper staff and there weren't any people to train you . . . . I was on with someone else for three days and after that I had the group myself. There was absolutely no training. . . . I didn't realize how difficult it was until after I began understanding what was going on, and then I could look back and see all that I had missed in the beginning—the severity of their illness and their really tremendous needs began to sink in. . . . I would never go back to a setting like that.

Mrs. Williams, who had been employed in a hospital for retarded children, had different kinds of problems:

> I was in charge of setting up the Activity Therapy Department and then once I got it set up, training the staff. Actually we all sort of learned together because I hadn't had the specific training either. I had about three days of training after I was hired. I spent about a month in which I was supposed to be oriented, and they brought in my first four assistants. . . . It was mainly a job of supervising and figuring out training programs . . . not too much actual work with children.

Mr. Waters found his one year of teaching an unsatisfactory experience:

> I taught fifth grade—oh, I enjoyed it, but it didn't fulfill the need. First of all, I had a class of forty and I saw a lot of kids with problems but I didn't feel that I could help them with their problems—I tried to in some sense, but I felt that I couldn't divide myself up among forty kids. And so it wasn't exactly what I wanted to do.

From these points of view the Children's program seemed to hold more promise.

Three of the four child care workers were recruited through private inquiry as to what positions in the area of "work with children" were available in the state mental health system, while the fourth heard of the Children's program from a friend who worked within the Mental Health Center and applied directly for a position. All had vague ideas as to what the program involved and what their functions would be within the program:

> Mr. Waters: What impressed me most was Mrs. Davis—even that first day from the conversation I must have impressed her in such a way that she made me feel that I could be of help here, and could really

fit in well and I know it made me feel so at ease—she didn't know the program herself so she just gave me a general idea . . . working with the group team seems very interesting to me and it seemed like it was something that I wanted to be part of.

Mrs. Williams: She (Mrs. Davis) didn't tell me specifically what my job was going to be, but she did tell me the basic set-up of the program. . . . I'm very favorably impressed.

Miss Wilson: It sounded like the kind of program that I would like to go into—I like the philosophy—I liked the idea that the child would be assigned to a group—but that it would be personalized—She (Mrs. Davis) seemed to be really interested in what was going on.

Role Perceptions

Given this backlog of experiences and career aspirations this group of employees faced a common task of defining the work of the organization as well as defining their particular contribution to the total operation. An employee wanting to "work with children" needed to negotiate with others for this right. All brought into the organization ideas of what they wanted to accomplish through this experience.

The primary factor differentiating the three psychologists interviewed was their degree of educational preparation and the degree of socialization into the professional role of psychologist. This tendency is reflected in their statements of their perceptions of their roles in the program as well as the way in which they saw themselves relating to others representative of other disciplines.

Mr. Packard: I see myself in a teaching role—this is a model that's being shown for psychologists . . . and I think this is where psychology ought to be. They've got a rich background in things that are supportive whereas psychiatry and social work seem to be going on a practical kick which doesn't have strong underpinnings in terms of research-supported evidence . . . psychologists are sophisticated in research techniques—it's sort of a cause with me.

His analysis of alliances between social workers and psychiatrists was expressed.

Here you have a social worker who is head of a unit coming in with what sounds like a different model, and then all of a sudden you hear about psychiatric consultation . . . and then you scratch your head and say 'Isn't that a new variation on the same theme?'—that's the message I'm getting.

Mr. Paulson similarly stressed the educative role of the psychologists: "It's an educative role—to deal with the observations and activity of the people involved . . . and to help those who work with the child understand what is going on." Mr. Peters, with the least education, saw himself in such a role only minimally as "kind of orienting—people with less training than you look to you for some kind of leadership. But I don't see myself sitting down and conducting training sessions." Instead he saw himself primarily as a therapist:

> My first feeling is that I would like to work with children in the program—in direct contact—play therapy, as well as having something to do with their development in the milieu. And, of course, I have a concept that I will be doing psychologicals which I enjoy—I get a feeling of gratification from making a correct diagnosis.

The psychologist's interests and satisfaction with the job highly correlated with his level of education as well as with future career aspirations. Although all four left the program during the time of the study, the three with higher levels of training left to take jobs they felt afforded them more opportunity for career advancement and development as psychologists, while the other, with lesser training decided to go to Europe with no formulated plans for any further work, other than tackling what "might be interesting or available in Europe."

The more highly trained psychologists had well-developed ideas of who should be treated in such a program as well as ideological commitments to specific treatment modalities, and, consequently, resisted conforming to an ill-defined treatment program that might prove hazardous to their future professional careers.

Role perceptions of social workers varied according to previous experiences as well as their appraisals of what would be expected of them in this new position; but primarily they defined their role as one of "working with families."

> Miss Selby: I would assume part of my job would be to help interpret family interrelationships, and to help make clear to them what you can expect and what you cannot expect the family to do. . . . I see the social worker as a buffer between the staff and the family . . . and, of course, the social worker helps with the transition of the child back to the community . . . she is in a position where she had been trained to bring together services and people . . . and, of course, I would also like to do some supervision and teaching.
> Mrs. Sanders: I like working with families and that is what I am best at—working with the families themselves and their children.
> Mrs. Samter: I don't know how the therapy part of this works, but I know that the child care worker is with the child all day and gives them support and someone to relate to, but as far as therapy goes I still don't know who is going to do it—if I am going to give therapy to these kids it is going to be different than if a psychiatrist would do it.
> Mrs. Shane: It was sort of vaguely outlined—that I would have some

opportunity to do individual treatment of children and of parents, and in doing social studies. . . . I have a pretty clear-cut idea of what I want to do . . . . I would like to have some experience working with kids in therapy.

Mrs. Simpson: I see myself as a team member—and also as a social worker—I will probably be doing work with families more than with children. I think there will be a chance to be involved with children. . . . I'm not sure it's as intensive an involvement in the treatment per se.

While Miss Selby saw her role as managerial and in the social work tradition, the lesser trained workers viewed this experience as an opportunity to broaden their repertoire of "social work" skills. Miss Selby's career lines were clearly outlined, within the social work profession, while the lesser trained workers had commitments to husbands and anticipated families as primary goals with social work career plans of secondary importance.

Social workers perceived their area of work as providing an opportunity to interact with people in a direct manner while simultaneously affording them a learning experience upon which further work in this area was contingent. Social work was viewed as interesting, as a way of contributing to family income while husbands were completing educational programs or were beginning business careers, and as a line of work that was enjoyable while simultaneously compatible with further aspirations as wives and mothers. Miss Selby, viewing her life from the perspective of a career, left the organization because she did not see mobility possible within this setting; she had not become a part of the planning body, her assignments were multiple and diversionary, and she was isolated in an attempt to keep her from disrupting what became defined as the "work of the organization." Miss Selby left to work with former colleagues whose career aspirations were more compatible with those she held.

All the child care workers were still employed in the program at the completion of this study and all were involved directly in working with the children—their initial desire. All expressed interest in further education, but none had formulated any definite plans with the exception of Mr. Waters who was attending graduate school on a part-time basis with an immediate goal of attaining a Master's degree in sociology.

As the program evolved the work became divided in the following manner: Psychologists were therapists to individual children and did diagnostic interviews and psychological testing. Social workers did family interviews and became family therapists, while the child care workers were involved in intensive work with the children. The nurse became one of the child care workers, while the teacher tutored a couple of the children.

Those who left the organization during the first year were the four psychologists, the social work supervisor, the teacher, and two child care aides. It may be hypothesized that strong identification with a professional group outside of the organization was one of the factors creating instability in the "professional group," particularly when other participants in the setting lacking professional credentials, were afforded equal status in the tasks assigned them. The professional image of those who already considered themselves to be "experts" interfered with efforts to indoctrinate them into this particular program. The teacher, for example, who had learned techniques of operant conditioning, was unwilling to accept at face value the analytic orientation toward treatment of the child, particularly in that she did not see any way of applying these principles in the classroom situation. The psychologist, who had been taught values of scientific problem-solving, was unwilling to accept the "intuitive" approach of the social worker.

The non-professional, having no such outside commitments and not socialized into a professional role accepted direction from those considered to be psychiatric professionals. During the formative stages the organization was staffed by relatively untrained individuals and by the program director who called upon outside consultants to tackle the job of training this body of workers. In this way there was a filtering out of all criticisms that could have been raised by those coming from divergent backgrounds. The significance of this tendency will be illustrated in subsequent chapters when the training and diagnostic processes are considered.

The Managers

Two types of managerial personnel were employed within the program; consultants and supervisors. Consultants were employed from outside primarily for educational purposes, and supervisory levels were developed internally as the program grew. The material in this section was gathered through observation and discussion with Mrs. Davis rather than in interviews. The lack of interview material for this group resulted from two factors: 1) it was never clear who was to become part of the supervisory staff, in fact, there was no internal supervisory group during the course of this study, and 2) this work was left largely in the hands of outside consultants, some of whom ultimately decided to become full-time staff members.

Consultants

Consultants served to supplement the role of the Program Director without disrupting the internal allegiances between staff and Program Director that were so vital within the early stages of operation. A resumé of the contributions each consultant made will serve to clarify the ways in which this system operated to the mutual benefit of the consultant and the Program Director. The first two consultants, the psychiatrists, had served in this capacity prior to the arrival of the Program Director. Both served as members of an advisory board within the state system for Children's and Adolescent Services. Through use of these consultants as resources, Mrs. Davis got vital information to guide her early planning. They, in turn, were engaged in private practice and had a need for treatment resources for children. As the program took shape, Mrs. Davis' need for these consultants diminished, and they were summoned only in times of emergency when Mrs. Davis needed to invoke the power of the medical profession.

The third psychiatrist, Dr. Cartwright, functioned to supplement the role of the Program Director by adding the weight of medical authority to the internal decision-making of the organization. Although a consultant, she became progressively more significant to the staff as evidenced by her invitations and participation in social activities conducted by the staff after business hours. Dr. Cartwright, because of prior alliances with Mrs. Davis, offered assurances that she would not jeopardize or undercut the relationship existing between Mrs. Davis and her staff. This factor provided her with entry into the internal organizational scene.

Mrs. Carroll, a social worker consultant, was hired early in the history of the organization to conduct training seminars in the Intake and Screening process. She had been employed in the same agency as Mrs. Davis, and, on this basis, was considered trustworthy. Her role within the program was expanded so that ultimately she became a full-time staff member responsible for the Intake service. Thus, her function progressed from that of training workers to do the initial work of the organization to becoming responsible for directing the coordination of this work with other parts of the program.

Mr. Carey was likewise a social worker, but his primary area of experience had been in conducting a day care program within a private agency. He was initially to consult with staff from the day care unit about problems arising from their interaction with the children. During the course of this work, the program he headed was terminated by the agency, and he also became a full-time staff member, responsible for the direction of the Day Care program.

A third social work consultant, Mr. Camin, was engaged in private practice treating children. He had completed a specialized course conducted within the Psychoanalytic Institute, and as a product of this experience, saw himself more as a psychotherapist than as a social worker. Although highly skilled, his mixed loyalties made his contribution to the organization of questionable value in the eyes of the program participants. Initially, he was hired to conduct diagnostic interviews with children as part of a staff training program, but in so doing, his diagnostic impressions were often conflicting with those reached by Dr. Cartwright in the diagnostic seminars. Further, his contact with the staff stimulated him to make several psychoanalytic interpretations about the structure of the organization. For example, he commented that "Mrs. Davis needs a man to share in carrying the responsibility of the program." In so doing he further appeared to be a threat to the internal power structure of the program. The staff increasingly expressed dissatisfaction with his "non-directive approach" in conducting seminars, and, ultimately he was encouraged to leave.

In this manner, consultants served to fill gaps that existed within the organizational structure and contributed the necessary skills to enable the program to develop without intruding upon the alliances established between staff members and the Program Director. The program, in exchange, afforded the consultants an arena of practice where they were the recognized experts. In addition to the consultation fees that served to supplement their incomes, they also received other side benefits. The psychiatrists, with private practices, encountered children they perceived to be untreatable in the setting of an office practice. They therefore had a vested interest in the development of a treatment resource to fill this void. The social work consultants, in contrast, used this opportunity to evaluate the possibility of full-time employment within the program, sensing the unstable nature of their current positions. On this basis reciprocal relationships between consultants and the Program Director were established.

Supervisors

As the program enlarged, it became necessary to introduce a middle-management level. Mrs. Davis could no longer deal individually with each of her staff members; there was a need for differentiation as new units were to open. Recognizing this problem, Mrs. Davis' first inclination was to hire supervisory staff. In this capacity, Miss Travis, a special education supervisor at a day school for emotionally disturbed children, was hired as "Acting Director for the Day Care Program." The initial employment of Miss Travis was a result of misinterpretation of cues exchanged between Mrs. Davis and one of her psychiatric consultants. The latter had referred her to consult Miss Travis about the requirements for special education within the program. While talking with her about this, Miss Travis indicated that she might consider changing jobs. Since the psychiatric consultant had referred her to Mrs. Davis, it was assumed that he was favorably impressed by Miss Travis. Mrs. Davis seized upon her as a possible recruit who might be incorporated within the program to meet the need for supervisory staff.

When Miss Travis entered the organization, she immediately set up a series of "planning meetings" based upon her perception of her role as "Director of Day Care." When she began assigning tasks to staff they expressed dissatisfaction. Miss Travis unwittingly was treading upon territory previously covered by Mrs. Davis, and staff suspected that Miss Travis intended to set up a "school" rather than their envisioned "treatment program." An early ideological conflict arose around the issue of education vs. therapy. The culmination of this conflict was the removal of Miss Travis from her position as "Acting Director" with Mrs. Davis again assuming control of this area of the program. Miss Travis was increasingly isolated from the operational direction of the program and was made responsible only for the direction of teachers employed within the program. The subsequent resolution of the need for supervisory staff was to recruit them from the consultant ranks on the basis of proven loyalty and ideological commitments in conformity with the norms developed within the program.

Ultimately the Program Director and the consultants were considered the specialists within the organization; other staff learned and accepted their direction. Any outside commitments or loyalties interfering with this relationship were perceived as threats and all intrusive foreign elements were weeded out. Employees who could not function in such a setting moved out; either because they saw no future for themselves in such a setting, or they were shunted to other areas of the organization and thus isolated from the staff and prevented from having any significant influence over program development.

While the majority of the staff lacked the desired professional skills qualifying them for the treatment of emotionally disturbed children they expressed willingness to learn and a commitment to values generated within the program. Consequently, they helped to foster the correct impression, necessary for negotiations with the external world. Furthermore, since their qualifications were not as complete as those of the professionals, and since they were primarily searching for an opportunity to learn, they were hired at lower salaries. This could always be used by the Program Director as an example of sound management, which was important in her relationship with a peer group of administrators competing for the same resources.

Mrs. Davis' position within the organization was buttressed on all sides. Assuring the Regional Director that she would provide the type of Children's program he needed to reinforce his position solidified that relationship. Successful negotiation resulting in the engineering of program boundaries identified Mrs. Davis as a powerful member of the Program-Director group. Recruitment of a staff dependent upon Mrs. Davis for career mobility with limited outside resources of power served to solidify her leadership internally. The consultants served to legitimate program activities to the larger child psychiatric community. A power base sufficient to facilitate program development was established, but what was the nature of the program to be developed? That was still to be determined.

Chapter VII

Casting

In any work organization, one managerial task that must be accomplished consists of coordinating the work and developing group cohesiveness among participants. In situations where the work of the organization, and that of each individual, are clearly defined the work itself serves as the focal activity for structuring group relationships. But in situations where no such basic definitions exist, the problem of developing group cohesiveness among the workers becomes accentuated.

In some types of work organizations people can come to work, fill their place on an assembly line, and leave at the end of their eight hours with little necessity for any interaction with their co-workers. In contrast, within psychiatric organizations, the importance of the group becomes accentuated. The characteristic working day of a psychiatric worker consists of hours of meeting with others, both on a formal or informal basis. A high value is placed on the importance of resolving differences among co-workers, reaching group decisions, and involving group participants in the planning operations of the organization. In the case of this psychiatric treatment program where little of the actual planning had been done and there was no pre-existent structure, emphasis upon group activities was accentuated. How then, given such an array of participants, did the group proceed in their task of developing a Children's program?

Since this staff was employed to develop and work within a child psychiatric treatment program, it would be anticipated that a focal activity would be discussion of matters pertinent to this task. Instead of discussing child psychiatric needs, much of the discussions centered around the interpersonal relationships of employees. Decisions such as the types of children that would be accepted and the nature of services that would be offered if reached, were reached as an outgrowth of competitive struggles between individuals rather than through more rational processes. A further factor, the political climate surrounding the program necessitated that conflict be confined and handled within the program. Thus, development of group cohesiveness within the program was the predominant theme. Such solidarity was achieved, as indicated earlier, through recruitment and retainment of a staff composed of individuals representing relatively homogeneous backgrounds of experience and training. Once within the organization, the training processes which ensued served to foster in-group identification.

In addition to these overt processes, group identification was fostered through a number of more subtle factors. The structuring of relationships within this program occurred at two levels: (1) an informal network of opportunities for socialization built into the system, and (2) formal processes of role-differentiation for individuals within the setting.

Roles, to some extent, are predefined by the participants as they enter the organization with a certain repertoire of behaviors learned in other contexts. This predefined "behavior-set" becomes modified in the new setting and results in role behavior appropriate to this new experience. The organization, in defining its structure, transmits and executes its work by allocating it to various participants. Some of this role distribution occurs when participants bargain around conflictual issues.

As the size of the organization expands, the need for formalization of the unwritten or informal agreements by which the participants govern their behavior becomes necessary. Concrete measures such as the allocation of space so that those who work together share a circumscribed physical area and the establishment of rules, procedures, policies, and schedules are initiated. Ironically only a small number of the rules are followed in the actual work situation. This repertoire of managerial ploys built into the organization are invoked only in special instances when they are needed to confront an individual with the demand to fit his behavior into the organizational structure.

Although the primary goal of the organization was supposedly that of treating emotionally disturbed children, the major portion of time spent in meetings and outside was devoted to a discussion of the managerial problems of the organization with a secondary emphasis on problems of training employees and diagnosing clients. Throughout the span of this study there is a noticeable lack of interaction specifically relating to the types of treatment methodology to be used.

Structuring of Relationships
Between Participants

A noticeable characteristic of psychiatric settings is the amount of time people spend in talking to one another. A second observation is that rarely is the content of their communication directly related to the work of the organization. A frequent criticism leveled against psychiatric professionals, particularly by others in the medical field, is that they "never do anything over there—they only talk." This tendency is perpetuated by some myths arising from the assumptions underlying the practice of hospital psychiatry itself; that is that all problems occurring between individuals can be resolved if people talk about them, and secondarily, that the fate of patients is dependent upon the quality of the dialogue, the "openness of communication" between participants involved in the treatment of patients. During the course of this study it is estimated that, on the average, each individual spent approximately seventy-five percent of the "working day" involved in some type of group dialogue while only the remaining twenty-five percent was spent in direct work with clients, either through phone contacts or interview situations. Frequently the amount of time available in working hours was not sufficient and the communication would continue in informal gatherings outside of the program area per se. It may be argued that one of the reasons for such a pattern was that there were no children in treatment during much of this time, and conversation was a way of filling the time; but, on closer analysis of the content of the communication, it appears that much of the dialogue served the purpose of structuring the types of relationships possible between participants within this work setting. Lacking concrete, definable tasks around which they could organize their relationships, the individuals involved discussed a multitude of issues that provided some grounds for them to relate to one another in a work situation. It may also be pointed out that, given the political context in which the program was developing, the primary emphasis became that of survival while the actual treatment of children became a secondary concern.

Informal social groups are essential and effective in supporting the organization's goals and practices since they create important group identifications. Realizing this, Mrs. Davis early in the program, designated one room to be used as a "staff lounge." According to Mrs. Davis, "Staff need to get away from children—I plan to put a coffee urn in here, and a couch and comfortable chairs so they can relax." This room became the morning gathering place for coffee and doughnuts and an abundance of conversation. The function of informal discussions around such issues as marriage, politics, and race relations was that of establishing common grounds on which subsequent alliances could be based. One of the favorite topics of discussion engaged in by the younger women in the program were such things as their apartments, the houses they were buying, clothes they had bought, places they had been on weekends, and a multiplicity of similar topics related to their personal lives. Miss Selby and the psychologists were excluded from these conversations. Mrs. Davis and her secretary, who had seven children, assumed advisory positions in these discussions.

Since Mrs. Davis was black and the rest of the staff was white, a topic of discussion introduced about a month after the initial group of employees was formed was that of the "racial joke." These "jokes" were mainly exchanged between Mrs. Davis and her secretary, with the rest of the staff assuming the role of involved listeners and occasional participants. Typical types of anecdotes told by the secretary were:

> Yesterday my child came home from school, and a Negro boy that sits in front of her had knocked her color crayons off the desk. She called him a dumbbell to which he replied that his mother had told him never to let anyone call him a dumbbell or a nigger. My daughter responded by saying, "Well, is dope all right?"

The types of stories told by Mrs. Davis in response to these anecdotal accounts of the secretary were centered around her children.

> One day my little boy came up to me and said, "Mommy, can I get a racer?" to which I responded, "I don't know—we will have to see . . . why do you want a racer?" He responded, "So I can join the racer riots."

These anecdotes served the purpose of initially testing out relationships of participants in terms of racial differences. After these initial interchanges, lasting for about two months, the racial joke ceased to be a topic of communication.

Another development related to race revolved around staff's response to the assassination of Martin Luther King, Jr. The week prior to the assassination the staff had engaged in a dialogue about race riots. (Mrs. Davis was not present at the time of this discussion). Miss Selby expressed her opinion that "some of these leaders that talk about being non-violent are really passive-aggressive and end up by stirring up a lot of trouble." This led to a discussion of open housing in which staff consensus seemed to be "it's all right. Just so they don't live in my neighborhood." The morning after the assassination, the tenor of the conversation changed and they talked about "what a terrible thing this is," and "He really was a great man." Mrs. Davis entered the room during this conversation and reported her reactions. "I listened calmly to all the broadcasts last night, and then it hit me—on the way to work when I got on the expressway and I saw all of those lights on the cars—I cried like a baby." The sharing of these experiences again served the purpose of establishing other's positions vis-à-vis the individual.

Discussions of politics served a similar function:

Miss Selby: I'm delighted to see everyone floundering around now with nothing to build a platform on (since Johnson withdrew and they can no longer criticize him).

Secretary: Bobby Kennedy really gained popularity in Indiana.

Miss Selby: I don't think that the Kennedy family is the best choice for this position—I have a suspicion of people who have had wealth for generations, and furthermore I think he is an opportunist jumping into the campaign after McCarthy's success in New Hampshire, and then the way he acted following King's assassination.

Secretary: I don't think he was necessarily an opportunist—that's politics and that's the way the game is played.

Mrs. Davis: Kennedy has gained an amazing amount of support in the past days, and I don't feel that he is using King's assassination to gain support, but that perhaps these happenings will precipitate a re-examination of his feelings, and that he will come out with some positive programs, particularly for the poor of this country.

Miss Selby: But they are so opportunistic. The Kennedy family employs a public relations firm to keep the memory of Jack alive.

Secretary: If it weren't for the fact that state employees are not allowed to campaign I would be out setting up a campaign headquarters for Kennedy.

Miss Selby: You don't understand me—I don't have anything against wealth, but it's this emphasis on establishing an image.

Mrs. Wakefield: Let's face it—if a guy is a dynamic hard-driving person he is going to get wealthy, and that's the only kind of guy who is going to make it into the presidency.

Miss Selby: I wish we had a system like the British where the campaign was paid for by the government.

Mrs. Simpson: Rockefeller might run.

Mrs. Davis: If he ran I would vote for him. I don't think it is necessarily bad to be wealthy—a person who is wealthy can do one of two things—he could be like a Rubirosa who spent his wealth having a good time, or he could do something for mankind.

Miss Selby: But a wealthy person is too easily out of touch with the problems of poor people.

Although discussions such as these had little to do with the work engaged in by the participants within the organization, yet such dialogues served to establish a context in which alliances and coalitions could be formed that would later be re-enacted in discussion of problems more immediately relevant to the work to be done. And, further, although there is no way to positively validate this impression, one's status in the course of informal discussions often portended his success in other areas. Acceptance of ideas introduced in meetings was based more upon the position of the individual in the informal structure of the organization than on the merit of the ideas per se.

Participation in these informal groups proved so important that boundaries were established between those employed within the program and those employed within the larger organization. These groups, in their discussions, underwent a sort of self-imposed isolation in the lunchroom and in other informal gatherings lest they lose their feeling of being a respected part of the group.

Allocation of Roles

The formal allocation of roles within the setting served further to differentiate and structure relationships between participants. Original role definitions were made on the basis of job titles assigned the individual at the time he entered the organization. Subsequent differentiation was based upon the needs of the program for specific types of work at specific times, as well as the tendency for individuals to "specialize" as a way of adding to their contributions to the organization. The process of role differentiation also reflected the way in which status was defined within the program; in particular the escalator effect by which participants elevated progressively in status while others simultaneously moved downward in the organizational structure.

The introduction of each new employee into the setting necessitated role-delineations of the other participants. A Staff meeting* three months after the arrival of the Program Director illustrates the way in which such introductions were traditionally made:

> Mrs. Davis: Before we start, I would like for you to meet Mrs. Askew—she's an institutional worker currently in training but she will be a child care aide for us, and Mrs. Alyn who is also an institutional worker, but who will be a child care aide and will be joining our staff. Now I don't know that you all know one another—Mrs. Williams who is going to be a child care worker—she's now an activity therapist, Miss Selby—a senior social worker and coordinator for the mentally retarded program, Mrs. Simpson who is a social worker, Mrs. Grace, who is our researcher—sociologist. Mrs. Wakefield who is currently an activity therapist and who will be a child care worker, and Mrs. ——— who is our secretary. Mrs. Carroll will head up intake, temporarily—this is really my job, but I'm a little too busy with other things.—She will be here five days a week in the morning.

The first means of identification of participants within the organization

*The types of meetings held during the course of this study were:
1) Staff Meetings held at least once a week through the entire period.
2) Intake training seminars started in the third month of the program.
3) Diagnostic seminars started in the sixth month of the program.
4) Day Care Planning Meetings started in the eighth month of the program.

was by job title, either the one currently held or the one into which the individual was to be reclassified in Children's Services. Initial introductions and role-definitions were quite simple in that the initial recruits had all worked within other areas of the state system and had a common understanding of what the job titles signified.

As needs arose within the organization for specific types of information or work to be done, role allocation was modified on the basis of those needs rather than on the qualifications of particular staff members. An example of this tendency is shown in a staff meeting one month later when Mrs. Davis expressed the need for information about potential resources within the community.

> This is the kind of data that I am asking for—what areas do you serve, what kinds of services do you give, what is your agency? . . . If we have this it is an advantage, and we are a step ahead. . . . Now I would like to get some work done on this as soon as possible . . . . I would like Mrs. Newman to work on this—of trying to look at the resources. Now I intentionally placed Mrs. Newman on it because she may not have as much knowledge about what is available and this is one way of learning also. I wonder if Mr. Packard and Mr. Peters could work on this also—the three of you.

Later, when it became obvious that it was necessary to go into the community to investigate resources directly, and Mrs. Newman expressed some fears about this, it was decided that this was "men's work"; and, consequently, all of the men in the organization were assigned to the "resource committee" with the women attending to problems relating to the internal organization.

As the need for clearer communication lines became evident, further delineation of roles regarding persons to whom staff could talk about specific problems was made.

> Mrs. Davis: As I said in the beginning there are some changes being made, but until these changes are made we will operate thusly, with my assuming the responsibility for the staff meeting as well as supervision of the clinical staff—and that includes everyone who is not clerical—I would expect you would talk to my secretary about administrative aspects like ordering equipment—we want to keep it centralized as much as possible. In regard to the waiting list (for retarded children), Miss Selby has assumed responsibility and therefore she will be making assignments of three staff members—Mrs. Williams, Mrs. Wakefield and Mrs. Simpson for interviews and contacts with waiting list families. Mr. Peters will share responsibility with Miss Selby around the waiting list families—he is going to develop something in the area of group work—group meetings with parents of the retarded. Mr. Peters and Mr. Packard will be planning to schedule some of the children for psychologicals but that will not be immediate.

The initial differentiation of staff communication lines between Mrs. Davis and Miss Selby were on the basis of "clinical matters" as opposed to problems of the "mentally retarded." As the organization continued, work with the "mentally retarded" developed into a euphemism for ridding the organization of undesirables. Staff assigned to this area were confronted with the overwhelming and insolvable problems of children on the waiting list, and thus diverted from what came to be defined as the primary work of the organization, involvement with emotionally-disturbed children.

As the complexity of the organization increased, certain staff members became "specialists" in some areas. For example:

Staff Meeting:

> Mrs. Davis: I've asked Mrs. Williams to assume the major responsibility for clarifying our geographic area and keeping us up to date—so if we run into any problem about geography, you go to her . . . Mrs. Wakefield has been working with keeping some kind of record of cases that come into us . . . so I'm reminding staff that any new case that comes in or request for service, put it in the box for Mrs. Wakefield.

With the opening date for Children's programs imminent, the need to differentiate the type of work staff would be involved in with children became increasingly apparent. In particular, differentiation between "child care workers" and "therapists" was necessary. A dialogue from staff meeting in the sixth month of the program's development reflects this tendency.

> Mrs. Carroll: There is a question in my mind about the people who will be doing therapy with children—being involved in the group process when there has to be some disciplining done. I really don't think this works out so well. . . . In therapy you have to treat the child with a certain amount of permissiveness which you cannot carry over to the group and into situations where disciplines has to be exerted. So if you had someone involved in doing therapy per se with the child and they were doing something in the group, then they would always have to be certain that they would call in a group worker to handle a problem where discipline was involved.

Through this process, agreements about the way in which differentiation of phases of work was to occur were reached, and established until some newcomer questioned these pre-established understandings.

The arrival of Miss Travis illustrates what occurred when a high-ranking program official entered the organization and challenged unknowingly the pre-existing system of agreements. In a staff meeting, Mrs. Davis made the announcement that Miss Travis would be joining the staff: "We are fortunate—we are going to get a Miss Travis who has 13 years of experience at the —— school heading up their educational department. . . . This is the kind of leadership that we needed for day care, especially around education." With these credentials given as support for Miss Travis' competence, a series of day care planning meetings were established with Miss Travis presiding. At the initial meeting she discussed her method for making assignments:

> Now I would like to know something about your interests—what area of the program you would like to work in—whatever your title or job description happens to be is less important to me than how you would like to function in the day care program. . . . Now Mrs. Tatum is pretty firm; she will be a special education instructor, and Mrs. Newman will be the nurse . . . but what I'm anxious to know is who has ability or thinks they can manage each type of activity.

Based on these considerations, Miss Travis made assignments such as "arts and crafts supervisor," "workshop supervisor," "swimming and gymnasium supervisor," and "group leaders." Staff became increasingly annoyed and dissatisfied because they felt they were not performing the work for which they were hired; staff expressed this dissatisfaction to Mrs. Davis. She responded that initially in her program planning she had specified that staff would be assigned to all areas and would rotate through all phases of the program via an elaborate plan plotting the percentage of time each staff member was to spend within each aspect of the program. A day care planning meeting included this delineation:

> I think we will have to make the assignments according to discipline . . . and staff will have to function in roles other than in their job classifications. We'll go first to Mr. Anderson—it's 10 per cent in day care, 60 per cent in in-patient, and 10 per cent in out-patient . . . in most of these, the percentage in the area will be pretty much the same, in that you take prime responsibility as the person that the child is going to look to— but you may learn to do some telephone intake, you may learn to do some screenings and diagnostics. In day care I would leave the job performance in terms of the percentage which is 10 per cent for Miss Travis to outline according to the program, and for in-patient I would leave this for the person who is in charge of in-patient . . . if there is a child you have assumed major responsibility for when this kid gets into out-patient you will continue this responsibility. Does this make sense?

The effect of this reallocation of staff time was to remove staff from direct responsibility to any one person, in this instance, Miss Travis. In effect, Mr. Anderson would be accountable to her for only 10 per cent of the work he was to do within the organization, with the remainder of his time diffused throughout other areas. In this way, Mrs. Davis regained control of staff rather than losing it to a delegated authority like Miss Travis.

Sometime later, with the recruitment of new leadership (delegating Miss Travis to a lesser role) and other developments, a reversal of official policy occurred on the basis of the following explanation given at a staff meeting:

> Mrs. Davis: In the beginning I thought that it was absolutely essential that staff be used in every area, and I still think that some of this is necessary, because in that way you know this program pretty much. . . . I think that some of this is a feeling in your bones—before we had children to say, you sit over to the side—you are an activity therapist—your role is thus—this could be very depressing. But you all ended up doing everything from ordering things to doing typing and everything else— now is the time for this—when we are becoming a day treatment center to spell out some of the roles.

Accompanying this reversal in policy, assignment of supervisors was also outlined:

> Now something that all of us have been trying to wade through to get some kind of organization in terms of who is responsible to who, and I have been trying to get this pulled together. What I have done thus far is spell out—we have Miss Travis, Mrs. Carroll and Miss Selby, and myself who make up the supervisory executive body of Children's Services at this point. Miss Travis is in charge of special education and is in charge of community special education in a consultant capacity . . . we will eventually have four special education teachers. . . . Currently Mrs. Tatum is under Miss Travis's supervision. Miss Selby is a staff supervisor and a consultant around emotionally disturbed and retarded children. Her supervisees are Miss Wilson, and Mrs. Askew. Mrs. Carroll is a supervisor in charge of staff training. Her supervisees are Mr. Anderson and Mrs. Saunders. Mr. Peters and Mr. Anderson will be supervised by Mr. Camin. The rest of the staff will continue under my supervision. . . . I've made an attempt to clarify the area around staff roles and duties and that is in terms of child care, and special education, psychology and activity therapy, etc. . . . I will give you an example— that the child care staff has a primary responsibility around his life here —and is the responsible person for looking at the child's total needs. As far as special education is concerned, it is to provide educational diagnosis followed up by the school, and some therapy with the child using education as a tool—this sort of thing.

The process of formal role allocation occurred simultaneously with the differentiation process occurring within the organization. The assignment of roles to individuals within the social system was based on consideration of current organizational problems as well as on the qualifications of the individual participants to fill these roles.

Professional Conflicts and Bargaining

While professional conflicts and bargaining are a predominant feature in certain psychiatric settings, the small numbers of "professionals" employed within this program, coupled with the fact that the organization was new and lacked clearly defined ideological commitments contributed to a picture where the conflictual issues were more diffuse than had been anticipated. One instance of direct conflict between the social workers orientation toward the family and the psychologists concentration on the individual illustrates the way in which such conflicts were manifested:

> Miss Selby: I'm going to take exception. I don't think children and adults are alike . . . . children's symptoms may disappear but the family context provides a part of the child's selfhood. Part of his sickness is outside in the family. . . .
> Mr. Packard: In intake you should be able to determine the crucial factor in terms of services we can provide—to be cured psychoanalytically will take a long time. All I'm saying is that our major service is that of removing the overt irritant.
> Mrs. Davis: That depreciates us to a certain point.
> Mr. Packard: If we make an adequate diagnosis and link him back to resources, that's not a depreciation.
> Miss Selby: I'm sitting here jumping out of my skin—if a person is brought up to the age of twenty without any help, then he needs to be analyzed—but if the child is treated now, he can be treated rather than develop a neurosis at a later date.
> Mrs. Davis: I agree with you about the family.

Sometimes friction occurred as senior staff members vied for the attention of the junior staff. An incident in which the provision of services for clients conflicted with the educational aims of Mrs. Carroll reflects this occasional dilemma:

> Miss Selby: We've got a patient out there—the mother was supposed to come and another relative is there and I don't know—I don't like to let them sit out there too long. I wonder if I should go ahead and then Mrs. Simpson, you could come in.
> Mrs. Carroll: Miss Selby, if you don't mind I'd rather finish this. Because I want to tie it up, and then she could come—it really wouldn't take too long, and I don't want it dangling up in the air.
> Miss Selby: I was wondering if she wanted to come—if we had a normal waiting place I'd let them wait, but there isn't any place.
> Mrs. Simpson: I'd like both of them . . . I'd rather finish.
> Mrs. Carroll: Well, Miss Selby would like you there and I would like you here.
> Miss Selby: It's just that the morning goes so fast—what I wanted to

know is whether I should tell them that Mrs. Simpson will be there or if she will skip this one.

Mrs. Simpson: I don't like to walk in on it.

Miss Selby: Let's skip it this time—because there is only so much you can absorb at one time—you get to feel like you have had it.

This situation led to the exclusion of Miss Selby from any further Intake Training Seminars on the grounds that "she was too disruptive" and increasingly Miss Selby was pushed into assuming responsibilities for the mentally retarded and deviously diverted from other activities.

In addition to this competition among the staff for alliances, disputes over the handling of clients ensued, primarily from the desire to prevent client consideration from disrupting the direction and development of the program. An early discussion centered around whether children should be seen in initial screening interviews.

Staff Meeting:

Miss Selby: We've got all this nice play area out there—we can just put some toys out there and the children can be seen there.

Mrs. Davis: That's one suggestion.

Miss Selby: This is generally done in clinics, I know, and I don't know if we've got anything better to do or anyone to do it.

Mrs. Simpson: I thought we were going to have the child seen too.

Mrs. Davis: What we are talking about is that the parent is seen in the first interview. . . . There will be many steps beyond this first interview, but today we have to confine ourselves to that. . . . But we give the parent an appointment to come with this child for a first interview and both the parent and the child will be seen individually and jointly, and one suggestion is that the parents be seen individually and that the receptionist might handle the child. Any other suggestions?

Mrs. Simpson: I thought that the parent and the child were going to be seen individually at the same time so you wouldn't drag it out, and I therefore thought that you would have two sets of interviewers in a sense.

Secretary: I don't think too much of the receptionist watching the kids —say there are four families in, and she's tied up with four squalling kids and the phone is ringing. . . .

Mrs. Alyn: There should be someone to watch the kids.

Secretary: Strictly for that—to take them for walks and to entertain them.

Miss Selby: It depends on whether you have a job classification for someone. If you have somebody, this would be preferable to a babysitter, but the thing—I think Mrs. Simpson put her finger on the question that I'm not clear about at all, and that's "What do we want out of the first interview?" Because, for instance, if we are going to want something like a history rather than a screening, then, you would want to spend more time with mother than you would otherwise. If we are going to want an approach to how this family operates then there should be very little time spent seeing them individually, so I think it depends on what we want to get, to some extent, and how much we will want to separate them from each other.

Ultimately it was decided that only parents were to come to the initial screening interviews. All decisions about accepting or rejecting the children for the program were based only upon contacts with the parents; children were seen only after they had been accepted. This type of ruling eventuated primarily from interaction in which professional conflicts were at stake, in particular, those surrounding Miss Selby, who thought that the child should be seen earlier during the screening process. On one occasion, Miss Selby violated this rule, and was severely criticized. However, when psychologists later did the same thing on the basis that "it seemed natural that I would see the parents and child together," there were no questions asked.

Professional conflicts and bargaining also occurred around decisions to accept or reject children for the program. Two particular instances illustrate the conflict between education and therapy, namely, the desire on the part of Miss Travis to have certain cases admitted because they were good candidates for an educational program and the rejection of these same cases on the part of Dr. Cartwright because of a perceived lack of treatment potential.

Diagnostic Conference:

Dr. Cartwright: You see my feeling is that you are not going to be equipped, at least to begin with, to deal with this—I'm not saying the public school can deal with them either, but they need certain definite techniques—so far sure you don't want to take a child with a perceptual problem as one of this group, too. Not in the early stages.
Miss Travis: I would be more apt to take a child with a percentual handicap if I knew what the problems were than a socially maladjusted —in other words, I would want to know what the problems are a reaction to.
Dr. Cartwright: Whether it is due to his inability to learn or to other circumstances.
Miss Travis: I would be more apt to take a child with a perceptual that than straight maladjustment.

Diagnostic Conference: Two weeks later

Miss Travis: There is something hopeful in this—that he doesn't have trouble when he is involved in group activities like at the swimming pool.
Dr. Cartwright: I took that another way—that when he is involved in action programs where he can release some of his rage through his muscles—you might be right—but I took it on a different level. You see when there is—when he can let out some of his steam through his muscles he is all right, but when he is just face to face with somebody,

he can't take it—that is, he—the lack of controls are so severe under these circumstances that he lets it out on whomever he comes in contact with.

Miss Travis: I would like some further exploration because I thought there were some hopeful signs in his psychological testing. . . . I know from some of my experiences, that children like this were able to profit. . . .

Dr. Cartwright: Let me make a prediction on this case—it isn't going to work. The unconscious connection between this boy's acting out and the mother's rage—her wish to do them all in.

Thus, professional role conflicts and the bargaining that occurred within the setting were significant factors in determining both the fate of the individual staff members and that of the clients.

Internal Management Problems

Informal processes, in the early stages of organization, were generally sufficient in managing interrelationships within the program as well as assuring that all members contributed to the organization. However, when new members were recruited or problems arose in which some participants were shirking their responsibilities, more formal procedures were instituted to bring such behavior "into line."

Rule Setting

The primary function of rules within the programmatic framework was the supervision of employee behavior to prevent attracting the attention of outside authorities thus limiting the possibilities of intrusions from that external source. Rule setting on this basis resulted in an abundance of miscellany designed to avoid trouble rather than to build up a logical, consistent, comprehensive body of guidelines to govern individual behavior.

Rule setting, therefore, occurred primarily in response to specific situations and ceased to be enforced once the problem was handled. The "oldtimers" in the organization had considerable advantage over the newcomers in that they had knowledge of the rules that had previously been made, and wherever necessary could make reference to them, as a means of control.

Early rules involved such things as staff working hours and the necessity of reporting their whereabouts at all times. These early rules were reiterated when specific incidents occurred that seemed to underline their importance. A staff meeting two months after the arrival of Mrs. Davis serves as an illustration:

> Mrs. Davis: First of all, I'd like to call this memorandum to your attention. The working hours are now 8:30 to 5:00 with one half an hour for lunch and two fifteen minute coffee breaks. . . . We have two sign-in and sign-out sheets, and they will be on the secretary's desk. . . . It is important that we know where you are.
> Miss Selby: I'd just like to emphasize this—yesterday a girl came in to the switchboard and slashed her wrists—the operator couldn't find the doctor who was on duty—that's why it is important that we have a way of knowing where we are.
> Mrs. Davis: I'm glad you brought that up—another time someone had an epileptic seizure outside of the administration building and they couldn't find the doctor.

Another example of this type of rule setting occurred when the staff requested permission to enter the building through the side doors rather than through the main entrance which necessitated their walking around the building. Arrangements had been made to install the right kind of locks on the doors and to make other necessary adjustments, when Mrs. Davis came in one day and informed the staff that this plan could not be followed. The preceding evening she had received a phone call from a friend who worked in a children's program in another state, who related an incident whereby someone had come into their program and kidnapped a child. Therefore, as a security measure, all staff had to enter through the main door. Rule setting on this basis occurred only if a situation arose that would call attention to potential areas of trouble, and was designed to avoid trouble if possible.

Relatively early in the program, Mrs. Davis outlined her expectations regarding staff behavior:

> If we are working with children, we've got to be able to talk about our problems if we expect to accomplish anything at all. I do not expect staff to act like children. I will not be unhappy if people bring up their problems and complaints to me, but I will be unhappy if they talk to other people outside the program and these things come to me via the grapevine. I have found out how active the grapevine is in this institution and do not feel that it is appropriate to communicate any of the problems about providing services to children outside the program area.

Staff was expected to discuss problems but only within the context of the program and preferably only to Mrs. Davis. This theme was reiterated at subsequent times:

> Certainly there are many times when things frustrate us, but if we are part of the system we are involved. . . . I think we have to look very closely at our responsibility towards its adequacy or inadequacy . . . and rather than spend a lot of energy looking at how much is not right—

> use that energy to try to make it in each of our small ways better—It's
> like what you have to say about your family—I can say what I like
> about my family behind closed doors—but don't you dare say anything
> about it, because I am a part of it—and if I say it is rotten it means a
> part of me is rotten too, so I really feel strongly about this—and any-
> time anything comes up in Children's programs, or in the Mental Health
> Clinic or in the State that you feel that you don't like, let's talk about
> it, but let's talk about it in here.

A strong value was placed upon keeping any problems "within the
family," and a frequent complaint from those working in other areas
of the center was that "staff in children's are so seclusive." This re-
striction of communication served to facilitate "impression management"
as Mrs. Davis dealt with the outside world.

Rules were also established to govern the client's demands upon the
program. An early staff meeting where the decision was made to see only
parents, illustrates the process:

> Mrs. Carroll: Normally in a clinic you see the parents first—you tell
> them specifically to come in alone, and then if you think the child fits
> within your program—that category of child that you will serve—then
> in the next interview you see the parent and the child together.
> Mrs. Wakefield: That's especially necessary here where there is going to
> be so much emphasis on the parent's participating and cooperating—
> because I know from the few phone calls I've gotten the parents sound
> like they just can't wait to come here and dump their child.
> Mrs. Carroll: They want to dump their child—you see I think you can
> give the parent a better picture of their child, and you have an oppor-
> tunity to interpret your service, and get the parent's questions, and let
> them know what the program is. . . . I think it does put an emphasis
> upon the involvement of the parent.

At a later meeting, staff expressed the opinion that if the child was
brought in for the first interview it complicated things, because sometimes the child appeared so different from the parent's description that
they found themselves wanting to "accept" these children. Rule setting
in this area thus served to facilitate decision making.

As the organization developed and moved from one in which inter-
staff relations were informal and contact with a client public was minimal
to one in which clients were being seen steadily and staff was performing
"actual work," a set of rules governing staff's relationships with clients
was designed to project an image of "competence" to those seeking services. Mrs. Davis' expectations for "professional" behavior was outlined
at a staff meeting:

> I would like to mention something about our general conduct. And this
> includes all staff. . . . In most of the settings where I have worked

everything was on a first name basis . . . . you can first name one another when it is on an informal basis, but never call each other by the first name in front of a client. I don't think it is fair for the client or for the staff. You are accustomed to addressing one another by the first name; you will have to be conscious of this . . . but I see no reason why any staff member should not be capable of this kind of discipline.

Further evidence of the concern for "impression management" insofar as a client public was involved was reflected in a discussion of the types of uniforms that should be worn by staff.

Day Care Planning Meeting:

Mrs. Harris*: I don't know what your feelings are—but I'm the one sitting here in a uniform. Once the children come, I think you may want to have something that looks a little more professional than shifts and sandals—maybe it's because I come from such a structured environment—but it seems to me . . . that your attire should be a little less casual. The people that are working directly with the children have to get down on the floor and play with the children. In the nursing school that was connected with the hospital where I worked, they came in street clothes and they had a place where they changed for the actual working with children. . . . They changed to sandals and shifts and things like that—but whenever we went back to psychiatric intake or anything that involved the outside community, we changed back into more formal attire.

Mrs. Davis: Let's talk about this. . . .

Mr. Waters: In day treatment, you are not going to have to worry about the outside people looking in on you—because there won't be that much outside viewing—the parents aren't going to be walking around—and here since you are meeting the parents on intake and out-patient—you will be dressed more appropriately for that.

Mrs. Harris: You should be dressed appropriate to what you have to do.

Mr. Waters: I said there isn't any need to change.

Mrs. Wakefield: Unless we are going to be doing interviewing and making home visits. . . .

Mrs. Davis: As I mentioned last week, staff will be involved in other activities that concern the total center whch means that you will have to participate on certain committees—and this will demand something. We did talk about smocks or something of that nature, but it may be that we should have some kind of clothing that you don't care about to change into. . . . I've thought about culottes or slacks—we can feel it out—some people are more comfortable—but you need to have something that you don't give a hoot about. Talking about what shows— this is something that I am going to take a stand on—I'm not against mini-nothing—I certainly think it is attractive and—but the fact that we are going to have disturbed children here—many of these children

---

*Mrs. Harris was a part-time member of the staff—a speech and hearing specialist.

have been over-stimulated before they get here. I do know of an instance where a staff person was attacked—it was too seductive. The kid had been exposed to things by his mother who was a prostitute and it shook him to pieces—we have to be aware of it, and so I think our dress has to be—it doesn't mean that you change your whole life style —it's just for work.

The importance of the uniform and accompanying rules concerning dress were emphasized when Mrs. Tatum was encouraged to leave the organization, primarily because of the short skirts that she repeatedly wore.

In summary, rule setting within the organization occurred when situations arose that called attention to potential problems and served to control members' participation within the organization through formal mechanisms, to govern their relationships to one another as well as to the client public, and finally, to handle problems of impression-management with the outside world.

The Structuring Process

An outstanding characteristic of the interaction patterns that occurred within meetings in this developing organization was the evident need to anticipate and structure the work that was to be done. Although much time was spent engaged in dialogue concerning this, rarely did things develop in the way that staff had pre-structured them.

Such things, as the type of clients to be served and the length of time needed to treat children indicated the early stages of this structuring process. The following interchange occurring in the staff meeting serves as an illustration:

> Mr. Paulson: The time scheduling in the program sounds rigid—I'm wondering if we maybe shouldn't make it a little more flexible.
> Mrs. Wakefield: My questions are about the length of time. We will have all different types of children—I don't see what we can do for an autistic child in this period of time—the majority of the children don't need years and years of treatment, but what if we get some that do?
> Mr. Packard: At the point of intake we need to make some assessment relative to pathology—we used to think in terms of sixty days. We need some conception of the time that a child will need at the point of intake.

Although time limits were specified, they were not necessarily designed to be followed. Later, in the same meeting Mrs. Davis defined the rationale behind setting time limits.

> The rationale behind the time limit is based on my experience in doing brief therapy. This was a long-term psychoanalytic treatment center, and this is what I was oriented to. The agency I was with switched to short

term and many of us got hung up on the time issue. We finally got the message that they were trying to orient us in a certain way. In reality, no one was going to be thrown out at the end of the time limit, but if you are oriented to get a job done in a short period of time, you make sure that your time is used to the fullest.

Structuring of limits on the duration of treatment for children was motivated by the desire to set a goal for staff to strive for rather than to actually govern procedure once the program became operational.

As the recruitment of clients became an issue, the structuring of procedures for information-getting was a predominant topic of discussion. Mrs. Carroll stated her view of what the course should be at an early Intake Training Seminar:

> I don't know how it is going to be worked out here, but on the basis of the material in the screening interview you make a decision as to whether you are going to seriously consider in more depth this child, and then you do a diagnostic which is more in depth than the screening interview, and it includes seeing the child, and then at the end of this period—once you have done that, you make a final decision as to whether or not the child is to be treated—but I don't think there is going to be time if they open the program in June to do some of this stuff.

Differentiation between screening interviews and diagnostics was frequently sketchy.

> Mrs. Carroll: First of all, let me say that a diagnostic interview ordinarily takes several interviews. We are thinking of it at this time as a joint interview with both parents together, in the event that the child has two parents in the home, an individual interview with the mother, an individual interview with the father, a home visit, and an individual interview with the child alone.

Although the persons who were to be interviewed were signified, differences in the types of information to be obtained from these different phases of the operation were never specified. Further, in all of the cases admitted or considered for admission during the time of this study, only one was processed according to this procedure.

Another problem reflecting the difficulties in the structuring process occurred when Miss Travis assumed the responsibilities of "acting director of day care." Her approach to structuring was to anticipate from the beginning the total number of children that would eventually be in the day care program. At the third day care meeting which she chaired, the structure of activities for the day care program was outlined. Diagram 4 depicts this structure.

This arrangement was projected, according to Miss Travis, on the basis of "8 children per group for 8 groups." The purposes of these various types of group activities was outlined by Miss Travis in a day care planning meeting:

> While four groups are in classes—writing and the basic school subjects —the other four groups will be in activities . . . it will be skill instruction, rather than using a drama group. In other words—very often groups will have crafts as a focus but it is focused only in terms of what they are going to structure therapy around. I would see these as more instructional. This is something you may want to talk about as you go along—but you may find that the needs are less for instruction and more for skills in learning to get along with people—but many of the children who come into these programs, however, need skills—he has a potential that can be developed—for example a child that has a capacity for developing his artistic abilities . . . . when this happens very often you have a very different self-conception—self-esteem.

It was this type of structuring that initially was called to the attention of Mrs. Davis as an example of the staff's fear that Miss Travis was more concerned with setting up a school than helping materialize the treatment program they envisaged.

A far different approach to structuring is illustrated in the diagnostic conference held with Dr. Cartwright:

> Mrs. Davis: One of the things that we were looking at as a staff is how we would plan for the child. When you look at the individual and the approach, you could have psychotherapy, and I broke it down in terms of quiet play and active play . . . shopping, music, games, and nature studies. Also an individual approach would be such things as—speech, occupational therapy, special education, and then we have another approach—any combination of these could be used—but there is the group approach either in class or in physical education, or prevocational kind of involvement—something in free play which might be dancing, drama, or indoor—outdoor free play—all within the type of milieu where staff attitudes and a consistent type of experience and program for the child is planned.
> Dr. Cartwright: You have to use a milieu approach, and then you have to be flexible enough to see and work with each child around his individual needs—and that to me is no easy job . . . but it would seem to me that you have to set up a kind of group program for every child.

In actuality, the children admitted to the day treatment program were assigned individual child care workers who worked with them on an individual basis, and then, as more children were accepted, Dr. Cartwright prescribed grouping of the children in certain shared activities. Staff did not always agree to the plans that were formulated and generally found ways of circumventing the prescribed structure.

DIAGRAM 4

PROPOSED STRUCTURE FOR DAY CARE PROGRAM

TIME	MONDAY	TUESDAY	WEDNESDAY	THURSDAY	FRIDAY
9:00- 9:30	Children Arrive .... Supervised Play				
9:30-11:00	Groups I, II, III and IV in Special Education Classes				
9:30-11:00 Group V	Swimming	Art-Gym	Music-drama, crafts-shop	Art-Gym	Music-drama, crafts-shop
Group VI	Music-drama arts-crafts	Swimming	Art-Gym	Music-drama, arts-crafts	Art-Gym
Group VII	Art-Gym	Music-drama, crafts-shop	Swimming	Art-Gym	Music-drama
Group VIII	Music-drama, crafts-shop	Art-Gym	Music-drama, crafts-shop	Swimming	Art-Gym
11:45-12:40	.............Lunch and Supervised Play				

Afternoon Schedule—Groups I-IV in Activities, while Groups V-VIII are in Special Education Classes

Emergent Problems

Much of the actual structuring of the program occurred around specific problems that arose. In response to a problem, or an anticipated problem, staff arrived at agreements as to how these situations were to be handled. The actions taken at these times became precedents for similar situations occurring at a later time. Consequently, procedures and rules of the program were often rooted in the solving of emergent problematic situations rather than in any concentrated attempt to formalize policy.

As previously indicated, although a procedure for evaluating parents and children had been developed, yet when the time came to admit children to the day care program, the need to have "desirable" candidates for admission superseded diagnostic procedures. An Intake Training Seminar one month before the formal opening of the program reflected the urgency of this problem.

> Mrs. Davis: What happened was that we got caught in a bind. The staff wish and my wish to get day care open—the availability of staff to conduct diagnostics and to conduct them rapidly—this necessitates a certain amount of pretraining and knowledge . . . and also Miss Travis's point which was an excellent one, not to open the day care on the same date as regular school, so that it would not seem that this was a school and not a treatment program, so when I learned that the date had been set for August 26—the target date—the only thing I could do was talk to Mrs. Carroll and the staff who was ready to conduct diagnostic interviews to speed it up so that we could get children— otherwise it would mean trying to get staff who are doing the screening interview ready so they could learn enough to conduct diagnostics, because this takes time, or we could hire somebody—some social worker who had had experience and could do it. So I agreed to do some with the help of the staff—Miss Selby had agreed to do some, and Mr. Peters—so that we will try to move with them more rapidly than normal.

The lack of adequate numbers of children for admittance to the day care program was now the predominant consideration.

Although throughout the early history of the program everyone had referred to the "day care program" at one phase of the operation, a problem erupted concerning whether the goal of the program was education or therapy. The dialogue surrounding this problem and its resolution took place in a day care planning meeting two weeks before the opening of "day care."

> Mrs. Davis: That is something that I would like some discussion about —how do you see our day care program. Now eliminate the word treatment and school and let's look at it.
> Mrs. Williams: I thought that the schedule we made the other day

rigidly divided it into what we do when. I don't know if some of the others of you have the same feeling.

Mrs. Wakefield: I felt kind of the same way—you know I look at it and the first thing that I think is that it is a school schedule. Which may be okay, but if it is to be a treatment center—I keep calling it a school. I think I told you about the home visit where I wanted to keep calling it a school, and then I'd say, "No, treatment program" but it was very difficult to steer away from it, because it seemed like the orientation was toward a school program. Part of it may be that I was thinking of something else—but it may be that we are all a little confused.

Mr. Anderson: We can have a schedule that looks like a school, where we start playing with the word treatment, as the way staff views what is happening. In other words, the staff views the child as in class, but how much freedom does the hyperactive child have to dissipate this energy—to leave the room and go with a staff member when he is supposed to be in class. You can have a schedule that looks like a school schedule, but what actually takes place is treatment—it is dependent upon the attitude of the staff—how much leeway they have—and how much freedom they have to let a child regress, to act out, to do what these children have a tendency to do. How much expression of their behavior is going to be allowed? That is what comes in.

Mrs. Davis: I think this is the point that Mrs. Williams and Mrs. Wakefield—all of you are expressing—that unless we bring it back— for instance, if he is supposed to be in an education class at this point. . . . There is one thing that I want to make clear—that the mission here was to set up a treatment center—not a school. It is not a school. We do need a structure but it is a treatment program. School will be part, and activities will be part, just as treatment will be a part—but it is only one part, and it will be for some and not for others. . . . I think this is the issue—How flexible is the structure?

In this way it was established that this program was to have the primary goal of treatment and not education and, at this point, Mrs. Davis assumed control of further planning for the day treatment program, thus relegating Miss Travis to the position of special education supervisor.

The anticipation of problems that would arise upon the admittance of children precipitated the formulation of rules and procedures. For example, the fear of "losing the children" stimulated this dialogue in a day care planning meeting.

Miss Travis: You might see what a deterrent pulling the shades all the way down might be—and if there are any other ideas we might come up with something else. . . .

Mrs. Davis: The only thing is this—and we really are not going to be able to make more admissions—beyond what we have when we start out because we will have no more staff than we have now—I would really question being able to lose a kid. I really do question this with this many people around, how could you lose one?

> Mrs. Simpson: We can lose each other. In one building—I'm sure we can lose kids—there are going to be so many places that aren't going to be used at this point—and with that few children there are a lot of places he can go off to. . . .
> Miss Travis: I think we can control some of this by locking certain areas, and also I think that we will lock the door going into the pavillion . . . and the windows, if the shades are down, and the windows are closed and locked—it's going to take even the fastest fingered of our youngsters to get the blind up and the window open, and we will have security screens eventually.

Decisions for locking doors and putting security screens on windows were made in anticipation of the possibility of "losing children."

At times, discussion of anticipated problems served another function— that of trying to conceptualize problematic situations that might occur around work with "poor, emotionally disturbed children." A discussion of the types of equipment and clothing needed for the activities in which children would engage reflects this tendency.

> Mrs. Davis: I'm sure that staff will discuss the kinds of things that parents will be expected to bring for the children. And gym clothing or outfits—sometimes short pants or blue jeans that you cut off—but at least this sort of listing will be necessary to give to the parents, and there is something that I kind of smiled at when Mr. Waters said that most poor children do have these kinds of shoes—I think you are right, but we are going to have a few—maybe not in our first bunch—who do not have them, but there are funds available through the Mental Health Center whereby if somebody needs something that badly we can get it for him.
> Mr. Anderson: They will supply us with them—there is no problem with that, but I don't like the way that they do it over there. They take any number of sizes and throw them all together and there's a big hassle and it's not sanitary.
> Mrs. Davis: And it's not only that—it's not respectful of the dignity of the human person—so that we can do it individually. . . .
> Mr. Anderson: What about swim suits—should we order them or ask them to bring them?
> Mrs. Davis: I tell you what about giving—I think we have to be very careful about what we give and what we supply. If any of these parents want to try to do for these children, I think that we put the burden on them as nearly as possible for supplying the necessary equipment for the kids.

Similar discussions concerning the ordering of play equipment and the anticipation of problems surrounding such activities as lunch time served to not only structure what people were to do in the situation but also to reflect the attitudes of staff toward the kind of clients they anticipated serving in the program.

In summary, a predominant underlying theme revolved around the relationships of individuals to one another within the program. Lacking any clear definition of the work to be done as a focal point around which they could organize, the program participants used a variety of other issues as a basis for organizing their relationships to one another. Management of social relationships from Mrs. Davis' standpoint was essential if the program was to survive. Rule setting, role-differentiation, and the deployment of personnel to certain parts of the program were some of the techniques she utilized. Successful management of these internal relationships was essential, not only for the functioning of the program but also to project a proper image to the outside world to assure a continued input of resources that were necessary for the program's survival.

Chapter VIII

Staging

A successful organization maintains contact with its external environment and patterns internal functioning accordingly. Business organizations must have accurate information as to the buying climate for their product; they must have knowledge of their competitors activities. The producer must also receive feedback that will allow him to ascertain the long range prospects for maintaining buyer interest in his product.

Since the success of psychiatric treatment organizations must be measured in terms of their ability to make positive alterations in human beings, a program must first of all be selective in developing a client population. Factors such as a cross-section of the types of persons seeking services, the work of other agencies providing similar services, and the public's view of psychiatric treatment all must be considered. Information must be gathered and, based upon this, the work of a psychiatric treatment program carefully staged.

Further, information is a valued resource in power maneuvers within an organization. In bargaining situations information may be introduced to support a position, and thereby gain advantage over an antagonist. Information may also be withheld in an attempt to control others. The person who has access to communication from multiple sources has power. In this case, the judicious use of information introduced by Mrs. Davis was a key factor governing program decisions as to what children would be served, when the program would open, and the nature of services that would be offered.

Of the total body of information available to this organization, only a certain part was introduced into the setting. Such information may be categorized as (1) positive, in that it was in conformity with certain shared beliefs held within the program, (2) negative in that it was in disagreement with programmatic goals or beliefs, or (3) neutral information. Positive information could be used as a means of further validating the "correctness" of a course of action that the program had chosen; the invoking of an outside resource to lend credence and support to an

111

internally developed idea or belief. Negative information, in contrast, could contribute to change in direction of the program as an attempt to bring programmatic goals into alignment with external expectations. Negative feedback could also serve to promote internal cohesiveness around programmatic goals in opposition to what was considered to be opposing forces outside the boundaries of the program. A considerable amount of information was not processed, and the program participants had only selected pieces of information available to them about the external organization.

In this program there was a variety of types of information available to participants. Mrs. Davis, in her contacts with the "outside world" had access to information about the state mental health system as a whole, as well as that specific to the Mental Health Center. She was the chief link between the program and its external organizational environment. As the arbiter and distributer of such information, Mrs. Davis used it in such a way as to pattern and shape the internal structure. The consultants further added input by referring to techniques of treatment utilized in other settings outside of the mental health system. Mrs. Davis thus controlled the amount and type of information by carefully screening and guarding the input of the consultants into the program setting. Such information tended to be instrumental in the shaping of ideological commitments.

Program participants had access to a different body of information. First they brought into the organization a body of information gleaned from past experiences, both personal and professional. A second source of data was the Intake calls from potential clients. Through these contacts the program workers had information about the nature of the client population in need of their services.

The input of information from these varying sources at times resulted in divergent views. What Mrs. Davis considered to be politically expedient solutions, based upon her sources of information, were not necessarily consonant with staff's perceptions of a client population gleaned through their contacts. Adjusting for these divergent views occupied a considerable part of meeting time. This chapter will outline discussions concerned with the establishment of geographic boundaries, projected opening dates, and potential treatment alliances as illustrative of the ways in which conflicting views were negotiated.

Geographic Boundaries

One of the early problems within a program's history is to locate itself within some context. Given a philosophy that mental health services were to be organized on the basis of geographic catchment areas, one would logically conclude that, although the geographic boundaries were changed once during the time of this study, these delineations would be one of the more readily definable factors. This was not so. Throughout the course of the study staff continually expressed confusion about the location of boundaries. Despite this constant preoccupation with boundaries, three of the children initially admitted to the program, resided in areas outside the stated georgraphical limits.

It may be hypothesized that such things as ambiguity about boundary locations served as a rationale for not providing services for children at an earlier date. And, although the discussions focused upon the location of the boundaries, the underlying issue was the problem of defining a client population appropriate to the goals of the program. If the geographic territory were confined to the ghetto areas of the city the likelihood of finding desirable patients, as defined by the program, was diminished. These factors, given the political bargaining arena in which the program was being developed, were important considerations.

The Program Director, in her discussion of the issue, was responding to political pressures. Geographic boundaries, to her way of thinking, represented her own territorial influence vis-à-vis the other Program Directors and so provided a bargaining factor. The program paticipants, on the other hand, had to deal with a client population demanding services. For them, geographic boundaries represented concrete factual information they could use in setting limits with parents and agencies demanding services.

An early meeting illustrates the way in which confusion over the location of boundaries was expressed:

> Mrs. Simpson: Are you going to get clarification . . . about boundaries?
> Mrs. Davis: Yes.
> Mrs. Simpson: We've been asking for this for a long time.
> Mrs. Davis: It's the total Region, but I'm not clear . . . . there is a great deal going on about reorganization, but we cannot sit back and refuse to do anything.
> Miss Selby: This is chronic—they haven't been able to make up their minds about boundaries in five years.
> Mrs. Davis: We have to do something.
> Mrs. Wakefield: Unit B has a Children's Program . . . and when I talked to someone there they thought that they served the whole Region too . . . . they would like to have some communication between the two programs.

With the reorganization, the geographic limits were changed and staff's concerns increased. A staff meeting one month later reflects concerns over the handling of clients who, now, with the shift of boundaries are outside of the area which the program is to serve.

> Miss Selby: Do you think that we will be bound . . . to operate as though we had new boundaries?
> Mrs. Davis: Yes, we will. . . . I think that we are at a vantage point in that we haven't started services—we haven't made any commitment to any persons that we are going to take them, so consequently, I think that we can confine ourselves to the new boundaries more easily than some of the operations that are going on here.

The staff meeting of the following week continued the dialogue:

> Miss Selby: May I make a suggestion. One of the things that has created this feeling of intense anger that we get from the community is that everybody is terribly flooded you know, by referrals, and they use the boundaries as a quick way of getting rid of people. You live there and you are supposed to go there—and then when the person calls there, they don't have the services that were implied by this quickie kind of referral—this increases the anger and one thing that I have been trying to do is to not make them on the basis of boundaries only.

The confusion about boundaries justified their inability to handle and treat clients who were asking for help rather than acknowledge that, regardless of the geographic location of the client, there would be no services available.

Two weeks later information about the new boundaries had finally been received and given to staff. The problem, however, was still not solved.

> Mrs. Wakefield: If you know that someone is definitely out of the area—then what do we do with it now?
> Mrs. Davis: I think that we would have to evaluate—if it sounds like something that would mean involvement in our day care program and they are truly out of the area, I think we would have to say that our boundaries have been changed. . . . If it's another kind of situation, however, that does not involve in-patient, or what have you, then I think we have to wait.
> Mrs. Wakefield: How much of this information will be given out to other agencies? . . . Because it seems that next year we will still be getting calls from people who still think the old boundaries hold. It seems like there is so much confusion—they know there is a change, but they don't know where it is—and so much of your time is spent repeating the same information.

Although geographic boundaries might be established, yet, other elements entered into the preferred way in which phone calls should be handled. If a client presented a disease that was of potential interest to the organization he should not be turned away strictly on the basis of geographic location. In later meetings, a discussion of how much information should be obtained from clients residing outside of the area provided further validation of the quest for a population of potential clients that would fit into the program.

Opening Dates

The setting of an opening date was in itself a bargaining tool. One of the reasons given for hiring Mrs. Davis originally was that she promised to open the program within three months. This date, along with five other such projected dates came and went before the Day Treatment service was opened.

A noticeable characteristic surrounding the setting of opening dates was that, although staff acknowledged the existence of these projected goals, these dates in no way affected alterations in their work behavior. The coming and passing of these dates caused little expressed concern on the part of the staff. The opening date was based more upon an evaluation of the tenor of public sentiment outside the program than on any consistent preparation toward attainment of an established goal within the program. In fact, when the opening date did arrive, problems arose in finding children to recruit as patients into the program, and no pre-planning for treatment had been accomplished.

Although a telephone intake service was in operation, and some of the clients were being seen on an out-patient basis, children were not accepted into the program until five months after the initial projected starting date, eight months after Mrs. Davis had been hired. External organizational problems were primarily cited as an explanation for these delays. Although much of the information obtained by Mrs. Davis about occurrences in these areas was at times withheld from the program participants, when they became uneasy about the lack of what they considered to be constructive work, these explanations were advanced to allay anxiety surrounding this dilemma. With the approach of the initial starting date Mrs. Davis explained:

> I think we are aware that we have moved a long way. It was three months as of yesterday since we did the first scratching of anything, and, at least, we have all of our furniture ordered and we will have all our job specifications. Incidentally, our job specifications have gone in . . . . the director of personnel . . . took the time to really push and explain our job specifications. . . . and they believe that they will get them through in a very brief period of time, so this will enable us to really have staff hired.

Mrs. Davis, in her negotiations with the outside organization gave "insufficient staff" as a primary reason for not opening the program sooner. It then became the responsibility of the administrative staff outside of the program if she was unable to meet projected goals. But internally these same arguments did not hold. Staff complained that they had nothing to do. Alternate explanations had to be advanced to deal with this problem. One strategy developed around the use of one of the pavillions which was currently leased to a private school for retarded children. Although there were other areas available where the day care unit could have been started, this particular area was chosen. This afforded a legitimate excuse for not opening sooner in that it could be argued by Mrs. Davis that, since this school had not moved their supplies out, the day care program could not be started. This again moved the responsibility away from Mrs. Davis to the administration of the Mental Health Center in that they would have to "evict the prior tenants" before Children's services could become operant.

> Mrs. Davis: One safety valve for day care is that —— school is still across there and it cannot be moved until the end of May or first of June. After it moves it will take 2-3 weeks for it to be cleaned up and in shape before we can move our furniture in—because of this we cannot promise anyone day care until the end of June at the earliest.

Thus, the difficulties in getting job specifications cleared by the Department of Mental Health and the inability to use a portion of the physical plant were used as convenient delaying actions in the initial developmental period.

Administrative changes and reorganization introduced another set of contingencies. The report of Mrs. Davis' initial encounter with the new Subzone Director was altered markedly when related to the group as opposed to her private commentary on the meeting. A staff meeting following her first meeting with the new Subzone Director contains this report:

> Now the (Subzone Director) had a conference with me on last Monday. Ah, I felt that the conference with him was very helpful because it certainly relieved some of my anxiety—about the new superintendent and director coming in. He does have some ideas that might help us control the quality of services that we give. At least control it so it is qualitative rather than a rush sort of thing. I think that one advantage he has in relation to his prior experience where there was a lack of control of the intake of patients, and maybe we can benefit from that. The only thing I can say at this point—our plans for opening in-patient services for June have been altered. In terms of time of opening—it will not open until the earliest—September. This does not mean that we

will not need staff—we need staff much before that but this will be for the purpose of training. As far as I know we will go ahead with plans for opening day care July 8, but it is essential that staff get adequate training in this area.*

Areas of disagreement such as the issue of management vs therapy, and the use of drugs to control children, between Mrs. Davis and the new Subzone Director were not reported. Rather, the encounters were used as a means for further justifying delay in the opening of Children's services; and, out of the total content of the meeting, information supporting current programmatic goals was selected to be reported to the staff.

Budgetary problems were another factor introduced as a reason for delaying opening of Children's services. In an early staff meeting, Mrs. Davis reported "At this point we have no major concern for money, but unless we approach it planfully we will have . . . we are assured 75 per cent of our budget, but the remaining 25 per cent may be cut." This possibility was translated into what it would mean for their planning. "The way it may effect us may well be in number—I don't see this as being a gross problem in that to begin with; we will hardly have more than ten children and we do not open until—and this was announced— on the track system until October." Initial plans were to have a day care program for 60 children. Changes in these plans were introduced when information about external problems was given.

Staff responded by reporting their personal feelings about another delay:

> Mrs. Simpson: I was just thinking that if we are going to have to change someday it's better to bring it up now—because I think this has happened before—you get used to working with a fairly competent staff and a fairly large staff, and then when the need came to deploy the staff things really fell apart because you had come to rely on the numbers as well as on the quality . . . . it's a lot easier to readjust to it than if you are not warned ahead of time.
> Mrs. Davis: That's an excellent point . . . because I think that this is one of the things that we are stressing here is quality. And we'll have to have it, otherwise, we've just got another kind of service going.
> Miss Selby: I was thinking that as we are opening program by program and not all at once, that if we are adequately staffed for any given program at any time what can happen, and frequently has happened, is that you'll be frozen as you are at the time—they won't subtract anybody, but they won't add anybody. . . . If we get day care going and staffed adequately, if they freeze us they will freeze us as we are—which would mean that we couldn't open in-patient until we get unfrozen.
> Mrs. Davis: There is this kind of freezing which is a safety valve that

*See Chapter IV for Mrs. Davis' account of this incident.

> we have. Nonetheless, there is the possibility—and I don't think that
> there is going to be any trouble with Children's—I feel' that there is a
> very real wish to get us going, and we have to have in-patient to back
> us up, and so consequently, I don't think that they can do that.*

Goal-setting which occurs in an organization located in a chaotic environmental context reflects the characteristic of attempting to anticipate unforeseen events against which goals may be plotted. The tendency to go
away more and more from the original goals can be witnessed. But although the ambiguity and confusion which proved troublesome to some
of the participants did exist, Mrs. Davis characterized some of these
happenings as "safety valves" which provided a rationalization for their
not having services in operation.

A further delay in the opening date of July 8 for day care programs
was reported:

> Mrs. Davis: Ah, now there is a matter that I'm certain has been on
> everybody's minds—and that is the July 8th date—and the possible
> opening day care. . . . This will not be possible. . . . One is the fact
> that the —— school hasn't moved. . . . Our furniture is still arriving
> . . . and it hasn't all gotten here. There has been a freeze on hiring
> staff that I did not find out until yesterday will not be lifted until July
> 1st. Consequently, we cannot hire staff except those to whom we have
> made commitments. . . . I think that we have to look back and realize
> that many things were not working for us when we started out—with
> no phones and desks . . . thus far we have seen people, offered services
> and we have moved, despite the fact that we didn't have anything, and
> we have operated despite the limitations. . . . July 8th will not be the
> opening date of day care. I would not want any children to come in here
> until we have lived in that day care building furnished. There is nothing
> more frustrating for a child—than to come into a place where someone
> is supposed to be secure and comfortable and find those adults confused
> as to where things are. We need to live with that furniture in that
> building. Ah, in the meantime, training is essential and we are going
> along in the process.

The delays surrounding the opening of Children's services were attributed
to such things as the lack of furniture, the probable inadequacy of the
budget, and the inability to hire people because of the repeated freeze
imposed on hiring by the Department of Personnel. Information about
these types of transactions was reported in staff meetings. However, areas
of disagreement between the Subzone Administration and Mrs. Davis
on issues related to the type of program that was to be developed were

---

*A job freeze supposedly means that no new employeees may be hired until
the freeze is lifted. During the course of this study, four freezes were imposed
but, in each instance, ways of circumventing these restrictions were found.

not mentioned. Further, the lack of staff "trained" to do the work and the problems of the internal planning for the opening of these areas were not alluded to, except in a tangential manner. In Mrs. Davis' terms, these external factors served as "safety valves" that could be used to take the pressure off for getting services for children initiated. Meanwhile, these delaying maneuvers provided the opportunity for the organization to gain information about the possible treatment alliances that might be established, as well as needed knowledge about the nature of the clients that were available to the program as a baseline for determining what options were open for them.

Management Problems Across Program Boundaries

While much of the interaction in meetings was concerned with the internal management of relationships between participants in the organization, increasing concern over the input into the program from the external environment and the output of the program into the external organization was demonstrated. Two specific topics of discussion illustrating these systems problems, were the discussions pertaining to transportation of clients into the program and the records and documents that were to be kept by the program. Hours of meeting time were often devoted to these discussions.

Transportation

An essential aspect of transportation discussions was the concern of staff as to the types of clients that could be recruited for the program. Issues such as fear of being inundated by too many children and a desire to keep them out, or, even conversely, fear that there wouldn't be a client public interested in the services of the program were reflected. Transportation discussion also permitted staff to conjecture as to where the children would come from and what type of children they would be. An early staff meeting illustrates this concern.

> Mrs. Davis: I do know what my hope is—to have maybe two central points in the city where parents who bring their children—the bus will leave from a certain point at a certain time—they may need to bring their children there by 8:15 and the bus will not leave until later— that means we will have to have some outposts—a facility where children can be in out of the weather, but where they can all get on a bus at a certain spot. I am positive it will not be door to door pick up at all.

As the intake calls began coming in, a concern over transportation as a factor in screening out potential clients became an issue, particularly in the light of anticipated boundary changes.

Staff Meeting:

> Miss Selby: One thing that I have been worried about in terms of the far south side—if we go ahead the next couple of weeks and continue to take these as we have taken them in the past—will we be in a position when the time comes for day care to provide them with transportation. Will there be enough of them so that we can count on following through on our commitment, you know?
>
> Mrs. Davis: We are not making commitments now, in terms of day care. We are not at this point saying—we are doing screening—there still has to be a diagnostic conference, and much more contact with the parent. We are not making any commitment—
>
> Miss Selby: What I was asking is will we be in a position to follow through with a commitment? Because I know that we are not making any commitments now, but it is a kind of—if we take these people and follow through on a diagnostic, and the diagnostic indicates that we feel this child will benefit and we still have some down there who are going to need transportation from us. That's what I am thinking and you almost feel that you should screen them out at the phone call unless we know that we can ultimately follow all the way through, you know what I mean?

At the time the structuring of the program provided the dominant theme in meeting interaction, dialogue about transportation was centered around types of buses, the number of children the various types of buses would carry, whether buses should be purchased or leased, and the general logistics of pickup and delivery.

Staff Meeting one month later:

> Mrs. Wakefield: I wonder if there has been any consideration of the size of the bus—what large number of kids will there be, and how closely will you have to watch them.
>
> Mrs. Davis: I think the size . . . is like a station wagon type of school bus—a van kind of thing.
>
> Mrs. Sanders: I think you can get about 10 in that—but the state law varies.
>
> Mrs. Davis: So our numbers would be anywhere from 8 to 15, and I prefer the vans because with our children I don't think we can use the big buses.
>
> Mr. Peters: Will there be more than one central pickup point?
>
> Mrs. Davis: Yeah, more than one—we may have two or three. But if we can—initially we will have to have about three but when we get in the full swing I would think that we would have a bus that could pick up ten at one point and another bus that could pick up its load at another.

With the approaching date for the opening of the day care program, staff concerns centered around whether clients could be recruited for the program. The staff meeting discussion later in July, reflected this concern as they again talked about transportation problems.

> Mr. Anderson: This is one thing that I want to bring up—I have been dabbling through the schedules of major bus companies and unfortunately we have run into a problem of major proportion in my estimation of getting clients out here if they don't have a car—the buses don't come directly by here.
>
> Mrs. Davis: You know, Mr. Anderson, I am—and you may be tired of me saying this, when I say I appreciate the work that the staff has done—these are things that wouldn't get done if we didn't have staff to work on it—and the clients who struggle to get here, and the staff too—I think that at some point we talked about making it so that we could mail out something about transportation.
>
> Mr. Anderson: What I did is type this up and we are giving this to all staff members who will be writing letters to people coming out here— all they have to do is to check this, and they can make the public transportation schedules very explicit . . . . the big point that I am concerned about is that you can get them only so close and not any closer.

Although hours were spent in discussion of transportation problems and extensive exploration of costs of buying buses, getting drivers, hiring attendants and similar related problems, Mrs. Davis announced at the day care planning meeting two weeks later, that these decisions had been made by others within the larger organization network months before she assumed her position.

> There was some negotiation around getting more buses for the mental health center, and this is what had been planned, and they had a projected view in terms of what kinds of buses would be needed, and it was the small buses. When I came, they consulted me, and I said to go ahead—they told me that it would take three to four months to get them and I said as long as we had buses—because we had to bring children from the inner city—ah, currently we will be able to—we will have only one bus available to us until at least January that we can use, but in terms of admissions this is going to be a gradual process anyway, so that I don't think that we are going to be at any great loss. I'm sorry because I think that the kind of rationale behind the kind of bus you want is good, but this is something that already had been started, but I think the most important thing is, and correct me if I'm wrong, is that we will be able to get the kids out here.

It becomes obvious that often the program had to function within decisions priorly determined by the larger organization of which it was a part.

Finally, discussions of transportation issues helped to form a basis for the staff's perceptions of the clientele they would be serving, as reflected in the following excerpt from the staff meeting following the opening of day center.

Mrs. Davis: I'd like to ask staff something about using the bus some-time in October—we will have about three children from the inner city that will need bus service—in all honestness, we have not had time to make an arrangement with a state-aided clinic to arrange for a pickup point as we had hoped . . . . at the same time, some of these children are coming from a long way. I would like to start the way that we hope to end up which is to bring your child to a clinic and pickup and deliver there. One of the reasons that this is that the children who would be picked up first don't have to ride so long, as if you picked them up at home—this is one of the advantages of a central pickup point—also you have the parent who doesn't have the kid ready, and having a central point was one of the ways of avoiding that . . . but my point is that if we don't have the time to work out something with the sites should we start something that we can't finish or should we ask the parents to bear with us for another couple of weeks and get the kids here until we get that central point.

Mrs. Williams: We should consider who the parents are—if they are the kind that will try to get out of as much as they can it seems like we would be getting into a bad situation, even if we tell them it is temporary, but, if they are the ones that seem willing to carry their own share then it is different—

Miss Selby: I have another concern and no suggestion to go with it—but a lot of parents will take their children to a central point and leave them—are we going to provide a babysitter there?

Mrs. Davis: That is what we talked about before—a staff person has to be there for them to leave the child with so that the site—their staff would not be burdened with having the child there.

Mrs. Tatum: You are going to run into the same problem in the after-noon—if they know that someone is there in the afternoon they may just leave the child there with the babysitter.

Mrs. Davis: My question is that if we have the bus on October 1st should we use it to pick up the children, or should we wait an additional two weeks until we can make arrangements for a pickup place? We may make it easy for the parents now and hard for us later.

Mr. Waters: How capable are the parents of getting the children here?

Miss Selby: I have the feeling that I would rather pick the kids up at home—

Mrs. Davis: One of the reasons I hesitate is that I want the staff to pull together and some of the children that we have are not exactly within the boundaries—if we drive outside of the area we can't take these kids —we took these children because we wanted to get started, and these children have already been bounced around enough; and if we ask our drivers to go outside our boundaries, we have just hung ourselves . . . as long as the pickup point is within our boundaries, it is all right.

Discussions of transportation problems branched into larger issues, such as recruiting clients for the program, managing the type of the clientele that would use the services of the program, and focusing the relationships of parents and program participants on their common concern for the children. Rarely were binding decisions reached; in fact, during the course of the study, buses were used and all pickups and deliveries were made directly door to door, even when clients did not live within the expressed geographic boundaries of the program. Furthermore, the provision of transportation, while originally concerned with the needs of the poor people from the inner city, became more and more a means of collecting clients from suburban, outlying areas of the city and thus ministering to a group of middle class children.

Records and Official Documents

The flow of information must be two ways. Information was fed into the program from the external environment. The program, in turn, had to feed back information about its work to the larger organization. The kind of information extended outward was extremely important in developing the program image.

The images fostered through the aid of records were first, the idea that the staff was doing "professional work" and secondly, that they were doing "legitimate work," that is, actually seeing clients. One of the difficulties of a program so long in the developmental stage was that of fostering an impression of "doing something" while there was little visible evidence to substantiate this.

The purpose of records, as Mrs. Carroll viewed them, was outlined in a discussion in an early Intake Training Seminar:

> Mrs. Carroll: Essentially what you are trying to do in the process is attempting in a sense—to present the record like a hospital record—when you pick up a hospital chart you see a description of a person's symptoms and the diagnostic information and actually this is very important because the person who handles this chart wants to get at, very quickly, what the problem is, what the diagnosis is. So that when you are doing this sort of thing you want to keep in mind that primarily you want to give a very clear picture of what the child is doing at this point . . . . it's a part of your realizing that this is a part of a disciplined approach that you are making to the situation. . . . You've got to be able to pinpoint and focus on the important material. . . . You bring your own professional expertise to this so that you know what is going on and be sure that they know that you know what is going on.

Indirectly, recording is a measure of the professional expertise of the worker.

The physical location became an issue as the opening of day care approached. Disapproval over the decision to keep records in the main record room of the organization rather than in Children's services was expressed. The question was posed in a staff meeting one month before the opening of Day Care:

> Mrs. Davis: The question submitted for the agenda is: "Will Children's records for out-patient be kept in Room 1175 (main administration building) and if so why?"
> Mr. Anderson: If we are going to be doing the out-patient services over here . . . . if I was doing therapy with the child . . . I would want the record readily available to me. . . .
> Miss Travis: If the major file has to be kept outside the pavilion would it be possible to at least have the major information kept here in a duplicate file, during the time that it is active?
> Mrs. Davis: There are essentials for accreditation—they do have rules about records being centrally located—but this does not mean that we cannot keep our own files here with information . . . but every record we have we will have to have in a central location.

This concern over sharing records with the larger organization was also felt by day care staff.

Day Care Planning Meeting:

> Mr. Waters: If we have one common sheet where people can enter their notes if they want—there may be nothing that happens, but maybe you have only one line—if it is on one sheet so that if something happens they can go there and have a day by day progress report on the boy.
> Mrs. Davis: I think that's a good idea—we need it centralized in case anything blows when somebody is away from here—somebody is going to have to be able to pick it up and see what happened. . . .
> Mrs. Tatum: One question—if there were things that I would like to report as a teacher—where would I put these notes? . . . Who should be responsible for the total chart . . . . shouldn't the person with case responsibility be responsible for this?
> Mrs. Newman: I would think it would all go on one place so you wouldn't have to go around looking for people to tell you what is going on.

Records were ideally viewed as a comprehensive evaluation and developmental picture of the child, and in that way the need for and importance of these records was agreed upon. It was almost as if the record held the clues as to what was to be done in a given situation. Thus, for program participants, the function of records was that of providing an effective tool for otherwise unstructured data which could be used as guidelines for subsequent action.

Mrs. Davis saw records in a very different light. For her, they were the means of substantiating and validating various points that she wished to make in her relationships in the "outside world." In connection with setting up a medical record committee, Mrs. Davis expressed some of her concerns:

Staff Meeting:

> **Mrs. Davis:** Somebody had a forty-five minute telephone call the other day, and I had to make a note some place that this sort of thing occurred because they are trying to work out something . . . to better reflect the kind of work that we do so we do need to be concerned about records . . . . so that if something is unusual in terms of time you might find some way of making a note to this effect so that one of these days when we go back to try to pick up this kind of data it will be available to us.
>
> **Miss Selby:** Actually there are some very specific ways of counting things, that if we are to defend ourselves we have to know—like they will count the number of patients, and calculate the number of staff hours needed to carry this number of patients, or they will count the interview hours, and be guided by the number of staff you have in evaluating what you are doing.

Subsequently, Miss Selby was given the responsibility of investigating the necessary record-keeping procedures. Her report was given in the staff meeting:

> The statistics are kept for the purpose of research and also so that (the Superintendent) can go to (the legislature) and say, "This is what we do with our time"—so it is important that we get this information to them. What you have are three forms—this first form is a record of interviews. . . .
>
> **Mr. Waters:** Actually what purpose does this serve other than just showing that you saw the person?
>
> **Miss Selby:** That is the purpose of the record—because you are—when the (Superintendent) goes to the (legislature) to ask for so many millions of dollars to run this place they check this to see if it is warranted. (The other two forms were concerned with reporting the diagnosis and disposition of the case.)

While records within the program provided a means of sharing information with the "outside world" they were also viewed as a defensive tool to be used to justify and validate the work being done within the program.

In summary, a predominant feature of the early stages of the program was the managerial concern with relationships at all levels, ranging from interpersonal one to one relationships, all the way to the direction of clients into the program and communication with the "outside world" via the record-keeping processes. Thus, hours and hours of discussion of issues that staff, at the time, often considered to be trivia served the function of dealing with internal and external management problems that were deemed pressing and, consequently, offered a legitimate excuse for the delaying of direct work with children.

Potential Treatment Alliances
and Resources

Success in the political arena of a bureaucratic organization, lies in a program's ability to assert its own unique type of work. The differentiation of a given program is contingent upon knowing the type of work similar organizations perform. Based upon that information, the type of program most likely to succeed can be evaluated. In this instance, evaluation of potential services offered by the state hospital as well as public demands for services provided a basis for deciding that this program's distinguishing feature would be the provision of quality services to a select few rather than quantity services which would meet the total demand. Quality in-services were defined on the basis of long-term therapeutic goals rather than short-range attempts at behavior modification. Having arrived at these decisions, the program then had to find a way of legitimatizing its position in the external world.

An early indication of the attempt to differentiate itself from other agencies is presented in an early staff meeting when Mr. Paulson made a suggestion about a possible treatment resource for a specific case. "An agency that might take this kind of a kid is ——— Mental Health Clinic who does quite a bit of diagnostic work. They may be able to take these kids on an out-patient basis. Perhaps we could form some kind of alliance with them." In the discussion that followed further development of this idea occurred.

> Mr. Paulson: Some of the places are better staffed than we are—especially in handling some of these things, and if they are going to be involved in doing the out-patient, a lot of times why shouldn't they also do the diagnostic work-up. Who are we to say we can provide this? Mrs. Davis: And another thing . . . in no way are we saying that you've got to come through us for diagnostics—If you can give the diagnostic—give it. If you are not equipped to do it, and there is no other facility within the community without the child traveling 70 miles you do it for him, and then we'll offer the consultation, if you want it, but if he wants a diagnostic and that's all, we'll try to start there. . . . I don't think we are going to try to impose, but I think your interpretation is absolutely correct.

The distinction then, was made between doing diagnostic work-ups or providing consultation to some other agency which would do that work. Diagnoses and consultation rank higher, in terms of prestige, than does the direct offering of services to clients. Thus, this early dialogue indicates an attempt to place this particular program in a more prestigious light than other organizations involved in similar work. Further evidence of this desire is provided in an interchange in the staff meeting one month later:

> Mrs. Davis: I am going to have a conference with (the Superintendent of Unit B) at which time we are going to try to make complementary programs in terms of what he will take and what we will take. We have our set program and policies, but I think there could be some shifts as to where we go and we are not that far apart, but we are in the process of trying to reach some kind of agreement.
>
> Miss Selby: It seems to me that unless we have identical programs we have to operate over the entire Region—otherwise kids get excluded on the basis of this little catchment area. . . .
>
> Mr. Packard: I want to raise the observation that at Unit B they— they, the program, from what I hear, in terms of treatment relies on behavioral conditioning which is quite different from what we are talking about.
>
> Mrs. Davis: Their treatment may be very different from what ours is going to be.
>
> Mr. Packard: You are not going to shock kids?
>
> Miss Selby: Are they using shock at Unit B?
>
> Mrs. Simpson: Rumors, rumors—don't believe everything you hear. . . .
>
> Mr. Packard: The point is the fact that you might be interested in knowing what they specialize in—they might be special in terms of treatment, like for the mentally retarded, operant conditioning may be more effective and they get better by use of this treatment modality.

Though this process of comparison with other agencies, the program began to identify itself as distinct from other agencies. In subsequent interaction there developed a struggle between techniques of behavior modification and psychotherapy with the predominating emphasis becoming that of therapy.

A further problem that occurred in relationship to the external world was the handling of contacts with those who called for services for children when the program had nothing yet to offer. Mrs. Wakefield posed the question in an early staff meeting:

> Mrs. Wakefield: What if a doctor or social worker call about a specific case . . . and we say no, we don't have a residential treatment program at this time, and they ask us for advice about where to refer them. . . . How far does our obligation go. . . . Like if the social worker asks us to find a place?
>
> Mrs. Davis: I think there is a difference—if it is a social worker, we might well be able to just say we don't have such a facility, but if it is a private physician we have to explore with him whether the family can explore the resources. . . .
>
> Mrs. Wakefield: Most of my questions were by social workers calling who would say, 'can you call unit B', or can you do this or can you do that—my first reaction was no—if there is anything that you can do as well as I can, then it is a different question.

Thus, one of the factors essential in handling the demands of the external public was determining what segment of the "outside world" was represented by the individual who made the contact. An incident occurring on the day in which the Mental Health Center complex was dedicated further reflects this problem.

> Mrs. Davis: I had a visitor going through and he came in and he hit a sore spot with me, and all of a sudden I found myself standing up and saying very staunchly—and I didn't find out until afterward who he was—but I still believe what I believe. He was saying about the in-patient unit, "of course these children will be heavily sedated" and whew, I hit the ceiling because I don't want for these children to be heavily sedated—This is one of these things—and each one of these guys that has some investments, some response from this drug business, but everybody has his own little business to peddle.
> Miss Selby: Did you see that business—that background information that we get from (that hospital) on that little boy—this is modern short-term therapy—drug him up and send him home.
> Mrs. Simpson: I think too that this is a lay person's point of view . . . this is the only way they can control him—they really don't have that much confidence in one-to-one therapy or your own ability to cope with them. If you give them a shot then you can handle it.
> Mrs. Davis: That's a good point because what you're saying—I was talking about a legislative person, and what you are saying is that they are lay people but you can't let the position that they are in influence what you do—certainly I'm going to stand by my convictions but trying to present it in such a way that it will create no ill will.
> Mrs. Carroll: Trying to keep peace!
> Mrs. Davis: Which is pretty hard after I had said, 'Not in these walls!'
> Mrs. Simpson: He was thinking about all the broken windows.
> Mrs. Davis: That's right—he was thinking about damage to the building.
> Miss Selby: That's one advantage in being in an old building—nobody worries about damages.

Staff that works within a state bureaucratic system rapidly learn to be sensitive to legislators and to techniques of "dealing with them."

The problem of the management of a public that shares a similar responsibility for the welfare of children is illustrated in a report given by Mrs. Davis on her visit to the local school district:

> There were certainly very strong negative feelings directed toward us. I hope that I was able to intervene a little in this—we will have other meetings to help work out our relationships and to help clarify what we might do, but there is one thing that I think that we will all have to be very aware of. In most of the telephone calls if any of you find that you are being asked questions to which you cannot give some kind of an answer, I think we'd better talk about it. . . . I think that one of the

things that we need to get across is that we do know where we are going although we may not know exactly the route where we are going we are still in the planning stage, but there will be a day care and we do know the age range because I picked up a kind of feeling from some of the teaching personnel—and I'm talking about those in counseling and social work—whereby they felt that the staff over here doesn't know where it's going. . . .

Mrs. Simpson: I think the confusion here comes not from not knowing where our program is going, but not knowing things like our boundaries, because this has caused some really sticky issues where you try very hard to explain your program, and give them definite answers and it comes right down to "Am I in your area—can you serve me?" Then you can't say for sure.

The difficulty of establishing relationships between agencies sharing responsibility for children was further articulated by Mrs. Davis:

One of our protections is that we do not accept a client without contacting the source—One other thing as far as schools are concerned—I think that the schools will have to be oriented in how they are to refer to us—ah, if we have a Child Study work-up on some child, and part of their recommendation is for referral to us, then the school should have—and if they don't have that is their problem—they should have to work out a method of referring to us. I see no reason why we should have to ask for authorization forms for information if they are sending the person to us. Because we are left with the baby when that does happen, and that is one of the reasons that the schools have been so slow in terms of getting central services available in the school system, because we have taken their job over.

Through contacts with external agencies, an organization not only learns about the demands that these agencies place upon it but, in turn, develops rules and obligations that can be followed in relating to the program. Experiences gleaned through telephone contacts in the early stages of the program thus served as stimuli for the creation of a body of rules and procedures to be followed, not only by the program itself, but by those who would obtain services. Through this process a series of reciprocal obligations was established to govern relationships with external agencies.

A further source of information gleaned from the "outside world" was through direct observation of other treatment programs for children and their work in this area. A report of such a visit was given in a Day Care Planning meeting by Mr. Anderson:

I thought it was very good—we found out a lot about some of the things—their classes are set up on the basis of the children and teacher's personalities being similar—so that you might have a particular child that cannot stand rigid structure, and a teacher who doesn't believe in using a rigid structure, and a child who needs structure would be put in with a teacher who believes in structure in a classroom situation. From what I understand they tried most of the other methods and this was the method that worked best as far as they were concerned. As far as the staff—they use whatever method of teaching or child-handling that works best for them—if they are oriented toward the Bettelheim approach they will be permissive with the child, and if you have a person that is oriented toward behavior modification then they function in that way, but they feel that to propose a certain set of structured rules about how you are to conduct your class is only going to—if a teacher feels that a certain approach isn't going to work the child is going to prove you right . . . but one of the things I noticed was that even those who say they are behavior modifiers—they are much more permissive than you would expect—that was my impression of one of the professors who said he was oriented toward behavior modification—when he was in the classroom he was considerably more permissive than people that said they were oriented in that way.

The program that was visited, in this instance, was one within the Mental Health Center where Dr. Daniels had previously been employed. Information about the nature of this program further clarified the developing conflict between a treatment orientation and an educational program. Instead of using these observations as a model to be followed, they were used as a justification of the supposed faults inherent in the educational approach to the management of emotionally disturbed children.

As the conflicts within the external organizational environment increased, reports of meetings held within the Region were given in such a way as to provide staff with the impression that their positions would be protected and that Mrs. Davis would see that Children's services survived. Supporting evidence is provided in a staff meeting in which Mrs. Davis reports on a Subzone Meeting:

> We are trying to establish complementary services so that we can be more comprehensive, and certainly with the tremendous need for services for children no one institution can do it. We also felt that it was difficult for (Children's services) to have our voices heard adequately— this is not because of a lack of interest in this, but there are tremendous problems around general administration—consequently, when we were in the meeting both (the Children's Program Director from the state hospital) and myself thought that we needed someone who was in a coordinating position at the subzone level for Children's—we were concerned about the resources and the court troubles we have—a variety of things that are on such a high level that it is very difficult for us to get the kind of attention with so many things happening in adult services . . . so we made a request to have a coordinator of Children's services . . . and I'm quite sure this is what we have accomplished. . . .

I am pretty sure that our route will be treatment—we call it rehabilitation to a limited extent because of a money factor but I think we are headed in the right direction.

Through this process of obtaining information about potential external alliances and resources and translating this into the organizations inner arena, the direction which this specific program was to take was clarified. Increasingly the emphasis was placed upon "quality rather than quantity" and "education rather than therapy," leaving the burden of responsibility for the masses of children upon the state hospital system, and determining a select segment of potential clients for the Mental Health Center.

Information about Potential Clients

Another factor which distilled the nature of the programs work was the input of information concerning potential clients. This information was largely gathered through telephone contacts initiated by an often distraught public, asking about services for emotionally disturbed and retarded children. The primary motive of handling Intake calls was ostensibly to provide individuals in need of help with the appropriate resources, but they also provided the organization with concrete evidence about the nature of the public demanding services. This knowledge helped provide a background of information for determining what segment of this population could be considered as desirable treatment candidates. Rather than predefining characteristics desired in children to be accepted into the program, the reverse process occurred. Based on the information collected through these telephone contacts, all potential trouble-makers were sifted out, and the residual group considered for acceptance into the program. This early concern with the character of the population to be served was reflected in an interchange occurring within a staff meeting:

Mr. Packard: We have to be realistic about what slice of the population could best be served—I think we have to take neurotic children. The more acutely disturbed we would be doing a disservice to, by taking them.
Miss Selby: But all of us have to face the fact that there are no services for these kids—you can't put a bandaid on a psychosis.
Mrs. Davis: Another responsibility we have—in the long run it is a disservice to expand inappropriately because it absolves the problem. Expansion will not be done here to the destruction of our program. We will keep records and statistics that say we had to turn away this type of child. Reporting and substantiating needs and raising questions about services that have to be provided is part of our job also. Then the state

can drag its heels but we won't try to cover up the problem.

Miss Selby: If we take kids that we know need residential care for two years and then we take them for six months, we do them a disfavor. . . .

Mrs. Davis: I call upon staff to be extremely honest in what develops in the treatment of children. It's the only way we can point out the validity—by realizing we are up a creek—that is not dishonest—we are not here to prove that it does work—if it doesn't we better admit and not go on with something that is dishonest.

Mr. Packard: I rebel against the term success—instead we need to determine the criteria. . . . I would simply like to say that our goal should be the remission of acute symptoms. Symptomatic lessening is one of the goals, and then planning in terms of linkage.

Mrs. Davis: With full recognition that this is only that and not cure.

Given only very vague definitions of the "appropriate child,"* the staff handling Intake calls was faced with the dilemma of what to tell those asking for services. This concern is reflected in a staff meeting:

Mr. Paulson: When you are on Intake you want to give them a clear idea of what we are going to handle here in terms of—this is a facility —we are visible—people know we are here now. They know we are going to have some kind of residential facility or day care kind of operation—(interrupted by Mr. Packard)

Mr. Packard: Until we get patients we will perhaps have to be vague even to persons calling in, you know. If the child seems to fit into our program we can do an evaluation, and then if a child is unsuitable for the program, then I think that we are entitled to have this flexibility of saying so.

Thus, one factor that served as stimulus for defining the clientele to be served occurred through the demands of a public for such definitions.

Lacking such basic definitions, goals were set for the beginning of certain phases of the operation:

Staff Meeting:

Mrs. Carroll: Then we'll be getting the first patient on May 20th?

Mrs. Davis: For diagnostic.

Mrs. Carroll: For diagnostic—but the first patient in the **program will** be—

Mrs. Davis: In day care June 20th.

Mrs. Simpson: And then in-patient will follow.

With these goals as stimuli, screening interviews were initiated, and from these contacts clearer definitions of the clientele to be served were reached. The seminars conducted by Mrs. Carroll and Dr. Cartwright reflect the

*A detailed discussion of the defining characteristics that were arrived at in determining the "appropriate child" for this facility is provided in Chapter X.

progress in reaching basic definitions that would govern decisions about the population that was to be served.

Mrs. Carroll, in her seminar described the process by which staff was to formulate their "impressions" of parents that were seen in the screening interviews:

> If you are doing a screening like this and you are doing it with some awareness of what you are doing so that automatically when you get through the material, your impressions start to—your impressions are coming all the time, but you sort of draw your impressions together . . . what you've drawn from the screening interview, and usually—I don't know how it is going to be done here, but usually the material is discussed in a screening staff. And determination is made at that point as to whether a complete diagnosis is going to be done . . . . this material will be important in determining whether a child will be accepted, and it also is important in terms of structuring the program and setting the tone for the program, so you do have to think about it in a meaningful way—and gather your impressions together.

Thus, contact with, and information about potential clients was perceived as "important in terms of structuring the program": the input of information obtained through the screening interviews was a prerequisite to the structuring process.

The opposite position, stressing a need for the predefinition of clients to be processed by the program is articulated in the first conference with Dr. Cartwright:

> Dr. Cartwright: That is the trouble family service agencies get into— they somehow feel that it is their obligation because they are a public service—they've got to take everything from soup to nuts—they get hoodwinked by the psychiatric clinics that this case belongs to them— big suicidal attempts and what have you that they can't handle—and I don't think that you should take that kind of a risk.
> Mrs. Davis: I think that it does—I'm not saying that it won't blow up —but I think there has to be a certain solidness of knowledge about what you can do well and some backup as to—you have to be able to have a base on which you are making your decisions.
> Dr. Cartwright: And that you don't know yet. Actually there is another problem involved here in terms of what your goals are—it's not only who fits here and who doesn't, but it's what your own goals are—if you have very fancy goals with most of them you can forget it—if you can help these children function on a minimal kind of basis that they didn't function on before then you have served a purpose . . . but one has to get off of fancy goals . . . and one has to quit imposing one's own view point of what kind of health they should have in terms of the kind of sickness you are dealing with. If you can get a kid to go to school, and act up a little, and learn up to his capacity you've done something. . . . You have to be realistic about what your expectations are. Now it may

> be that under the circumstances you may want to switch over to the parent—you may want to invest more in the parent basket than in the child basket.
>
> Mrs. Davis: This is where we have built into our program a heavy investment as far as parents are concerned.

While recognizing the need to be sensitive to the demands of the public for service, this interchange reflects a concern for defining the criteria which is to govern selection of the client population.

As the first projected opening date for day care approached, a lack of defining criteria was given as one of the reasons for postponing the opening. A discussion in a staff meeting at that time indicates the process by which goals were altered:

> Mrs. Davis: Now considering the fact of training, ah, and the need for workup—we can go ahead with the screening and diagnosis, and some of the outpatient and family groups—but how do you see the date of opening our day care?
>
> Mrs. Wakefield: First of all, how many staff do you think we will need —how many children will we be getting?
>
> Mrs. Davis: I think that it is going to be a small number initially— ah, we can learn and gradually add, but you know our maximum for day care is forty . . . what is realistic in terms of getting the staff and training—this doesn't mean that we are going to sit and hold our hands —it means we are going to be involved tremendously with parents and parents groups and some diagnostics for children, but not in day care. What is a realistic target date?

No decision was reached. The introduction of the "training seminars" underlined the need for a greater clarification of the nature of the clientele to be served, and until such conclusions were reached, the possibility of setting an arbitrary date for the opening of the day care unit was discarded. The conflicting needs for information about potential clients as a needed stimulus to govern program planning and the converse fear of inundation if defining criteria for a population to be served were not established but reflected in the continuing dialogue.

The work of the organization became increasingly complex as case material presented in diagnostic conferences revealed the shortcomings of referral material received from other agencies. Dr. Cartwright's critique, delivered in a conference reflects this tendency:

> What I'm feeling is that if you take a child—I think this is part of your job—if you take a child for a three month study period to make a diagnosis and you come out with a report like this (from another agency) you'd better look for another job. If you come out with a report like this you might as well skip the whole thing and not even start because this is no report. If you take a child you have to look at every corner

of his development and his behavior and try in every way you can to make up your mind if this is a candidate that is treatable or untreatable, and what is his diagnosis?

Through the input of information about other agencies, as reflected in the referrals that were sent to this program further goals were defined and stated. In this instance, the change in direction toward doing diagnostic work is evident. Further indication of this trend is shown in a day care planning meeting in which Mrs. Davis stated:

It is essential that we have medical-psychiatric consultation on all children who are admitted into day care . . . . we will proceed orally (in our reporting in diagnostic conferences) according to that outline so that Dr. Cartwright can relate herself to these areas in trying to decide whether or not this child can—in her opinion—if this child can be manageable in day care, and something in terms of prognosis, hopefully. It will depend upon the amount of information that is available. . . . Now there will be additional admissions conferences that will be held in terms of where this child will fit and how he will be programmed— that is not going to be done in the staffings tomorrow—but hopefully we can get something about prognosis—but we are trying to get kids here . . . on the date that is set.

Thus, the criteria for a potential client population was defined in terms of "manageability" within the day care setting, as well as some prognostic judgment of the potential treatability of both the child and the family unit. Those perceived to be unmanageable were kept out while treatability was not a necessary criteria for admission.

In summary, although goals were originally set for such things as opening dates and a population to be served, alterations in these projected targets were made on the basis of current information about the environmental context of the program, and appraisal of the current political situation. This turning-away-from or modification of original goals typifies large-scale organizations upon which a multitude of outside, as well as inside, forces impinge. Such adaptation and procrastination of goals seems to the participants to be necessary for the survival of the organization. The chaotic state of this external environment complicated the process and it may be hypothesized that these conditions contributed to the development of conservative trends that had an impact upon the final shape of the program. The stage was set.

Chapter IX

Rehearsal

All organizations confront the problem of training workers. However, the type and intensity of the training process varies from organization to organization. In a production organization, for example, assembly line work requires the worker to learn only what is relevant to his particular functions. The lower the individual within the organizational hierarchy, the less he needs to know of the total operation. In fact, one of the most common ways in which management works to control employees consists in keeping them ignorant. If an individual knows nothing more than how to pull a lever on a machine he is not likely to jeopardize this tenuous control of a job by agitating. The individual is confronted by constant reminders that he can be replaced; the less educated the individual the easier he/she is to replace.

In psychiatric organizations the problem of training staff takes on different dimensions. Producing a "mentally healthy" individual cannot be accomplished by pulling a lever. In fact, the definitions of what constitutes "mental health" are ambiguous and conflicting; the mental health worker has no clear guidelines to determine when his work on a particular individual ends. On the other hand, most of the teaching in psychiatric settings centers around symptomatology, or how to recognize mental illness. A mental health worker requires training in how to make judgments upon the sanity of other individuals; techniques of treatment are secondary to diagnosis. All mental health workers, from an untrained psychiatric aide to the most highly educated psychiatric professional, are involved in making these judgments. The chief individuating factor, instead of being the type of work people do within the organization, is the amount of deference paid to an individual's appraisals. A second separation is found between those who are considered qualified to teach and those who are considered in need of being taught. Although psychiatric professionals have been exposed to a number of conflicting views in their educational training, on-the-job training for the non-professional frequently reflects none of these conflicts. Workers are taught simplistic

137

approaches to making evaluative judgments. This then becomes one of the chief ways of maintaining control over an individual worker. He has been taught to make certain judgments that conform to those of other fellow workers. Rarely does the untrained worker openly question the judgments of the psychiatric professional. Rather he incorporates their viewpoint and makes it his own.

In this particular program the recruitment of a non-professional staff was important in maintaining control of the political battles within the larger organization. An untrained staff could readily be indoctrinated.

In contrast to professional educational programs, aimed at developing independent thinkers who consider many points of view in making clinical judgments, the training process adopted by this program consisted of teaching workers one main point of view. The novice worker was placed in the interview situation with the goal of obtaining pertinent information from the parent, and the novice in turn was subtly indoctrinated with the philosophy of the program during the review of these interviews. In these reviewing sessions, staff was taught how they ought to have conducted the sessions and how they were to make inferences from the material elicited from the parent. The outgrowth of this teaching process was a staff adept in the ways of rapidly stereotyping parents and children in the interview situation and manipulating data so that the information extracted from the interview would substantiate the stereotype.

Staff was also trained to make deductions from the information about a family's history of illness and problems between marital partners and relate them to the child's behavior. This search for a causality which would explain current problematic behavior took precedence over any other consideration.

The emphasis was upon training, as a goal in itself, while training for therapeutic work or providing services to children, was secondary. This type of instruction was functional in other areas of life. With staff composed primarily of young, newly married women, these training sessions combined counsel on marital relationships and child-rearing that served to prepare them for experiences outside the purview of the program.

Politically, the program could argue that they were developing new and innovative approaches in the use of untrained, and, therefore, less expensive, staff. Since staff was trained in only one technique of interviewing rather than bombarded with the various conflicting "professional" views, parents were exposed to the same routine by all interviewers and were satisfied. Furthermore, as long as children were not allowed in the interview situation, the reality of the actual child did not interfere with the stereotypes developed in the training process.

This chapter will trace the procedure used in training staff to anticipate situations and catalogue their experiences in a way compatible with the goal of propagating the work of the organization.

The need to structure, through hypothetical situations, the nature of the work of a newly developing organization is an essential form of interaction. When this organization deals with "disturbed" children as its clients the hypothesizing, for those who have had no experience with the emotionally disturbed, takes the form of relating anticipated experience to past experiences of normal children. Those who have had the experience of working with emotionally disturbed children, however, contribute by supplying the organization with their experience. Through this subtle course, staff is taught to identify the mentally ill child and envision the type of behavior that it can anticipate from him.

In addition to this subtle form of indoctrination, occurring throughout all areas of interaction, specialized training seminars, serving as the main arena for staff instruction within this organization, are organized along more formal lines. These seminars equip the untrained staff member with a shorthand method of categorizing his various contacts with children and parents, so that he can extract a meaningful structure from the chaotic "hodge podge" of data which he is given. Subsequently, on the basis of his having catalogued these experiences, he is taught to make judgments concerning the significance of this interaction, particularly as it relates to the future direction and treatment-potential of the family or child.

The training process in a newly developing organization is further complicated by the lack of any premolded structure into which the staff is indoctrinated. Consequently, the training process develops simultaneously with the growth and expansion of the organization, and, in some instances, it can be argued that the training process determines the emerging shape of the organization.

Anticipatory Socialization Processes

Discussions centering around such mundane matters as the ordering of furniture and supplies were often interlaced with statements about "what children would be like." A statement by Mrs. Davis, made while ordering furniture early in the year, reflects this early concern: "At first I thought that my selection would be the most economical one because I wanted plain table tops without any wood graining effects but I found that they were expensive—I want plain tops to cut down the sensory stimulation . . . . children who are having hallucinations and other problems don't need any more stimulation."

Often these discussions revolved around the justification of ordering given equipment on the basis of "children's needs."

Staff Meeting:

> Mrs. Davis: I want to bring some life into the pavilions—I think where you enter I want some big potted plants. Also I want an aquarium . . . also if you have any idea about bringing life into the pavilions I would appreciate any suggestions. Children need bright living things.
> Miss Selby: I've thought about some pictures but I don't want any of those psychotic pictures like they've got over in the administration building.

Through these early forms of interaction, the children were made the reference point around which decision making revolved.

In contrast to the frequently stated view that "children are nice to work with," Mrs. Davis anticipated that staff would at times become frustrated in their work with children.

Staff Meeting:

> Mrs. Davis: Every adult that the child comes in contact with we would hope would have some orientation in how to relate to children and also how to handle your frustrations. We will provide means for this, and although we have a day care center which runs six hours, we will certainly have the rest of the time . . . for some method of communicating feelings and what have you—we will have a structure here so that one will not have to wait the full six hours if they are extremely frustrated— there will be channels so that if a person has to get away from a situation that is frustrating and pull out and have somewhere to turn . . . . someone will be available so they can get rid of their frustrations.
> Miss Selby: It's better to get mad at each other rather than at the kids.
> Mrs. Davis: Yeah, this is the important thing, but I also want the message very clear that I do not expect anyone not to feel like smacking the kids, because this is natural in all, and we don't expect you to— in certain respects we expect a degree of maturity but there is no shame in feeling this way—in fact this is an element of maturity to know one's limitations—and when you've about had it—you do have to have a place where you can go and say, "I've had it."

Not only were children "loveable," it was concluded, but they were also capable of angering and "frustrating"; and, therefore, early in the developmental phases of the program, provision for directing these frustrations to an outlet other than the child was made.

Given a relatively inexperienced staff, the organization was concerned with transforming them into "disciplined workers." Mrs. Carroll expressed this necessity in an early Intake Training Seminar:

> I think that some of the things that you do can only be determined by experience. I think too, that in approaching this situation, that if you become overly identified with the fact that there is a shortage of services for children to the point where you feel that you have got to meet every child's need, you are doomed to failure from the beginning. . . . You not only have to be compassionate to be able to work with people as people . . . but you also have to be objective to the point where you are disciplined in your approach. You cannot do all things for all people—it is better to do for a small number than it is to try to cover the waterfront and not get anything done. This is a brand new program—it is a new approach to working with children—and I think that you are going to take a lot of things that normally you don't have to take into consideration in the regular kind of work with children—so there is going to have to be some experimentation—you don't like to think of doing this with people, and children in particular, but this is the way that it is going to work out.

An early expectation of the senior staff was that, given a definite procedure for selecting candidates admitted into the program, staff would be responsible for developing the necessary objectivity for evaluating the applicants and assessing their needs.

Another form of anticipatory socialization involved various viewpoints of the participants in the program as to what "children are like." A segment of a staff meeting in which an art consultant, who later joined the staff, expressed her feelings concerning the contribution art could make toward understanding and helping the child, serves to illustrate this form:

> Mrs. Davis: . . . one of the things that we will be doing with our children is that of dealing with their problems of identity, self-image, and basic trust, and I would like if you could give the staff some idea of how you approach this.
>
> Art Consultant: That's a subject that I can always talk about. I firmly believe that everything a child does is part of himself and reflects something of himself. In addition to gaining acceptance for himself from others, he needs self-acceptance—I think that in the field of art, aside from just the sheer creative aspects of art, which is more in the order of a cathartic experience, that the child might receive—I feel that everything that he draws, and when he projects even the slightest tangible evidence of his creativity, he is identifying himself with what he creates. . . . I feel that the most important things that one can do for a child is to allow him to say "this is mine," regardless of the caliber of the creation, and regardless of the limitations it may have. I look upon this kind of relationship as an attempt to have the child accept, on his own basis and on your basis, that which he is.

After this introduction, staff discussed the manner in which they would deal with a situation in which a child drew a picture which he wanted to destroy, while they wanted to hang it up. They concluded that the child should be allowed the freedom to do whatever he might wish with "his production"—even to destroy it. Thus, the idealistic presentation of the significance of art to the child was translated, by staff, into the handling of anticipated problems.

As the program moved into the phase of actual contact with clients (initially through the screening interviews), emphasis was placed upon the viewing of parents and children by staff.

Intake-Screening Training Seminar:

> Mrs. Carroll: I want to emphasize that when you are looking at pathology you are not looking at it to be critical or judgmental—Why are you looking at pathology? Why do you want to know about pathology? Why does the doctor when he is treating a patient want to know about it?
> Mrs. Simpson: If you don't know what is the matter you don't know where to start.
> Mrs. Carroll: You've got to know what the difficulty is in order to be able to treat it—I want to emphasize that I have worked with young students who feel that I emphasize pathology too much. And they really feel strongly about this. But I try to convey to them that this is not judgmental—that this is the means of making an evaluation, and you've got to do it. But you've got to do it with the thought in mind that really what you are going to work with is the strengths, so you want to look for the strengths as well as the pathology, but you have to know the pathology first.

It was argued that staff should first look at the pathology of the parents as a means of determining tentative treatment for the child. This, in turn, justified the view that the gathering of information on parents was essential since they were often the villains.

Further expectations for therapists in their relationships with children were outlined in the diagnostic seminars conducted by Dr. Cartwright:

> It terrifies the child to attack you and you have to be stronger than the child— . . . when you are the therapist and you think that you are to be kind to them and good—and you are not going to be unkind and use your hands or sit on them . . . but sometimes they will want to do this to you and you can't let them. I had a case presented to me where the therapist every hour had his tie torn off—his suit torn up—and I listened to this case and all I said to this worker was "I think you've got to get some consultation in this case. I've never been attacked by a child— and either there is something in you that is going to permit this kind of stuff and then it is going to happen whether you set it up or not— then very often it happens when you are not set up to control the child,

and you are so mixed up in your feelings that you aren't supposed to
do anything, that you get yourself attacked for no good reason it's not
good for the child and it's not good for you."

Therapists were expected to control children, and, indeed, the measure
of their competence as therapists was to some extent guaged by their
ability to execute this control.

Techniques for dealing with the specific needs of certain types of children were also outlined:

Diagnostic Conference:

> Dr. Cartwright: You see psychotic children do very well under circum-
> stances of structure the only thing is that they have no structure as
> human beings, so they depend on things outside remaining the same—
> they can sit for hours and do a puzzle as long as no one interferes with
> the puzzle . . . . the problem with these children is their ego develop-
> ment and you want to attend to that.

As additional children were accepted into the day care program, staff
realized that the needs of the different children were sometimes in-
compatible and expressed concern about this.

Day Care Planning Meeting:

> Mrs. Wakefield: This has been something that has been on my mind
> too—is that the first two children that have been accepted, as Dr. Cart-
> wright has diagnosed them, function at a psychotic level—and what is
> therapeutic for a child who is psychotic is not always therapeutic for
> someone who is mildly disturbed or kind of neurotic. So how many
> people are we going to have like this? And what does it mean to deal
> with a psychotic child, you know? How many people can work with
> them, and how are they going to be mixed?
> Mrs. Davis: Let's relate first to the fact that we've got to have some
> balance—and I want to relate to something else—and that is the kind
> of understanding that these children are ill and I think we have to do
> our own soul-searching as to our attitudes. We can talk a great deal, but
> we've got to feel compassion and understanding—I think that number
> one we have a structure, and then we've got to break it down because
> I think that it is according to whether we want to maintain the struc-
> ture or help the child . . . and the priority has to be to the child, and
> not to the structure. . . .
> Mr. Waters: We were talking about the classroom situation before, and
> the way I feel about it is say a boy does run out of the room—now for
> one boy that might be therapeutic to let him leave, and for another it
> might be therapeutic to tell him to stay in his seat— . . . I was under
> the assumption that you have to play each kid by ear—each kid is
> different and you would have to sit down and debate what is best for
> each child.

One of the expected possibilities, despite the evolution of an elaborate program structure, was that each child would be different and that staff would have to respond to these individual needs.

Experienced workers provided explanations for variations in the flow of work that also served as a guide in anticipating certain "busy seasons."

Intake Training Seminar:

> Mrs. Carroll: Have intake calls slowed down? You should have a spurt when school starts. People will begin to call—why?
> Mrs. Wakefield: Because they are getting their kids back to school.
> Mrs. Carroll: There is also a remission of any requests for psychiatric help during the summer, and I always have the feeling that people can get outdoors and away from themselves. . . . The same thing is true if you are working with adults in the summer, they get kind of antsy— they really aren't concerned about what is going on inside. And I think it is because they can get outdoors and there are more ways of getting away from their problems than there are in the winter—when families are thrown together willy-nilly and they can't get away from the child. . . . Also I have been in agencies where you get more calls on Monday than you get on any other day of the week and you know that is because people have been together over the weekend and they can't stand each other any more.
> Mrs. Simpson: Christmas time, too.
> Mrs. Carroll: Right after Christmas—it goes down before a holiday season and then it goes up after New Years. . . . People get so involved with the holidays that they get away from themselves, and then you get a heavy onslaught with the beginning of the year because people do get very depressed—here's another year starting and I am no further ahead than I was last year.

The result of this type of formulation was some degree of predictability, even though it was based upon unvalidated conjecture upon what was, for the new worker, a totally unpredictable situation.

A further type of anticipatory socialization ensued with the encroaching date of the arrival of children into the day care program. At this time certain staff from other departments, such as housekeeping and dietary, were brought in for some orientation to the program. During these meetings specific concerns about anticipated incidents were expressed:

> Mrs. Carroll: I think that if a child attacks it is because you have something that he wants for example if you had a mop and he wanted it— and he starts to grab the mop, and you refuse to let him have it, but I don't think that kids attack unless there is something like this.
> Mrs. Davis: Their tolerance for frustration is often very limited, but a staff person will be with the child.
> Housekeeper: What would she do if the child wanted the mop?

Mrs. Wakefield: We will be with the child—the staff will be with them —so that if the child wants a mop the staff person would ask you if they could have the mop to kind of let you know what is going on. There may be some reason that he can't have it, but just so there is some communication.

Mr. Waters: Probably if a child is really causing a problem and a child care worker or someone is trying to calm him down and there is part of the housekeeping staff there, it might be that they should leave the area temporarily until he gets calmed down.

Mr. Andrews: Now that we scared them—but with the caliber of the staff that we have I don't think that there should be any problem—I would think that these children would have a friendly relationship with them.

Through the anticipation of such incidents, informal solutions and modes of behavior were agreed upon and served to orient staff to possible solutions.

Another anticipated problem was that many of the children treated by the staff would be "treatment failures." This expectation was outlined in a Diagnostic Conference with Dr. Cartwright:

Dr. Cartwright: I like to get people in there pitching to see what they can do with the child, but I think that you've got to have in the back of your mind that you can't make miracles with this kind of a child, but that doesn't mean that you can't try.

Miss Selby: One of the things that happens when you work with people is that you develop a kind of inner protection against the pessimism because you can develop a feeling that you can always try, and the one's that you succeed with are what keep you always trying.

Dr. Cartwright: No one has the formula in these cases—I haven't anymore experience say, than you do about whether he is cooked or not —I have a little more experience may be. . . . But I would take him to try to see what can be done. You have to try—but I think you should come out with something that you can say—this is what is wrong with these studies and hospitalization is that no one comes out with anything. . . . You are going to have to make up your own mind about what areas you can help him in and what areas you are going to leave alone. . . .

Mrs. Carroll: And if you don't start with this attitude, then you get sucked in.

Dr. Cartwright: And you make believe. I have seen therapists who have sat for years and nothing was happening.

Mr. Anderson: If you don't start with a real approach you have fantasies that you are going to make tremendous progress with the child, and you are going to be God and he is going to be wonderful—and he's not.

The themes that trained the staff to anticipate the type of child encompassed by the program, to know how they would respond to him, what types of problems might arise, and what the likely outcome of their actions might be, were recurrent throughout meeting discussions. In effect, these dialogues served as a rehearsal for a performance that was yet to take place.

Formal Training Processes

Although training was emphasized in all areas of the program during the early developmental stages, one specific activity, the Intake Training Seminar, was specifically designed to train staff to perform the needed work for the organization. These training seminars served the purposes of, first, instructing staff in the procedures of getting information from potential clients, and, secondly, categorizing this information in such a way as to guide subsequent action, both their own, in terms of the immediate situation and the organization's, in terms of supplementing the information that would be used in subsequent diagnostic evaluation.

Information Gathering

The first phase of the training process was concerned with indoctrinating the staff in, what was considered, relevant information. The second Intake Training Seminar provided a list of subjects that staff was to gather information about.

> Mrs. Carroll: In talking about the child's background what are the things that you touch on—what are the things that you would raise question about in relationship to the child's development? What are the things that are important to a child's emotional health from the very beginning what is the first thing that you want to know?
> Mrs. Wakefield: By whom and how he was cared for—if he was wanted.
> Mrs. Carroll: Why would you want to know that—what does this tell you?
> Mrs. Wakefield: Very often they did not—and this effects how they feel about the child.
> Miss Selby: Was he planned?
> Mrs. Carroll: You first want to know if this was a planned birth—what else do you think would follow after that?
> Mrs. Williams: You would probably want to know if it was a difficult birth or if it was normal.
> Mrs. Carroll: What would you want to know about the child as an infant? I've said something to you about the child's basic temperament. . . .
> Mrs. Williams: If when the child was born he was real aggressive and the parents would have liked a passive baby and vice versa—this would effect how they handled the child. . . .

After going through the list of information pertinent to the initial contact with parents, the question of parent reaction to this type of treatment was raised.

> Mrs. Carroll: Now, in asking these questions—what do you suppose? We'll come back to the questions but initially what do you think a parent's attitude is when you are asking all of these things? Do you think they understand why you are asking it?
> Mrs. Wakefield: A lot of them would maybe think that it was a waste of time.
> Mrs. Williams: Like, gee, you're getting awfully nosy—
> Mrs. Carroll: How would you handle a parent's reaction if he didn't understand what you were trying to do?
> Miss Selby: It would be better if you prepared the parent for what you were going to do before this reaction. . . .
> Mrs. Wakefield: If you pick up the feeling that they are uncomfortable or that this is kind of silly—if you sense this you can say something that although it may not seem important it is important—you need to reassure them.
> Mrs. Carroll: If you were geared for trying to get this information on the first interview and you had a parent who was extremely anxious about the child's behavior when he comes in—if this child is acting out and creating a great deal of difficulty—sometimes you have to devote the initial interview when the parent is so upset to handling his anxiety, and you can do this by giving him suggestions as to how to cope with this child at this time. Sometimes even a little interpretation when the child is exhibiting extremely bizarre symptoms, for instance if he is a firesetter—parents will be extremely disturbed if he is a firesetter, hopefully—But if the child is a firesetter and he has set fires that are dangerous to the home it helps sometimes to give the parents an interpretation or an explanation of firesetting generally. . . . Why interpret when a person has very bizarre symptoms—what are you doing? How would you feel if you heard voices or if you had hallucinations?
> Mrs. Wakefield: I would be frightened.
> Mrs. Carroll: You can't find a cause—what you do is try to diminish the anxiety and show them that there is a cause and effect in these symptoms—you have to be careful that you don't carry it too far—because really you don't know that much about it, but you have some notion of what basically is behind firesetting.

Staff was oriented to the techniques of information-gathering and the handling of anticipated problematic situations, by means of such hypothetically structured situations.

Having completed the initial interview, the next step was to summarize and write a report of the interview and, in so doing, outline one's impressions. The difficulty in formulating impressions was expressed in an Intake Training Seminar:

Mrs. Wakefield: I have a lot of difficulties putting down impressions. . . .
I don't know if I am expected to be more specific, or if I am supposed
to diagnose this kid, but I find myself hesitating to write down my
impressions . . . because I feel that I don't know how to organize—I had
a lot of ideas, but I had a lot of difficulty getting it down where I
would give some of my feelings clearly. . . .
Mrs. Simpson: I have the same problem.
Mrs. Carroll: That's because you don't trust yourself. You haven't done
it long enough to feel secure—you've got to practice. . . . What is the
purpose of this? . . . of setting down and discussing this in learning how
to do it. . . . Your thinking is reflected in what you put down here.
You are not just sitting and recording every word the mother said . . . .
your thinking is indicated by what you pick up and what you think is
important in the complaint. . . . What you jot down, so why not bring
it to a logical conclusion—just put down what the meaning of this is—
you will make mistakes initially, but you've got to make mistakes to
learn. . . . You are not a secretary—you are approaching this in a professional way, and in order to operate in a professional way you've got
to take some risks in expressing your thoughts. Maybe you are wrong,
but maybe you might be right, too.

Through this process staff were trained to go through the "right steps"
in the information gathering process and in order to compensate for
their lack of professional education, they were given a base from which
they could draw inferences and make logical conclusions from the information gathered from the parent in the interview situation. In order
to attain a stronger basis upon which they could make decisions, they
entered the next step in the training process which involved the discussion of "actual cases." On the basis of this training, the staff would be
taught a system of cataloguing these various types of experiences.

Development of a System for
Cataloguing Experiences

Since the staff lacked the professional background and educational
preparation that would qualify them to make clinical judgments upon
the clients they would be seeing, Inservice Training Seminars were established to compensate for this void. These seminars were conducted
weekly by Mrs. Carroll and were attended by all "junior staff members."
Initially, cases presented were those seen by Mrs. Carroll. In the second
phase of the training process, however, junior staff members sat in on
actual interviews conducted by Mrs. Carroll, Mrs. Davis, and Miss Selby
and were required to write up the content of the interview. The third
phase involved the actual interviewing of clients by junior staff members
themselves, the writing up of the interview, and the presentation of the
material to the seminar.

Types of Situations

The importance of being able to accurately evaluate a given situation was first stressed in Mrs. Carroll's seminars. The rationale underlying the argument is outlined in the second training session:

> Mrs. Carroll: Why do you want to know this? You know that as he goes through certain stages of development he needs certain emotional satisfactions and the meeting of these needs or the frustrations determines the child—the basis of the child's illness—it's where it starts. . . .
>
> Mrs. Williams: In treatment don't you sometimes go back to the stage where the problem developed and sort of work with the child from that stage on—to try to—because he got to this stage where his needs weren't met, and that he needs to have met in order for him to develop.
>
> Mrs. Carroll: And what else would you want to know? That will be very important in screening because here you are trying to make a judgment as to whether a child is ill.
>
> Mrs. Wakefield: You mean how treatable a child is?
>
> Mrs. Carroll: This would give you some prognostic indication as well as some knowledge as to the severity of the illness . . . . you almost know if you know enough about children and their illnesses—you can speculate as to why—as to when this child was frustrated and how he was frustrated—and when the illnesses first began and the circumstances surrounding them. For example, with a phobic child you know that the mother has a great deal of hostility against the child, and this usually starts early in life . . . you direct your questions in terms of wanting some of the background information in that particular way, and you get the information by directing it in this way, and it shortens your interview. . . . The more you can zero in on certain areas and get the information you need to substantiate your speculation about the child's illness and basically what is wrong—whether he is neurotic or psychotic —the more confidence the parents have in your ability to help . . . because they pick up the feeling that this is not mystifying to you.

Staff were so trained that they could, upon hearing certain symptoms indicative of specific types of illnesses, infer that certain events occurred in the developmental history of the child. This training provided them with a focus for the interview that not only made the procedure shorter but conveyed the idea to the parents that "they knew what they were doing." In effect, the procedure was to first make the diagnosis, and then collect data to substantiate this diagnosis.

The first phase then, was to accurately appraise the situation almost from the moment the parents presented themselves in the interview situation. An initial problem of assessment occurred when a given client had been to a number of agencies prior to his coming to this particular program, but the referral material from those agencies had not as yet arrived. In order to maintain the impression, for the parents, that staff knew what they were doing, they had to arrive at the same initial impression as these other agencies. Mrs. Carroll posed this question: "You have a situation where there is a long history of contact with other agencies—you don't have the material . . . and you go into the interview knowing she has talked to a jillion people about herself and the child— What would you be most concerned about in gathering this material?" Mrs. Simpson suggested that they should "try to get her to tell you about the places she had been and the contacts she has made and what her picture of all these places was like in terms of what she thought had been done." Mrs. Carroll suggested that it would not be appropriate to put too much emphasis on this:

> I think you would want to know mainly what she thought came out of all of these contacts for the child and for herself . . . in addition you don't want to push her too far in asking questions that would be probing and cause a lot of anger in her—Why not?
>
> Mrs. Simpson: Probably because she would have a lot of hostility.
>
> Mrs. Carroll: You want to keep the anxiety level low—you don't want this woman to become too upset . . . and you want to be able to get what you need out of her . . . . this is the way you direct yourself to anyone you are working with.

Obtaining information about parent's experiences with other agencies without antagonizing them by excessive probing became one of the many functions of the staff.

A second problem in the assessment of situations occurred in cases in which the parent was not able to provide an integrated account of the child's behavior. Mrs. Carroll posed this question in her seminar:

> Now you've got a parent who comes in and begins to describe a child, and he gives you a feeling instantly that this is a particular kind of child with particular kinds of difficulties. . . . He goes rambling on and starts talking about something that really is at a tangent with what you want to get. . . . You are trying to get to what is going on with the child at this point.
>
> Mrs. Simpson: You would ask him a leading question.
>
> Mrs. Carroll: If it were a phobic child, you know what is characteristic of a phobic child, so you would ask about this.

The "leading question" approach was decided upon as the most effective and, therefore, the one to be implemented in obtaining from the parent a unified account which could be fitted into a particular diagnostic category of the child's behavior.

Another problem arose when the parent's account of the child's behavior did not correspond with reports sent by other agencies.

Seminar:

> Mrs. Carroll: Their description of him is much more—shows him as being much angrier than the mother describes him in the material that she gave. I also had asked her if he was ever depressed, and she said that she hadn't noticed it, but in this report it indicates that he is frequently moody—that he sits alone and stares out into space. He was playing with matches last summer—was carrying a knife and attacked other children.

Again the proposed solution to this situation was to infer from the referring material that the mother was "hiding something" and to ask "leading questions" to obtain the missing information.

A fourth type of problematic situation arose when the parent would not readily volunteer information about the child.

> Mrs. Wakefield: I think the one that I'm afraid of is the person who comes in and you have to drag every word out—that to me is so much more difficult. . . .
> Mrs. Carroll: That's part of directing your material . . . . now some of this is resistance and part of it is that they don't know what you want so you have to make it clear to them the kind of material that you need. . . .
> Mrs. Wakefield: I was thinking about one appointment that I made— when she called she told me that as far as she was concerned the child had no problem at all and she was very shocked to get this report from the school. . . .
> Mrs. Carroll: What do you think you do if a parent says they don't know there is anything wrong with a child. . . . In this kind of situation you have to do something with her feelings about having the child singled out by the school before you go any further.

Another type of problem situation arose with the parent who "is very unsophisticated":

> Mrs. Carroll: For instance, this parent doesn't know from anything— they haven't read the books and they don't know the theories—all they can relate to are the things that are most troubling to them or to the school . . . . then what do you do?
> Mrs. Wakefield: One of the things that you could do if they were very unsophisticated would be to compare this child to one of their other children, or find out what is different about this child.
> Mrs. Carroll: You help the parent to see the child more clearly— many times they are so anxious they only see one aspect of the child, but they don't see the child as a whole because they see him doing what is uppermost, and what is disturbing becomes the focus, and you want to settle the anxiety so you get a clear picture of the child.

Part of the interview strategy, then, involved getting the parent to have the same view of the child as that held by the staff worker.

A question that frequently arose concerned the difficulty of determining whether the child or the parent was in need of treatment. An example of this is given in an Intake Training Seminar:

> Mrs. Simpson: This seems to be a situation in which there is a re-action—and I think this was the way the worker in adult services was looking at it—that the child was reacting to a crisis in the family and that it could be handled either through the child's reaction to it or through helping the mother cope with her own feelings and reducing her anxiety. . . .
> Mrs. Carroll: I have a suggestion about handling this interview—you might have started by just letting her talk—a little about her situation and her feelings before moving in on the child. . . . I think it is important to convey to her your recognition of the fact that she is very troubled herself and that you are interested in this.

Throughout these seminars, staff was given instructions in evaluating a variety of situations and, on the basis of these evaluations, general directions as to how they were to manage these situations. In addition to the specific categories, general directives were given to govern all interviewing situations.

> Mrs. Carroll: I think that the trick in interviewing parents is always to keep in mind that no parent wants his child to have a problem, and that even though the parent may play a large part in provoking the child . . . that he is doing it out of his own difficulty so you shouldn't put him on the defensive—you don't approach him as if he deliberately did this—and I think that this is one of the difficulties that people have in working with children is in relating to their parents—they get very hostile toward the parents and they approach them as if they had deliberately set out to hurt the child.

Although the implicit model that staff was "trained" to follow was one in which the parents were the crucial factor in the creation of illness in the child, they were not to permit these feelings to interfere in the interviewing situation. Increasingly, however, and despite instructions to the contrary, parents were made to be the villains in the situations.

Types of Parents

Since the method of evaluating potential cases for admission to the program was first through a screening interview held only with the parents who presented their view of the child's behavior, an essential factor in the interviewing procedure was that staff be able to quickly evaluate the type of parent with whom they were dealing. Such things as the physical appearance of the parent as he came through the door into the interviewing situation, his mode of dress, and his manner of speech were identified as critical points of observation.

Mrs. Carroll: But what about this woman who looks very meek? Sort of like a little girl, really—well she's got nine children at home, and she looks like the tenth child, essentially the way she appears physically as well as the way she presented herself. What about the quality of being overwhelmed? The confusion as she talks the anxiety that she feels toward her child—the helpless kind of quality about her?

Mrs. Wakefield: When you look back over what she had gone through. These marriages and all of these children. Not just this child, but all the other things—I can see why she is overwhelmed.

Mrs. Carroll: Yeah, I think you have a suspicion that this young woman with nine children, although all the children are not her own—she is married to a man with three children, and she has five of her own, and one of theirs. You have the feeling that this woman with the kind of dependent air about her is always overwhelmed, and you wonder how such a woman can take care of nine little children. This in addition to this very hostile, aggressive boy. . . . She's the kind that you would have to feed in order for her to feed the child, with the knowledge that the excess that you give will be passed on to the child. You can't just zero in on the child, and ignore her.

In addition to the immature, childlike mother, another type of mother to which staff was sensitized was the one with underlying psychological problems of her own.

Mrs. Carroll: She seemed to have a sort of flatness about her . . . . what are you picking up immediately that gives you some diagnostic clue as to how she relates to the child—how does she see herself, and how does she see the relationship?

Mrs. Wakefield: I would think that when a person comes in and cries and weeps at least it is a feeling, and it's coming out in the open. It would be upsetting to me, but at least you would be getting something from her, and then this woman talks about all her problems, her hospitalizations, and all of her children, seem to have problems, and nothing comes through.

Mrs. Carroll: I don't know how much you know about depression and what this represents, but it is anger turned inwards . . . . you know that this woman has had several hospitalizations the precipitators of her hospitalization being that she was extremely depressed . . . . you know this woman has a great deal of guilt, and you know that you have to cap this instantly. You don't want to stir up the guilt—you want to allay it as much as you possibly can—in order to keep the person from being too upset by it.

As implicit danger, in interviewing parents, was not accurately assessing their emotional status and unwittingly "uncapping" their psychoses in the interview situation.

In the case of some parents, the child's symptoms supposedly "gave them away":

> Mrs. Carroll: Now she had a child who is a soiler—what do we know about the mother of a soiler?
> Mrs. Wakefield: That this is usually a very angry child that controls the mother in this way.
> Mrs. Carroll: And what kind of a mother normally is most aggravated by this kind of a symptom in a child?
> Mrs. Williams: A mother who is very rigid.
> Mrs. Carroll: So thinking about this, what about Mrs. P. . . . . She was extremely well groomed and attractive; she talked readily but did she talk spontaneously about feeling or did she just give a recital of facts?

In the above case, the staff were not to let the mother's favorable appearance mislead them into erroneous evaluations of the situation. A parent could present himself as looking either too good or too bad— in both instances the responsibility of the staff was to determine the underlying factors of this initial impression created by the parent.

Staff were also instructed to consider the life situations and backgrounds of the parents who presented themselves in the interview setting. Particular problems arose around interviewing lower class black patients.

> Mrs. Carroll: She seems more intelligent—but the man wasn't literate. . . . As I continued to talk to him I did get information from him that did indicate that he had special feelings for the child. . . . If you have a situation like this where two parents come in and one is taking over the interview—what do you do with the parent who wants to take over?
> Mrs. Wakefield: You direct questions toward the other parent directly.
> Mrs. Carroll: Directly to the passive one and you try to draw them out. . . . Many of these parents are this way—uneducated and unsophisticated and you have to be aware of what is normal for them versus what is normal for you. What kind of a household is this? The woman works and has all of these children, and how does this influence how she sees him? How much overcrowding is there in this house? How much financial pressure is there? What is going on between this man and woman that makes the marriage difficult for her which makes it much more difficult for her to give to this child. All these things you need to keep in mind because this does have an influence on what is going on with the child and his treatability as well as that of the parents.

Thus, staff not only had to consider the way in which parents presented themselves in the interview situation but also the environmental circumstances in which these parents lived.

While the uneducated parent created one set of problems, the educated parent posed a different problem in the interview situation. One such case involved a child who had been excluded from all special education classes but whose parents insisted that he should be in school. Their response to this exclusion had been to write letters to their state senator, the governor, and the director of the Department of Mental Health in an attempt to get help for their son. The dilemma presented by this type of parent is reflected in a training seminar:

> Mrs. Carroll: You have to try to get them to start thinking about it—about the child's behavior. I do think that more specifically you might throw out some statements that apply to autistic children and try to see whether or not they see some degree of this type of behavior in the child . . . there are things about autistic children that are very striking which they may see and which frighten them very much . . . and use this as a means of trying to explain to them that the big problem about the child is that he is sick—that he is just too sick to fit in a classroom and that he needs special facilities, and this is a facility for treatment of disturbances in children—and that your concern is about this child—your interest in him would be related to the fact that he is sick.

The goal of the interview, in this case, was to enable the parents to see that the problem was one of emotional sickness and not, as they would have preferred, an educational one.

In all cases, the goal in interviewing parents was not only to get a description of the child to guide the diagnostic evaluation but to simultaneously have the opportunity to evaluate the psychological and social problems of the parents and, thereby, determine their "treatability." The presumed "treatability" of the family was the significant determinant in decisions relating to the admission of children into the program.

Types of Children

From the interviewing material, a typology for categorizing the behavior of children was also derived. The purpose of this system of categorization was to provide some means of assessing the needs that these particular children were apt to have. A case discussed in an early seminar serves to illustrate this process.

> Mrs. Carroll: I think that if you see soiling as the key to this child's problems then this material can be focused around soiling—of course he is infantile, but primarily he is an angry child and expresses his hostility this way—so that in treatment this child should work through this anger.

Staff was also alerted to the fact that if parents presented one side of a child's behavior, there were very likely other facts to which they should be sensitive.

> Mrs. Carroll: If the parent describes a child as a very angry child—and this is what you are going to get . . . a parent that tells you constantly what the child does out of his anger. Then what do you look

for—you look for the opposite side of the child. Can the parent tell you the opposite side of this on his own?—and what do you do to get a total picture of what goes on with this child?

Mrs. Wakefield: You ask if he seeks affection, or is gentle and clinging. And then you ask if a child steals and what he does with it.

Mrs. Williams: And also how he reacts after he has been angry—and if he is guilty and tries to get back in the good graces.

Mrs. Carroll: You also want to know if the child ever had depressed moods—now most of the time the parents have noticed this—they notice at times that he goes off by himself—they haven't labelled it as depression and sometimes the child will talk about how bad he is.

The evaluation of the "good" aspects of the child's behavior was seen as essential in determining whether staff could tolerate this kind of a child in the program situation.

Cultural factors were also considered to be complicating factor, in assessing the problems presented by the child.

Mrs. Carroll: An over protected child doesn't react this way . . . . a child that you hold as close to you and you don't let them get away from you is a child that normally finds it very difficult to get away and go out in the world—he is going to be very dependent and insecure and anxious. This is a child who is very frightened but it is covered by a veneer of bravado, but you know a 10 year old who runs away like this —you know that some of this stems from the environment—in this setting kids are tough—in the slums a kid at seven is really a man in the sense of knowing how to take care of himself . . . but even in this environment you would not find a child who would run away as often as this one does . . . you would know she had not over protected this child.

A further factor, in assessing types of children was that of determining the degree of sickness associated with various forms of deviant behavior.

Mrs. Carroll: What would you feel about a child who wants to get out of school? You'd begin to question in your mind if this was a school phobia? If he had a school phobia this would help to determine whether or not he was schizophrenic. Schizophrenic children don't have phobias so this would be diagnostic. You would want to know how the parents reacted to it, and if it was successful.

The major focus of the Intake Training Seminars conducted by Mrs. Carroll was on developing typologies and ways of cataloguing situations and assessing individuals with which staff would be confronted in the interview setting. Children were a secondary consideration in these dialogues. However, on the basis of these interviews and the conclusions that staff were trained to reach, diagnostic decision making occurred.

Value Judgments

Throughout the Intake Training Seminars, there was not only content about types of situations and people who would present themselves in the interview setting but also a running commentary that served to indicate the way in which staff made value judgments about the types of interaction that occurred between parents and their children. An initial type of dialogue that occurred within a training seminar serves to illustrate this tendency:

> Mrs. Carroll: First of all, what about M's birth—M is the eldest child of this young marriage. She was 18 and the husband 21. What would you expect about them as people at this point?
>
> Mrs. Simpson: They are not very mature.
>
> Mrs. Carroll: Were they ready to have a baby?
>
> Mrs. Wakefield: They probably weren't even ready for the marriage.
>
> Mrs. Carroll: Now she conceives this child and she says that they really didn't plan to have this child, but she really didn't care whether she got pregnant or not—what about this?
>
> Mrs. Simpson: I think that every woman, no matter how well planned it is, has some feeling about another person coming into this marriage . . . and the younger you are the more traumatic this is going to be. . . .
>
> Mrs. Carroll: This is a fairly infantile woman, and you would speculate about why she had to have a baby. She just didn't have a baby because she didn't know how not to have one. You wonder why she wanted this baby—did she want it for herself, and her husband—why does she want a baby? Because it was her idea, I'm sure. She talked about enjoying the pregnancy, and I think that if this was the case you can speculate about her really wanting the baby to satisfy her own infantile needs, and to satisfy her needs through taking care of the baby as she would have wanted to be taken care of.

Later in the same seminar:

> Mrs. Carroll: She is a real martyr, if I've even seen one . . . and you would think that if the husband wasn't like this he would be an alcoholic, because this is the type of woman who typically marries an alcoholic . . . . she told me that he beat her to a bloody pulp, and you wonder why she continued to live with him, and she said, "Of course I couldn't separate, you know—because I had these small children."

Not only did these training seminars provide the staff with the necessary background for the screening interview; but they also furnished a social commentary on life in general, which further served to establish relationships between the participants within the organization.

One predominant theme of these discussions was the inevitable chain of human events, particularly in the area of mate selection. This inevitability is reflected by Mrs. Carroll.

Mrs. Carroll: Of course, you know, you choose your mate out of your own neurosis, and of course the unconscious factors within you are stronger in terms of attracting you to a person than are the conscious factors, so if you are seeing two people who are having problems in marriage, as you talk with them you can see how their behaviors mesh together in terms of what each is seeking from the other in meeting his or her neurotic needs it's a fascinating thing—and you find that people duplicate their parents' marriages . . . and they go on repeatedly unless the chain is broken by their getting some insight into this . . . . the chain will never be broken until this person gets some insight into himself and how he functions—how he frustrates himself in choosing the kinds of partners he chooses.

A further theme revolved around the cultural values represented by the clients:

Mrs. Carroll: Often times you will see in these kinds of family setups in Negro families . . . that the woman is stronger because her opportunities are greater than the man's—the Negro male is particularly depreciated by the society that he lives in, and the culture, because the mother is the mainstay of the family—and you will get a repetitive pattern where the mother is a very strong woman, and everybody congregates around her and the man is on the periphery he is there to produce children and he doesn't have much function in the family, and often he disappears, because he feels so little like a man—and so depreciated—and the girls—they will almost have more automatically to give to the girls in terms of strength . . . . the woman is the stronger one in the family, but the girls are given more opportunity—they stay in school longer and they develop more skills and talents, and even in slavery they were given more opportunity.

A later meeting continues the same theme:

Mrs. Carroll: This is the mother who had three illegitimate children previously—what would you expect that she feels?
Mrs. Wakefield: I'm sure that she doesn't have much self-respect and she tries to cover up by being neat and attractive—but underneath—
Mrs. Carroll: You get the impression that underneath, sexuality in a woman of this culture is acceptable. An illegitimate pregnancy is not responded to in the way the middle class person would.

Further social commentary on black family structure was contained in another meeting:

Mrs. Tatum: Mrs. Carroll, am I correct in assuming that in these families—I am not familiar with this one, but I have heard that in families like this that are on ADC the brothers and sisters have sexual relationships with one another.
Mrs. Carroll: I don't think in most cases this is true—there is certainly a lot of stimulation in these families, you see—I think their

abhorrence of incest is just as strong as anybody else's in that incest is something that is universally condemned . . . but there certainly is a lot of stimulation . . . . they sleep in the same room with their parents . . . if a woman is not married they see the boy friends come in and out . . . they begin to act out their sexual impulses very early . . . and you would have a suspicion that in a case like this, that the kid might be sexually stimulated by the mother . . . . we would have to investigate further to see what the sleeping arrangements are—you'd have to have some idea of how seductive she was with the child, but you would know that whatever he is running away from it is provoking a great deal of anxiety.

Through the use of these generalizations, staff were ideally able to make judgments that were accurate appraisals of the total situation. Mrs. Carroll expressed the satisfaction she experienced when she was able to make these accurate appraisals:

It's fascinating how you can pick up all these little things, and how together they weave to make—for instance you may be talking with someone, and if you have enough of a feel about this, and you know enough about how people behave and what indicates what, you might say something to them that seems to them like you are clairvoyant—they say, "How did you know this?" or "How did you know that?" It's not that you are clairvoyant but that you know how people interact and what is behind certain kinds of behavior—that this man has told you what his relationship with his wife is like—and in addition . . . about his own resentment toward his mother . . . and you know about his tendency to operate in this way, and that they support one another in this sort of behavior . . . . they almost determined from the beginning that this was the kind of marriage that they were going to have because each of them is repeating what he saw in his own home as he was growing up.

The reward held out to staff was the knowledge that the apparent unpredictability of human behavior was not really so; that if they became "professionals," they would be able to extract meaning from what now appeared to them to be a chaotic world, peopled with individuals possessing a multiplicity of problems.

The training process that occurred within this program took place on two levels: an informal level not actually designated as training in which individuals conjured hypothetical situations and discussed ways of dealing with these anticipated problems, and a formal level through which staff were taught to draw inferences from and categorize the behavior of the parents and their interpretation of their child's behavior. In this way, a staff that wasn't trained in any particular psychiatric profession and had a limited background in work with children was taught how to do the basic work of the organization, while theory remained secondary. The impact of such an educational process was that staff was indoctrinated into only one predominant perspective, without being given the opportunity or the encouragement to consider alternate ways of viewing the problem. Professionally trained staff who came and went during the course of the early development of the organization felt that this method of indoctrination was questionable, but because of this attitude they were rapidly excluded as participants to the "training seminars."

This type of training process promoted ingroup solidarity by insuring that all the staff remaining within the program were engaged in the training process. And, by making the training process self-contained, boundaries were reaffirmed and maintained. In the political arenas of the organization, the ability of the program to maintain autonomy in the training of its staff was considered to be an asset, by virtue of representing economical management techniques. Finally, since it could always be argued that staff needed to be trained as a preliminary step toward providing services to children, concentration on the training process provided further justification for not opening Children's services at an earlier time.

The stage was set. The Children's Program had established its position within the larger organization and thereby had access to the needed resources. Staff had been recruited, training processes served to indoctrinate them into a common ideology and value system. Only one factor remained undefined; who were the children to be treated?

Part IV
Program Characteristics

Chapter X

The Children

One final measure of success in an organization surrounds the sale-ability of the end product. Products sell for a variety of reasons; in some instances the quality of the article is the basis for the buyer's purchase. But in other instances the product appeals to some aspect of the buyer's imaginative or fantasy life. In some cases salesmanship convinces the individual that to keep up with others he needs this particular item. No matter what the basis of the article's appeal to the buying public, a marketable product must be produced. In addition, the end product of the organization often serves as the concrete element by which the organization can appraise its success. By figuring the costs per unit of production in relationship to profit margins, an organization calculates its financial status.

But what of the end product in a psychiatric treatment organization? In this case, what is the marketable commodity? The buying public expects psychiatric organizations to change people, so that when they return to the larger society they will "adjust," that they will no longer be troublesome. However, if psychotherapy truly focuses upon the individual's needs the end result might be freeing the individual from fears that have restrained him; he may not necessarily be less troublesome to those about him. The end product envisioned by society and that desired by psychotherapists may not be in agreement. Furthermore, lacking any clearly defined indications of when psychiatric work is completed the psychotherapist must successfully promote an image of accomplishing something. He seeks to convince both the patient and his family of the improvement he has witnessed.

A newly developing psychiatric treatment organization thus confronts a dilemma. On the one hand, the clients who seek services have been defined as social deviants; society expects changes in these individuals to comply with its definitions of sanity. But in many instances abilities to change the individual are lacking and, on closer examination, it may not be the proscribed patient who needs changing as much as the social

163

order. For example, psychiatry is beginning to recognize that in most instances a problem within an individual indicates a family problem and that the family should be treated as a unit. As the family changes, so does the individual. But the family who comes to a psychiatric agency usually comes with one member they define as troublesome. They expect the individual to change, not themselves. The family evaluates the work of the agency on the basis of their abilities to change the designated patient.

Psychiatric organizations, to get around this dilemma, must develop strategies that will allow them to appear successful. First, the psychiatric worker seeks to maintain his self-image and strives to achieve a feeling of accomplishment. Secondly, the accomplishments must be communicated to the public which evaluates psychiatric services; this includes other psychiatric services as well as the consumer public. Thirdly, the individual psychiatric patient must see an improvement in himself and thereby become a living example of how psychiatric treatment helps. How can a psychiatric organization demonstrate this type of success?

Although this study does not include an analysis of the treatment process and the end product, the first step toward management of this problem involves the selection of a client population.

The key administrative decision, considering the political context surrounding the program, proved to be the definition and selection of children for the program. The recruitment and selection of staff and their control, the ordering of supplies and materials, and the maintenance of boundaries between the program and the larger organization could all be manipulated if the difficult factor of actual children within the program did not intrude. Eventually, however, it was necessary for the program to provide visible evidence that it was, in fact, providing a service for the treatment for children. Consequently, the very population which the program was supposed to help—the children—simultaneously posed a threat to the equilibrium of the organization, for they did not fall under the same set of controls that were applicable in other areas. The children, as part of their program, necessarily used facilities such as the swimming pool and gymnasium in the central administration building which made them visible outside the confines of the Children's Program. In addition, provisions for ancillary services, such as Housekeeping, Dietary and Maintenance, allowed a number of employees with loyalties to other parts of the organization to filter into the program area. The parents of the children, involved in therapy as a necessary requirement for treatment of the child, also posed a potential threat by representing ties to the outside community that transcended boundaries controlled by the program. Finally, treatment of the children necessarily involved some relationship with other agencies, such as schools, which were similarly interested in children.

Although the initial aim of the program was to help children who were having problems at school, or problems capable of being treated on a short-term basis, these were not the children ultimately chosen. It may be hypothesized that the alternative chosen, that of accepting mainly schizophrenic children, was based upon political factors rather than upon any logic inherent within the program. Specifically, any person, be they a psychiatric professional or a layman, on viewing an autistic child, would find it impossible not to notice that such a child was "not right." Admission of autistic children provided visible evidence that there was a need for the services and therefore validated the existence of the program.

Secondly, schizophrenic or autistic children, while severely disturbed are not generally as aggressive toward others or destructive of physical property as are other types of children with behavioral problems. Accepting this population limited the problems which the other sort of child might have posed for the ancillary service staff.

The parents of the children, most of them having become desperate and exhausted in their plight of seeking help and having already been fruitlessly involved with a multiplicity of agencies, were willing to do anything to receive assistance for their disturbed child. These factors brought them increasingly under the control of the program.

Finally, since most of these children had never been able to function in other settings such as schools, contacts with these agencies and the hazard of having the work of this program brought under their purview was limited.

From all aspects, the program made a politically expedient choice in selecting a population of children that were primarily schizophrenic or autistic. However, this politically expedient decision ignored the fact that, according to experiences of others, this population of children are the poorest candidates for treatment. This, too, turned out to be an asset, since the chances of successfully treating this type of child are so slim, the likelihood of having negative criticism hurled at the program was significantly decreased.

Diagnostic decision-making then, in many of its facets, became a means of building a protective shield around the program to limit the possibilities of criticism and to create a picture, for the eyes of outsiders, of an organization which was instituted to perform a needed function and was, at least to some degree, successfully fulfilling it.

As the psychiatric treatment program for emotionally disturbed children developed into an organization, it ultimately had to evolve a decision-making procedure concerning the clients which it would serve, as well as some definite ideas about the type of psychiatric treatment which it would provide. Although extensive amounts of time and energy were accorded to other topics of conversation, everything revolved around the predominant idea that eventually children would be admitted to the program and some type of treatment would be given to them.

Assuming these vague directional ideas, a series of decisions had to be reached. First, there was the need for a staff considered qualified enough to make these decisions. Given such a staff, the program had to reach some type of agreement upon the nature of "the appropriate child" for a psychiatric treatment program such as the one being established. The dimensions of the child's illness, his age, the area in which he lived, and the type of parent he had, were all factors which entered into this defining process. These visions of the "appropriate child" were made in the light of the estimated demand for services that this organization would eventually offer. A further dimension included the process by which an "appropriate child" could be identified, and, finally, once such a client was found, what would be offered to him within the psychiatric treatment program.

Diagnostic decision-making took place in an atmosphere governed by an underlying set of ideological premises against which the presenting symptoms of the child were measured. Based on these considerations, decisions about whether or not to accept or reject the child were made.

Factors Governing the
Diagnostic Process

From the beginning of the organization's history, the staff was preoccupied with the types of children that would receive treatment in this particular program and how they were to function in identifying this group. An initial problem was that, according to the tradition of psychiatric practice as a subspecialty of the medical profession, none of the staff employed within Children's services were qualified to make the final decisions about who should be accepted or rejected into this treatment program: these decisions could only be made by a medical doctor. As the program moved toward a projected opening date, Dr. Cartwright was recruited as a consultant to conduct diagnostic seminars. The primary focus of these seminars was to decide which of the children that had come to the attention of the staff would be admitted for treatment.

The Psychiatric Consultant

Finding a consultant whom the staff considered qualified enough to judge the crucial matter of admissions would be treated and establishing that consultant in a position of authority was one of the first problems. The difficulty arose from the fact that she was not an express member of the organization. In this instance, Mrs. Davis's previous contact with Dr. Cartwright, had taught her to respect Dr. Cartwright's competence as a child analyst and ability to make this level of decisions. This confidence, however, was not shared by other members of the staff who had previously been involved in seminars of a similar nature with Dr. Cartwright. This doubt was reflected in a staff meeting after Mrs. Davis outlined the credentials which she considered as qualifying Dr. Cartwright to fulfill this function within the organization.

> Mrs. Davis: Dr. Cartwright will be here mainly for the purpose of helping us develop our knowledge and skill in diagnosis of children and with the parents. . . .
> Mrs. Simpson: When Dr. Cartwright comes can one of the things that we discuss be some of the things that we feel that we would like to get from these diagnostics to really get a feel for how she conducts them. Because I know I used to sit in on her before and I felt that I was completely overwhelmed and I—I think part of it was that I was an observer. I really wasn't there to participate; that's part of it, and also I wasn't comfortable in the group, because it was just such a competitive type of thing. I'd like to get more of a feeling for how she sees it, and how she is going to structure it—this was during a time when there was all that controversy and I went in not really knowing much about what interviews were for or the conferences and I came away from it, and everybody was hating everybody else. Part of it was the feeling that was underneath it—and I would just like to understand where we are going before we begin.

Dr. Cartwright, in her first meeting the following week also recognized the problems that she had previously encountered in other areas of the organization.

> You shouldn't feel that you have to defend yourself—the whole emphasis is on the process and I should only state that my last experience here was that I was often accused of it like it was a dirty word—of being an analyst. I am an analyst that's true, but I'm a very practical and experienced person, and I'm also a human being so I hope that for those of you that have whatever fantasies about analysts, that you will deal with yourselves about this, because I hope I don't have to blow up again as I did eventually in one of the staffs about being sick and tired of being called an analyst when I wasn't saying anything about analysis—and that's my only pitch, because I had never come across

that one before—that is I got my major training from a social worker who was practical, and I don't get fanciful and in outer space with my dynamic training—I'm pretty much on this earth—at least most of the time.

While being an analyst was considered a necessary qualification for conducting diagnostic conferences, these same qualifications had proved to be an impediment in a previous encounter. Dr. Cartwright, in presenting her credentials to the group, assigned a secondary importance to her background in analytic training and stressed the practicality of her decision-making as the primary qualification. This was also coupled with a statement that made staff reluctant, at a later date, to question the types of decisions that were made, because these questions would be interpreted as an attack upon Dr. Cartwright's worth as an analyst. In this way the stage was set to prevent the staff from challenging decisions made within the diagnostic conference.

Defining the Work

Before Dr. Cartwright was hired as a consultant to the program, staff had spent an extensive amount of time discussing and defining their conception of the appropriate child for this setting, as well as the way in which such children would be identified, particularly during the screening interviews which would provide direction for their work in this identifying process.

Estimation of the Need for Services

An early consideration was the estimation of the number of potential clients to be considered for this treatment program. Mrs. Davis outlined what she considered to be the need for Children's services in an early staff meeting.

I do think that because there is such a gross need for children's services, we can certainly, and we would have to specify what we can do because it is a drop in the bucket compared to needs. I think that the roughest kind of estimate I would get in terms of high risk for children was about 2500 a year needing hospitalization. Our projected kind of hospitalization is not a drop in the bucket of what we can do here for this population so we will have to narrow it down . . . . we will have to define what we can do realistically in terms of our staff, its experience, and general development.

The following week Mrs. Davis provided an estimate of how many children might be admitted from the geographic catchment area under the new system of reorganization: "I have a breakdown in a broad and speculative kind of way of what we would get . . . which is about 600 children per year. . . . just a drop in the bucket compared to the number of children that need services."

This projected need became the basis for justifying the establishment of criteria to govern the selection of patients. A staff meeting contained a discussion of factors that might be used to delimit a specific population that would be served.

> Mrs. Davis: What we are trying to do is to make certain that our day care, out-patient, in-patient you name it, is available, but we know realistically it can't be available to everyone who needs it. Consequently, we can limit by age, we can limit by geography, etc. . . . but when we would have to define how many we can take from these areas or what kind of children we will take, and the basis on which we decide to take these kinds of cases. For example, if you live in (a particular community) and there are absolutely no facilities for diagnostic workups, then we might provide diagnostic programs.
>
> Mrs. Carroll: But diagnostics aren't any good unless you've got someone to treat after the diagnostic. . . . There are plenty of sick children, out there, and everybody knows it. But what's available for treatment?

Given the facts that there were a large number of children in need of services and a need to establish a criteria to govern the type of child that would be considered appropriate for the program, staff spent extensive time engaged in discussions as to what they would consider an appropriate treatment candidate.

The Appropriate Child

An initial consideration, expressed in an early staff meeting, focused on the possible kinds of children that might be considered for the program.

> Mr. Packard: The population of autistic children is very small—behavioral or adjustment problems make up the largest numbers of children that represent a high area of need for treatment.
>
> Mrs. Davis: Do you think that some number of these could be helped through a program like we have here?
>
> Mr. Packard: I think we could help with some of these adjustment problems . . . the need is for services for children who are having severe problems, but who can be helped. Large numbers of children need help in going through crisis situations in the school system. The first problem is that of identifying the referral source.

The following week, staff decided that the best way to determine the types of children that might be served would be to discuss actual cases that had come to the attention of the staff through telephone intake calls.

Staff Meeting:

> Miss Selby: About this case . . . the man who called is a friend of the family . . . . the child has been suspended from Catholic school where mother had placed him because the public school had bothered her (about him) at work.
> Mrs. Davis: . . . I think you are saying that the friend of the family was concerned but that the mother was not concerned and not interested in becoming involved. That rules it out.

A basic criterion governing the selection of a child was parent involvement.

A second case, presented in the same meeting, illustrated the importance of potential clients having had contacts with individuals within the program.

> Miss Selby: Now this is an eight year old girl—the mother is unable to find a reason for her actions—
> Mrs. Davis: Is that the H——? . . . that one is appropriate.

This particular case had come to the attention of Mrs. Davis through one of the agencies where she was currently doing consultation and was therefore considered to be "appropriate." As third case illustrated another problem.

> Miss Selby: Here's one that we will not want to take . . . . this boy fights at school—he hurts himself, and his mother is upset because she doesn't know what is wrong with him. . . . He bites other children, he attacks other children—he went into the classroom and then went into the corner. He either has these outbursts of attacking or he withdraws.
> Mrs. Davis: What are they requesting?
> Miss Selby: Just help—this is a Sister from the school. . . . I didn't consider this appropriate because he bites.
> Mrs. Davis: We could take a biting child . . . the hyperactive one is a different kind of thing. So he bites and kicks—
> Miss Selby: But he bites people.
> Mrs. Davis: . . . but that's not inappropriate if he is biting and kicking.
> Miss Selby: Well, he is eight so that isn't so big.
> Mrs. Davis: The main thing we are trying to clarify here is what we will take and what we won't, using the calls we've gotten thus far. We will take kids that are physically aggressive . . . and this is one of the reasons we are putting the age the way we are, because it's one thing if you are going to get an adolescent who is physically aggressive and try to contain him.

In considering an "aggressive" child, age was the primary determinant.

It was decided that the age limits for the program would be from six to twelve years old.

These early defining processes were ignored when Dr. Cartwright entered the scene. In the introductory conference in which Dr. Cartwright was introduced to the group, indications of this change in direction were given:

> Dr. Cartwright: See, I think in the beginning processes there will be much greater refinement in the thinking about what types of children can you reach under what kinds of circumstances—there isn't anybody that has that kind of information, so it is learning.
>
> Mrs. Davis: Are there a few that could definitely be identified that could be helped in this brief period of time—I ruled one out and that was the autistic child.
>
> Dr. Cartwright: I have a fantasy about that—I think that some of this could be—you could use the autistic children to see if they are cooked or not cooked . . . you could use autistic children to see if there is any response . . . and I think that you could see under a diagnostic basis— not on a one-shot interview—what happens under this kind of circumstance . . . and then you make up your mind whether this is a candidate for custodial care or intensive residential treatment, again knowing very well that we haven't got the resources to send him to. . . . One thing, autistic children are a lot less trouble than some of the other ones.

Later in the same conference Dr. Cartwright amplified the rationale underlying her thinking:

> Dr. Cartwright: The kinds of patients that are referred for in-patient care are generally two types—either psychotics or they are acting out— and both of these types, unless the psychotics are very quiet, don't fit into places like this with open doors where they can get lost, and break windows and that kind of stuff.

One criterion for selection, then, was the omission of the truculent, potential trouble-maker. This was finally coupled with the idea that the legitimate work of the organization would be to provide good diagnostic evaluations of severely disturbed children rather than the short-term treatment outlined in earlier discussions.

The Screening Process Defined

Not only was it essential to have some idea of the type of child that would be accepted into the program but also to have some consensus about the procedure used in this type of selection. "Screening" was defined by Mrs. Davis in a staff meeting:

> Now on the first visit it will primarily be an interview—no testing or physical examination. It will be solidly screening it will also be an

interpretation of our services . . . and also to get the message across clearly what the responsibilities of the parents are, and what our expectations and requirements are.

The purpose of screening, as outlined by Mrs. Davis in the same meeting was to "determine whether or not our services are appropriate to that particular child's needs, but equally important was the determination of whether or not a different service or resource might not be closer to a client's need and how it could be made available." Although screening was manipulated to exclude undesirable candidates from the program and refer them elsewhere, this proved difficult, since, at this point there were no criteria on which these judgments could be based. This difficulty was discussed in an Intake Training Seminar:

> Mrs. Carroll: If you find yourself in a situation where you know from the information that the parents have given you at this point, that the child will not fit into the program . . . you would be expected at that point to start the parent in another direction. . . .
> Miss Selby: This will be difficult at first because we have no program to measure against.
> Mrs. Carroll: But you have to screen out some people—you have to be able to decide which children you are going to take right off the bat, and in the process of doing this you will find situations where obviously on the surface this child doesn't fit here . . . once the program is firmly formulated and you know what you have to offer you can do this more expediently—but still you have to have some awareness about what to do with that child if he obviously is not going to be served here.

The worker who conducted the screening interview played a crucial role in the decision-making process. Through this initial contact with the parent, he was in a position to judge the "appropriateness of the child" for this program, and in this way control the flow of cases that eventually would be brought into the diagnostic conferences for further consideration.

Diagnostic Decision-Making

The process of deciding who would be admitted to the program and who would be rejected was contingent on a multiplicity of factors. One primary factor was the time at which a particular case was brought to the attention of the diagnostic seminar. A case presented before the program was in operation would most likely have been rejected and an elaborate rationale built up to justify the inappropriateness of the child for the program. However, if a case were presented just prior to the time of the program's opening, its chances of being accepted were increased, even if the child's symptoms had been judged inappropriate. The intensive screening process had been so successful that there were not enough children in the program. A second factor of increasing importance in the decision-making process was the evaluation of the potential aggressiveness of the child. If a child was judged to be hyperactive and destructive, the recommendation most apt to be made was that the child required a "structured" environment, and the only place this particular type of structure could be provided was within a state hospital rather than in this specific program.

A third factor to consider was which member of the staff presented the case to the diagnostic seminar and whether his particular interests lay in the direction of seeing a child either accepted or rejected for the program. For example, a child that was deemed a good candidate for the educational program was often rejected because of the underlying conflict presumed to exist between educational and therapeutic goals.

A further consideration involved the presumed treatability of the child; although, as time progressed, this became less of an issue while increasing emphasis was placed upon "diagnostic work-ups" as a primary function of the day care program.

Symptoms as a Consideration

Most of the children who came to the attention of this particular program had been seen before by various agencies. As a result of these prior contacts, an abundance of diagnostic material from other agencies was fed into the program and provided some basis for making decisions. Some of the children had been known to other agencies for varying lengths of time, some as long as six years, and had undergone repeated diagnostic studies to determine their pattern of maladjustment with recommendations for treatment by another agency. Some, after having gone to the other agency, underwent more diagnostics and were again recommended for treatment in yet another facility. Some children had accumulated as many as six diagnostic work-ups without yet having received any treatment. Frequently, much of the diagnostic material from the varying agencies was highly contradictory, and that pattern often continued within this program. The recommendation for "a really good diagnostic" was frequently made because material from other agencies was considered unreliable.

Within this framework, much of the emphasis of the early diagnostic conferences with Dr. Cartwright centered around the type of information necessary to make these diagnostic judgments. An example of this occurred when the first case was presented to Dr. Cartwright by Mr. Peters.

Diagnostic Seminar:

> Dr. Cartwright: You also—then you go into the presenting complaint—
> the time that it began, plus the handling will make some differences as
> to the hope in a case like this. For instance, the whole issue of running
> away—you see either children run away from something or toward
> something.
> Mr. Peters: In both cases the children ran toward something. . . .
> Dr. Cartwright: The other thing that I would like to know in cases
> like this is what precipitated the actual incident . . . and also you want
> to know how she functions across the board in areas that are im-
> portant. One of the areas we know is that she didn't do well in school.
> The other area would be what are her peer relationships? What are her
> adult relationships like across the board? Does she relate to adults in
> a clinging dependent kind of level or is there any other kind of re-
> lationship? What are her capacities? . . . What does she do? . . . Is
> there any evidence that she sublimates at this point? . . . This is the
> kind of picture you want to get as a cross section . . . so that you might
> get some idea of where you might be able to sink in even though this
> is a chronic problem.

Early in the diagnostic conferences, staff was instructed to obtain certain
information that would be helpful in making decisions.

A frequent type of interchange within these diagnostic seminars related to Dr. Cartwright's impression that children had been wrongly
diagnosed and misunderstood by others with whom they had prior contact. A conference in which they were discussing a little girl provided an
example of this type of dialogue.

> Dr. Cartwright: You see she had a problem of total existence—and
> she is being misinterpreted all over the place, including the psychiatrist
> and whoever saw her, and described this child as withholding, as doing
> all sorts of things—this child functionally is psychotic.

Accompanying these diagnostic statements were instructions as to what
a child like this would need.

> What this girl needs—for a baby to grow up the child needs an
> auxiliary ego—the mother through her relationship to the child helps the
> child grow up—here you've got a child who doesn't have much of an ego
> who needs—in some way human beings . . . so you are faced with all
> kinds of things . . . she needs for the adults to be an auxiliary ego to
> help her because she has no controls or no capabilities to control her-
> self. . . . Again my major point that I am trying to get across—and
> even the psychiatrist who makes the fancy report about the defenses she
> has—she doesn't have many defenses—and without defenses her ego
> breaks down, and what comes out is a result of a broken down ego—so
> you can't look at her as a child who is out to get your goat—this isn't
> the same—it's a completely different problem.

Although these children manifested an all pervasive lag in most areas of development, staff was instructed to look for the "hopeful" signs:

> The aunt says the child wants attention all the time—if this is true it's a hopeful sign. That is if she were completely autistic at this point she would be completely cooked . . . what is hopeful about this child is that she did develop speech.

Thus, in gathering information that would govern the diagnostic decision-making process, staff were not to trust other diagnostic statements that had been made about the child and were to attempt to evaluate the total child. In so doing, they were to look for the "hopeful" signs that might be submerged in the pathology.

In some instances, however, the impression left by previous diagnostic material was considered too favorable; and so the dialogue focused on the hopelessness of the case rather than on any favorable signs. In these instances, it was generally concluded that the information presented was unreliable.

Diagnostic Conference:

> Dr. Cartwright: Torturing a cat and animals may be something that kids engage in at certain periods of their life according to a developmental stage—but I don't think this is all of the story. Their diagnostic is incorrect—they call him psychoneurotic . . . and then on the next page they talk about delusions of strength and supernatural powers— this doesn't jibe—if you look at the total personality of this boy—this is why in a case like this it is important to see when some of these things began because some of the torturing and sadism toward animals is not an uncommon kind of thing in an obsessional neurosis . . . . many children who are not psychotic feel so inadequate and weak they are preoccupied with strength—but my flavor of this whole story is that this boy shows severe defects in his ego . . . . there are some further signs of deterioration—firesetting—so he is getting worse.

A different case presented three weeks later contained a similar theme:

> Dr. Cartwright: This is one of these typical cases that I find myself getting more and more resentful of because people are shipped from one place to another and no one takes any responsibility and no one makes a diagnosis—and my own feeling is at this time there isn't much more that you can do . . . . this is not a severe neurotic disturbance because I can dissect this and show you at every level of development that this is an atypical kind of development—he doesn't relate to peers, right? He doesn't achieve at school—his object relationships are primitive—he's a wetter and a soiler—I don't see any of this on any kind of neurotic base, but on a lack of control. He is a fire-setter—I couldn't make anything neurotic out of that.

Mr. Anderson: (The hospital report) says that "there is functional retardation with schizophrenic reaction" and yet the other diagnosis seems to indicate that there is organic mental retardation with severe problems.

Dr. Cartwright: If you are retarded, you may be disturbed because of the way that the environment reacts, but how far you go with someone who is retarded will be determined in terms of [how] retarded they really are so that when you are applying for something—the first thing that high class institutions will want to look at is an I.Q. because they don't want to waste their time for psychotherapies, which is the usual thing in in-patient psychiatric set-ups . . . and the second thing is that you can go only as far as the protoplasm will let you go, and that's true of both retardation and organicity you can have both of these categories and a superimposed disturbance—but you aren't going to be as successful with somebody who is retarded . . . but the way I read the material and the way he conducts himself in the interview I would seriously doubt that this is his problem . . . that he may not have an I.Q. of 180 is also true. . . . I would quibble about only one thing and that is the diagnosis of schizophrenia. . . . I'd like to look at him more in terms of a dynamic diagnosis so I would call this child "borderline— severe ego defect" because schizophrenia has a kind of an implication which diagnostically is hard to substantiate in these kinds of children.

Out of a massive amount of material collected from a multiplicity of referral sources certain factors were sorted out as being relevant, either as "hopeful" signs or, conversely, as indications of the "serious pathology" represented by the child's symptoms. In the three cases illustrated above, the first was considered an "appropriate" child for admission to the program with the others rejected because of the severity of their "ego defects" and disturbed personality configurations.

Parents were considered another significant factor in the diagnostic decision-making process. Two cases presented in a conference just prior to the opening of Day Care serve as illustrations of contrasting cases. In the first case the symptoms of the child were described by Mr. Peters:

Mr. Peters: His behavior is that he bites his hands, is preoccupied, plays alone, dances about, claps his hands, laughs inappropriately, and has very, very limited speech . . . . he rarely uses words to indicate things that he desires—he points—he seemed to me to describe times when he was even at a loss to point to things that he wanted but he felt he wanted something and that he couldn't communicate what it was. Ah, the biting of the hands is to a point where he has worn a callous between his thumb and forefinger.

Dr. Cartwright: You've got some very early symptoms in there which indicate severe pathology . . . . he was a headbanger and a body-rocker —and he was also a loner so there already if he was a happy healthy child, it doesn't jibe with it . . . there is indication of very early and severe pathology. . . . He is interesting in that he sounds like some of the classic cases that Loretta Bender used to demonstrate on the stage at Bellvue.

In this case, it was the father who had originally brought the child in; and, although the child's symptoms clearly indicated a severe degree of illness, the father's obvious interest and the consequent potential of the parents' involvement in treatment were key factors governing the decision to accept this child.

The second case, presented the same day, serves as a direct contrast; the child was not considered "ill," but rather, the "sickness" of the father was felt to be a factor contributing to the atypical behavior of the child. The diagnosis of the father was the prime determinant for the rejection of the child in the program.

> Mrs. Carroll: The complaint of the school is that the child is extremely hyperactive, doesn't do any work, day dreams at times, makes noises, seems to be unaware that he is disturbing other children. Now the mother claims that the child is very difficult for her to handle because of his constant demands for attention—he becomes defiant when told to do something and refuses to follow the simplest instructions—She complains that he lies—apparently he makes up fantasies—and he pushes her to the limits until she punishes him and then he becomes very contrite and says that he wants to be good. . . . I do remember the mother saying that she and the father had been—that the father was hospitalized, that she had been to a psychiatrist in terms of what she was going through in her relationship to her husband, and she said that she began to realize how insecure she was and how ineffectual she was both as a wife and a mother.

A combination of "interesting" symptoms on the part of the child and parents who demonstrated the interest and inclination to become involved were important considerations in the decision to accept or reject a child. Manifestation of milder, less interesting symptoms on the part of the child and personal problems on the part of the parents which were verbalized in the initial interview were negative factors in the consideration of the child.

A further factor in presenting symptomatology that was considered of importance was a differentiation of elements that were considered to be organic as contrasted to functional.

> Mrs. Sanders: (This boy) is seven and there is some question as to whether he has a perceptual handicap or not—he was referred here by the school. . . . He was taken out of the classroom situation because he was gagging . . . at this point they decided he couldn't adjust to the classroom situation . . . so he stayed with a tutor one hour a day. . . . They can work with him on a one-to-one basis but they would

> prefer to have something done about his anxiety level that would enable him to go back to school . . . he seems to be an anxious boy—this shows up in his hyperactivity and he has a lot of bizarre speech and he pretends that he is a machine a lot of the time.
>
> Dr. Cartwright: There is a question about whether his behavior is neurotic or psychotic or is a consequence of his organic problem—whether his psychological problem is the major one. . . . I think there is no question that there is an organic problem here . . . but I have never seen this kind of preoccupation in terms of—that he is a machine—I haven't seen this in just an organic and I am inclined to believe that this is indication of psychosis, and this is a separation problem.

Screening and evaluation of potential patients were devised so that preference was given to the child who manifested a psychotic rather than an organic problem. In the above case, it was judged that the psychological problem was predominant over the organic problem, and, on this basis, the decision was made to accept the child into the program.

The Decision-Making Process

The first case admitted to the program was diagnosed as psychotic with the primary determinant governing her admission being her prior contact with Mrs. Davis in her role as consultant in another agency. The rationale underlying the decision to accept her into the program was presented by Dr. Cartwright:

> Mrs. Davis: She is one of the few fortunates who has an aunt rather than the mother—and actually the aunt has a great deal of feeling.
>
> Dr. Cartwright: I think this is where the strength comes from because she had some sustenance during these years . . . I think you really have to gear yourself toward the aunt as the first thing . . . I have a feeling that this is a mixed case—that this is psychosis and deprivation that is all mixed up . . . in this case you can see how much there is still fluid and that can be lifted with an adequate approach, and that you can determine if it will take forever or never. I think this is a good case for you, because you do see the fluidity in this girl and this is a good case to test out how far you can go.

This child was considered a good case in that they could still see some "fluidity"; and further, they did not have a pathological mother to contend with but rather an interested and involved aunt who was responsible for the child.

Other children were considered in need of treatment, but it was decided this was not the place for them.

Diagnostic Conference:

> Dr. Cartwright: My question is what are you going to do with this child
> —and to answer this you've got to know when this all began. I know
> for instance that his anxiety is the kind of anxiety you see in psychotics
> . . . this case is both dangerous to himself and the outside—in this case
> you'd better be careful about the kind of decision you make . . . . what
> is most important in this case as far as you making a decision, has to
> be that you must very carefully find out what kind of behavior he
> engages in. You can't put a boy who sets fires, who runs away, who ties
> children up, who bites children—you can't put a child like that in an
> open unit—I don't think that you are the place for him. . . . Somebody
> is going to have to decide if this is a candidate that is treatable . . . but
> you don't want to start an in-patient unit with this kind of pathology—
> if you are going to take psychotics—take the quiet ones—because it
> just isn't an appropriate place.

Although this child was equally in need of treatment, the nature of his
symptoms governed the decision that this was not the "appropriate"
place for him.

For others who were considered equally poor candidates for treatment,
a crucial consideration was the possibility of working out a type of arrangement with the school whereby these children might be retained in
the school setting. In one instance where there was an interested school
social worker involved, it was decided that additional intelligence testing
might serve the purpose of getting the child admitted to a class for
socially maladjusted children rather than his current assignment to a
retarded section.

Diagnostic Conference:

> Dr. Cartwright: I don't know what his I.Q. is, but I seriously doubt
> that he is as retarded as he functions—that he is severely disturbed is
> obvious—and this case has to be approached through the family. . . .
> It seems to me that the first effort should be to maintain him in the
> circumstances and see if a (family service agency) can take on the
> family while you (the school social worker) continue with the child . . .
> and then if he could be transferred to a better school situation. . . .
> School Social Worker: It all hangs on the I.Q. business—when they
> see a boy referred for social adjustment and he has an I.Q. below 75—
> Dr. Cartwright: When was he tested the last time?
> School Social Worker: A year ago.
> Dr. Cartwright: What about testing him again?—and getting—testing
> him with much more of a pitch—what the test doesn't indicate—most
> tests when there is a low I.Q. say that there is a scatter—you see if you
> had that kind of evidence and if that is what you strove for in testing
> him to demonstrate that this is not an adequate I.Q., then you might
> beat the system.

Repeat testing in an attempt to get a higher I.Q. score was one of the means by which those children who were perceived as potential "trouble makers" were steered away from the program.

Other children were not taken for fear that taking a child from a particular school district or agency would place the program in a position where excessive demands might be made upon it by these other organizations.

Diagnostic Conference:

> Dr. Cartwright: You see what you have here is that you are already being exposed to the dumping syndrome. . . . You've got to be very careful that you don't fall into this . . . . you see there are plenty of sick children all over the city—and the facilities out here are less than there are in the city—and so all the schools and all the agencies are now going to come running with all of these cases and say you take them, and therefore you are going to have to set up—you are going to have to go back to some of these schools and discuss what they have available, because you could get a thousand cases tomorrow . . . . there should be clear indications as to why children come here, and not just as part of the getting rid of—solve my problems—because you can't give any guarantee that you are going to solve their problems.

A guiding rule in the diagnostic decision-making process was that no matter how sick the child might be, if he remained within a school setting, he would not be accepted into this program.

A further factor of significance in determining the fate of a child being considered for admission to the program was the nature of his symptoms in comparison to those of others who had already been admitted.

> Dr. Cartwright: If this child is extremely provocative you don't want to take too many of those in at first—these are the kinds of patients that you are going to see but you for sure don't want to start with one who is racing around the room, and the other who is going to get everybody to beat up on him, you see—so I think you have to be very careful what your original patient population is . . . . You see you also would want to worry about the little ones and the big ones—particularly if you have sadomasochistic ones, because your little autistic ones are going to get beat up.

This theme was continued in another case presentation the same day:

> Dr. Cartwright: Now one thing I want to warn you against in taking in certain kinds of children in day care—you don't want to take too many of these roamers at once—take a few quiet sit down schizophrenics because otherwise you will be dancing all day long. You have to be careful in terms of your population, which you are going to find out, because they are all going to change after they come in—that you make sure that you take some that are stationary and that not all of them are twirling all over the place.

The case under consideration was presented as being a "quiet type of schizophrenic child." When Miss Travis observed, "This is the sickest child whose history I have read" and asked the question, "Is your recommendation that we take him into the day care program?" Dr. Cartwright responded, "I think that these are the kinds of children that should go into day care—the only thing is that you are going to have to stack the population. This is a good candidate, depending upon the parents, I would say." The degree of atypical symptoms and the need for therapy were not the significant criteria for selection. Rather the inhibited, quiet behavior of this child was considered of value in balancing the population.

In other instances, it was recognized that the child was in need of help, but that the precarious equilibrium of the rest of the family made it too hazardous a venture to become involved with the child.

> Dr. Cartwright: He is not a particularly good case—because he has a severe ego disorder—a dangerous ego disorder—he's a firesetter, ah, and he's got a low I.Q. . . . I would not feel that this kind of child is a good candidate for day care even if you could sort out these parents.
> Mrs. Simpson: I think that we had more or less ruled out day care but thought that we might offer the mother something now, and then later take the boy into in-patient.
> Dr. Cartwright: . . . still you've got a child here who is seriously disturbed and is a hazard, and if you are going to get involved with these kinds of families you'd better have it in the back of your mind what you are going to do with the child when he burns up somebody, you see. Because you have to realistically evaluate what you have for the child when the chips are down . . . it looks like the mother needs something, right? But if you involve yourself with these people you fully have to consider that at any moment you might have to do something with this boy. That's reality . . . I don't think you'd better take on this package.

The decision to reject this boy was based upon the perceived illness of the rest of the family, rather than on his symptoms alone; and the knowledge that adult pathology is even more difficult to deal with than child pathology enforced the decision that accepting this child would be detrimental to the program image in general.

As the date for the opening of day care approached and the program found itself without an adequate number of children, this additional consideration became instrumental in the decision-making process.

> Dr. Cartwright: The problem in this case is that they made a diagnosis that this boy has an organic problem but he also has an emotional problem above and beyond his perceptual problem. He for sure documented his early traumatic history—you know how he was locked in . . .

and his licking on things and his early types of behavior are very sick. . . . Again with your newest desperation that you haven't gotten any patients for day care one could be flexible. . . . This is the kind of kid, that in terms of his responsiveness in the past, whom I would not be against taking in day care treatment . . . . he isn't as hazardous as the last one.

Although it was finally decided to wait until further investigation before making a decision about this child, the fact that his case was presented at the time when the program was in need of children greatly enhanced the possibility of his being accepted.

Further confirmation of this tendency was demonstrated in instances whereby children, who, had they been presented for admittance into the program at an earlier time would have been rejected, were accepted even though their symptoms did not fit the criteria of "acceptability" previously established.

Diagnostic Conference:

This case demonstrates something else—it is perhaps the most thoroughly worked up case you have and for that it is worthwhile—but you see again the etiology is unclear. Despite the work-up you cannot make up your mind where the organic problem came from or the severe psychological problem except for one small thing—these parents are very interested in having this child educated. And that usually doesn't begin at age 6, so there would be a question of what did the mother pick up that made her respond in this way, because you have organic signs and you have definitely psychotic signs, but again he has been worked up many time, and each time it has come out for a recommendation for school and now at age twelve residential treatment is asked for. . . . I am very pessimistic at what you can do when you pick something up at this age . . . and this is a case that is worse because you pick up that the parents are not cooperative—I think in this case you should take it on an exploratory basis . . . but with a child of 12, I'm terribly pessimistic. There is no need for further workup—it is all in the record and it is clear—the only question is how do you reach them? A family that has denied for twelve years that there is a problem.

Despite the diagnosis of organicity, possible retardation, psychosis, the age of the child, and questionable treatability of the parents, it was decided to accept this child into the program. There was a need for children to open up the program.

The diagnostic decision-making process followed no clear cut set of criteria, other than those arising from the immediate situation. Out of the total population of children who were considered in need of psychiatric treatment, only seven were accepted during the time of this study. The choice of these seven was based upon a multiplicity of factors. First, the initial intake phone call provided an opportunity for the Intake worker to make a judgment as to whether this request was appropriate for any consideration at all within the program. These considerations were primarily based upon interaction within the program that focused on identifying the "appropriate child" for this program. Although there was some discussion of the type of child that this program would treat, these earlier understandings were often reversed as witnessed by policy which determined that if a child was retained in the school, the program would not accept him, thus ruling out a large group of children who were experiencing difficulties in school and for whom short-term help seemed indicated.

Ruling out this population narrowed the potential clients down to those excluded from school; and, ironically those excluded from school were primarily diagnosed as schizophrenic or psychotic with accompanying organic and perceptual problems or children having "ego defects" with the latter category of child always ruled out in the decision-making process. The exclusion of the child with an "ego-defect" was always based upon his potential destructiveness and the recommendation most frequently made was that this child needed a "secure setting"— a state hospital.

This process served to define a population of children appropriate for this program which in turn served to foster the political goals of the organization. These children were unquestionably sick and a problem to other social groups in society. Providing day care services for these children could be justified as an innovation in the psychiatric field, since these children are usually treated in long-term in-patient settings. Staff participating in the treatment of these children turned out to be committed to the impossible task of "helping these children." Finally, the hazards of admitting these children for whom the program was in principle set up, proved too great. A modus vivendi was achieved.

Chapter XI

The Production

How can the work of an organization be discerned? In any organization there are at least three perspectives that warrant consideration. First, an organization seeks to promote an image of what it accomplishes via the medium of written reports. A business organization communicates by way of annual reports to the stockholders. These reports serve to give an accounting of the work of the organization in the hope of eliciting continuing support from the stockholders.

Workers within an organization may have a far different view of the functioning of the organization than do the stockholders. The top-level managers, for example, may know of such things as intrigue, bids for power and control, and mismanagement of funds. The lower-level worker may be aware of the inferior quality of the goods. No matter what their place in the organizational hierarchy each participant appraises the work of the organization. When people have worked together over a prolonged period of time, commonalities of opinion are likely to have developed. But rarely does the insider divulge his views to the consumer public.

A third view of the work of an organization may be obtained through actually studying what the organization does through a review of all phases of the operation. Objective measures of the output of an organization are likely to be at variance with the subjective views held by the participants.

At the end of the first year of this psychiatric program written reports provided one indication of the actual work of the organization. A second measure was that of the views held by participants within the program. A third measure consisted of tracing the decision-making process surrounding each child for whom services had been requested.

Written Reports

Although innovation and change from the original baseline of the program proposal are apparent in patterns of staff interaction within the

185

program, written documents revised during the course of this study do not reflect these changes explicitly. Rather, the revised documents are characterized primarily by an expansion of the rationale underlying the need for a particular type of children's service, accompanied by a deletion of certain restrictive clauses contained in earlier documents. In effect, the later program proposal defines the needs and identifies potential treatment resources outside of the program, while being less definitive about the specific funtions of the program itself.

A review of the revised program proposal written nine months after the initial proposal illustrates this bias. After quoting at length from studies within the Department of Mental Health as well as exploratory contacts with community resources, the goals of the program were stated as follows:

> It is to these inadequacies in existent services for emotionally disturbed, mentally retarded, and mentally ill children that the proposed program of Children's services addresses itself to. While diagnosis and consultation remain an important part of our services, our primary focus will be on the actual rehabilitation of the child. Our goal is to restore, establish, and maintain mental health and social functioning in as brief a period as possible, so that the child is able to return to his community milieu or remain in that milieu in as mentally and socially well-adjusted or adapted condition as current "therapeutic" methodology is able to produce.

Although the officially stated goal of the program was the provision of rehabilitative services to the child, statements made most frequently during those seminars dealing with the consideration of clients for the program were similar to the following: "He is a good diagnostic case," "You can take this child in to see whether he is cooked or not," and 'You can't treat a child like this in a short period of time."

While earlier program proposals had set specific time limits on the length of treatment offered in day care and the types of children who would not be accepted, the revised program proposal contained no such specifications. Rather, the program proposal stated that:

> In the initial stage of Children's services operations, priority will be for the child ages 6 to 14 who is in High Risk of Institutionalization as defined within the Region; Children's services embraces the concept that persons are more effectively treated within and without removal from their natural community. Further, prompt attention shall be directed to forces that impinge upon his functioning. These forces shall be directed or redirected to the task of supporting, enabling and maintaining the mental health of the child and his family.

The two specifications state that the children must fall in a given age range and that they be in "High Risk Institutionalization," a very ambiguous phase that is in no way defined. The effect of such a statement was that of publicly conforming to the overall goals of the larger organizational structure, while not committing itself to any defined population of clients or to any specific treatment methodology.

Further indication of the ambiguity of public statements is reflected in this definition of the Day Care program and its function.

> The Day Care program is an integral part of the spectrum of comprehensive mental health services for children at (the Mental Health Center). It is the treatment modality of choice for children who require a greater amount of intervention than is feasible through an out-patient service, but who do not require full-time hospitalization, in-patient residential treatment or institutionalization. The central focus will aim at meeting the mental health needs of the mentally ill, emotionally disturbed, and mentally retarded child between the ages of 6 and 14, who are unable to adjust to or benefit from local programs. The goal of the Day Care program will be to return these children to full participation in the community.
>
> The children will participate in a planned program of structured and unstructured activities in a therapeutic milieu at the Center for up to six hours a day five days a week. Objectives will include (1) fostering improvement and developing effective skills in interpersonal and social relationships with peers and adults; (2) developing skills, gross and fine motor abilities; (3) mastering basic academic skills, remediation of learning disabilities and developing positive attitudes toward learning; (4) learning and practicing personal health, safety and care skills necessary in daily living; (5) developing and practicing effective communication skills; (6) developing a positive self-identity and self-image; and (7) developing capacities for self-expression.

The objectives stated in the revised program proposal could apply to any child in any setting. Furthermore, they were unrealistic for the population of autistic and psychotic children who were ultimately accepted into the Day Care program.

Official documents, instead of portraying the true nature of the program, reflected, rather, the perceived expectations of the outside world. For example, contained within the revised program proposal is terminology that indicated that the program would conform to overall organizational goals and that its purpose, in terms of children, is to make them into "normal citizens." The program proposal in no way communicated anything of what actually had occurred within the program. It provided no guidelines for action within the program itself but rather served to promote an impression that would conform to external expectations. The major change reflected in the revision of the program proposal made during the course of this study, is an increased sophistication in the political realm rather than a refinement of the program itself.

Staff Perceptions of Program Structure

A further measure of the structure of the program that had evolved throughout the first stage of organization was obtained through responses to a questionnaire administered to all personnel employed within the program at the end of the first year, excluding supervisory personnel. The purpose of this questionnaire was to investigate commonalities or differences in staff definitions of the work to be done and the public to be served by the program. A total of nineteen questionnaires were completed. The responses to the questions were grouped according to the length of time that the individuals had been employed. Of the group completing the questionnaires, nine had been employed less than two months, four had been employed from two to four months, four had been employed four to six months, and two had been in the program for more than six months.

It was assumed that staff would agree on the geographic boundaries that the program would serve as well as the age limits of the children that would be accepted. These assumptions were not validated by questionnaire responses. The greatest specificity as to the location of geographic boundaries was shown in the responses by those who had been employed less than two months. Two respondents who had only been there for two days showed greater awareness of the area that the program would serve than did others who had been employed over six months. The newcomer in the organization probably learned such things as geographic boundaries and similar concrete facts in an attempt to structure an ambiguous situation, while the staff member who had been **employed over a longer period of time and had experienced changes** in the area to be served reflected the resultant confusion and also the tendency to use other criteria of a more abstract nature in defining the population which would receive treatment. The Intake worker who was confronted with the public and was charged with the responsibility of either scheduling appointments for screening interviews or referring calls elsewhere had specific knowledge about geographic boundaries as this was one of the criteria which governed her decision making. The tendency of those employed for the longest period of time to use more abstract measures is revealed by comments such as "probably things will remain concentrated in the city, though I do have some feeling that the suburbs may supply us initially with the majority of kids." Responses such as this seemed to indicate that these staff members were aware that, in spite of specific boundaries, other factors frequently intervened. Ambiguity of responses to questions for which there were specific answers also reflects staff's perceptions that although these criteria were defined they in effect did not govern decision making.

Although all staff members agreed that the lower age boundary was six, the upper age boundary was not as clearly demarcated. Differences of opinion as to the top level ranged from twelve to seventeen years, with staff having been employed the longest specifying that direct services would be given to children from six to twelve and indirect services to those from twelve to seventeen.

The most frequently listed criterion for admission was that the child have some type of emotional disturbance, but rarely was this further defined. In only three instances staff specified that children should not to "too sick," i.e. firesetters, homicidal, or suicidal. The second most important criterion, as reflected in the frequency of responses, was the involvement of the parent in the treatment process. Age limits and geographical boundaries served as further differentiating factors, with the remainder of the responses centered around specific factors that would rule children out for the program. The responses on the questionnaire in no way paralleled the actual process that occurred within the diagnostic seminars.

TABLE 1
STAFF'S PERCEPTIONS OF CRITERIA FOR ADMISSION TO THE DAY TREATMENT PROGRAM

	Frequency				
Criteria Listed	-2 mo.	2-4	4-6	6- mo.	Total
1. Must have emotional problem	5	4	3	1	13
2. Parents must cooperate	4	3	3	1	11
3. Must meet age limits	4	1	3		8
4. Geographic requirements	4	1	1	1	7
5. Retardation may be secondary problem	3	1	3		7
6. Child should be able to benefit	1	3	1	1	6
7. Short-term problem	1	1			2
8. Child must be excluded from school	3	1	1		5
9. Child must not be physically handicapped	3	1			4

When asked to state the rationale behind what they had defined as the criteria governing admission, the nine newly employed staff members identified efficiency factors as the primary consideration underlying the admission of this group. Such things as "studies show that this is the highest area of need," "so that we can make efficient use of our resources", and "it's easier to run a program with some criteria" were listed. Those employed from two to four months differentiated this program from that of other treatment organizations. For example, "State hospitals are for those in need of long-term care" and "these criteria are set up so that we can work intensively and meaningfully with those we can help" were given as reasons for the criteria being established. All of those employed over four months described the rationale as based upon the relationship between parent and child and made statements such as "you can't treat the child without treating the parents." There was a marked differentiation of responses in providing a rationale for the criteria established by the program, with the newcomer focusing upon the efficiency factors involved in delimiting a population and those employed for longer periods of time concentrating on ideological commitments.

When asked if they agreed with the criteria governing the selection process for children to be admitted to the day care program, sixteen of the nineteen expressed agreement. The three who disagreed questioned (1) the restrictive nature of the criteria since they felt that the program should feel some obligation to take more of a cross-section of the population, (2) the fact that only one person made the decisions, and (3) the basic theory underlying the medical model which guided decision-making. The questioning of the criteria was made primarily by the new employee, rather than those employed for longer periods, again indicating differential socialization patterns.

In response to the question regarding criteria that the family must meet, all respondents specified that the family had to be involved in the treatment. Such things as the family's being intact or other similar specifications were not mentioned.

Staff expressed vague ideas about the criteria governing admission of children to the program as well as the characteristics desired in the parents. Lacking these definitions, they had little basis for structuring their contacts with parents or children according to any logical frame of reference. The child had to be "emotionally ill," fall within a certain age range, live within a specific area, and have interested parents; but other than that there was no consistency in ideas about "appropriate" treatment cases. While in practice the aggressive child was ruled out at all stages of the process, staff did not refer to this factor in listing criteria governing admission to the program. Instead they responded by listing criteria derived either from meetings where rationalizations were advanced to justify admission or rejection of a child, or from factors derived from written documents. Although there was a well-defined process of selection operating within the program, staff responded as though there was an implicit agreement not to acknowledge how the system in reality operated.

Given this ambiguity, the next question that followed was the consideration of how staff structured their work without the guidelines of these basic definitions. In response to the question, "What is the major goal that you wish to achieve in taking your first intake call from a client?" newcomers emphasized "making a proper referral elsewhere" with little consideration of clients for this program. Those who had been employed longer periods of time stressed "information gathering."

When asked to list the information that they wished to obtain from a client in the initial call, identification of the problem was listed most frequently. Table 2, enumerates the information which they considered important to obtain.

TABLE 2

INFORMATION LISTED TO BE OBTAINED
IN FIRST INTAKE CALL WITH CLIENT

	Frequency
Understanding of the problem	5
Obtaining identifying data	10
Making appropriate referrals	10
Review of previous treatment obtained	5
Social history	4
Provide information regarding our program	3
Assess parental attitudes	2
Establish communication with the client	1

Although staff saw one of the primary goals in the intake call to be the identification of the problems, the ambiguity surrounding criteria governing admission to the program presented a dilemma in terms of decision making. When asked how they would make a decision regarding which individuals would be brought in for a screening interview, they expressed considerable confusion. One determinant which was used most frequently was that the child fit the age and residence requirement and that his problem "be appropriate to the services provided here."

The frequency of the response that the goal of the intake call was to make an appropriate referral is an acknowledgment of the awareness on the part of the staff that a minimal number of those seeking services would be admitted to this program. One primary concern focused on the need of working out alternative routes for treatment. This concern with making appropriate referrals was also related to a concern for maintaining an image that, although help would not be offered in this setting, still staff was concerned about the needs of people requesting help. This further served to protect the program from encroachment from the outside.

The purpose of the screening interview was similarly identified as that of obtaining more information about the problem. Only three of the nineteen staff members specified the nature of the additional information that they wished to acquire in the screening interview. The additional information which they specified as important was (1) "a basic understanding of how the parent perceives the problem," (2) "a first impression of the parent," (3) "evaluation of the current situation," (4) "family dynamics," (5) "the workability of the child and the suitability of the parents," and (6) "background information to establish etiology."

Most respondents did not make any clear differentiation between intake calls and screening interviews except for the emphasis upon identifying data in the intake calls. On the basis of this information, it may be concluded that there were no clear-cut guidelines governing the decision-making process at the Intake or Screening levels other than the individual perceptions of staff members as to the nature of an "appropriate problem."

Definitions of the "diagnostic process" similarly reflect differences of opinion and lack of clarity among staff members. Table 3 provides a compilation of concepts reported to explain the "diagnostic process." Eight respondents followed the definition of the diagnostic process given in the Intake Training Seminars which specified a sequence of interviews with parents and the child, while four expressed the idea that the diagnostic process was continuous from the time of the initial contact with the program throughout the entire treatment process. Four confined their definitions to one specific situation in which a consultant saw the child, who had already been accepted for treatment, in a "free play" situation; diagnosis was viewed as the function of one particular individual, with little relationship to the work of others.

TABLE 3

STAFF DEFINITIONS OF THE
DIAGNOSTIC PROCESS

	-2 mo.	2-4 mo.	4-6 mo.	6- mo.	Total
1. Specific sequence of interviews	4	2	2	1	9
2. Ongoing process concept	2	—	1	1	4
3. Identification of the process with individual conference with child	1	2	1	—	4
4. No response	2	—	1	—	3

The importance of diagnosis was closely related, in their minds to the treatment of the child. Ten of the nineteen respondents made statements such as "you cannot treat effectively without a good diagnosis," or "You can't treat a child until you know what you are treating." Six indicated that they did not know why diagnosis was stressed, and three of the four who considered the diagnostic process to be confined to one specific interview situation, saw this activity as a check on other diagnostic impressions. For example, "You need to be sure that the perceived problem is the real one and that we can help solve it," and "You need to have a firsthand impression of the child" were given to support this view. In general staff appeared to believe that success in treatment was dependent upon accurate diagnosis.

Although diagnosis was seen as an important key to success in treatment, staff identified numerous problems in the process. Table 4 presents a listing of problems identified.

Staff reflected little confidence in the diagnostic procedure. Responses to questions concerning the Intake, Screening, and Diagnostic phases of the work indicates that staff responded according to rationalizations previously advanced during training and diagnostic seminars regarding the relevance of these phases of the work. The ambiguity and divergence of responses indicate that staff did not see these factors as directly relevant to the work; rather, these were steps to be followed with the information gathered through this sequence having little relevance to the actual decision-making process.

TABLE 4

IDENTIFICATION OF PROBLEMS IN
THE DIAGNOSTIC PROCEDURE

	Frequency
Unreliability of the process	5
Difficulty of making differential diagnosis	4
Diagnostic process too brief	4
Child not seen in his natural setting	4
Lack of communication of diagnostic findings within the organization and from other agencies	4
Diagnosis made on the basis of disciplinary biases	2
No test data used in making decisions	2
Lack of agreement between participants	2
Lack of procedures to guide process	1

In response to the question on the type of therapy to be provided, the newcomers gave the most explicit answers, primarily centering around concepts of milieu therapy. Four of the eight responses from those employed 2-6 months mentioned primarily individual relationships leaning more toward an analytical ideological stance, two listed types of activity groups provided, and two characterized it respectively as "up for grabs" and "babysitting." The two respondents who had been employed six months or more defined it as "milieu therapy" without explicitly defining what they meant by this term. It may be hypothesized that the newcomer responded from the framework of learning that he carried with him into the organization and thus reported the "ideal." Those employed an intermediate period of time had been inculcated with some of the psychoanalytic ideology and responded from this framework coupled with some knowledge of the reality of the situation; while those employed the longer period of time and now completely immersed in direct work with children did not perceive the question as relevant.

Staff responses, differentiating therapy and child care work, are reported in Table 5.

For most staff members, particularly newcomers, it was important to be able to differentiate the functions of child care workers from those of "therapist". Newcomers focused more on concrete facts, such as the length of time spent with the children, relations between peers as opposed to parents, and "generalized" vs. "specific" therapy. Those employed for an intermediate period of time posed a dichotomy of inter-action, i.e., conscious behavior vs. unconscious motivation; while these employed for the longer period of time saw little need for differentiating.

TABLE 5

STAFF DIFFERENTIATION OF CHILD
CARE WORK AND THERAPY

Child Care Work	Therapy	Frequency
Deals with conscious behavior	Deals with unconscious motivation	7
Generalized therapy	Therapy more specific	5
Works with child over prolonged period of time	Works within limited time period	2
Focused on child's relationship to peers	Concentration on how child related to parents	1
Little differentiation of roles		2

Direct involvement with parents or children was reported as being the most satisfying aspect of the work by ten of the nineteen respondents who had experienced direct contact. Those who had not worked with clients reported such things as "staff development seminars," "anytime that I've felt that I was doing something constructive," and "I've only had fleeting moments of satisfaction" in response to this question. Six did not respond at all to this item.

In contrast, least satisfying aspects reported by respondents showed much greater variation. Table 6 lists least satisfying experiences reported by the respondents.

Greatest dissatisfaction was expressed by newcomers who particularly complained of having nothing to do and not knowing how to handle that work that was given them to do. This together with the perceived lack of structure, inadequate communication, and lack of understanding on the part of their supervisors, contributed to their unhappiness.

When asked how this experience compared with their anticipations, eight reported either that their anticipations were fulfilled or that they hadn't known what to expect. Five reported that they had expected to be involved in more direct work with clients, three had anticipated more structure than they had found, two had anticipated that there would be more professionally trained staff than there was, and two complained

TABLE 6

ASPECTS OF THE WORK REPORTED AS
BEING LEAST SATISFYING

Slowness of the program developing and having nothing to do.	5
Being on intake and not knowing how to handle the calls.	5
Sitting in meetings.	3
Lack of structure.	2
Poor communication.	1
Lack of understanding between supervisors and supervisees.	2
Not having sustained involvement with child.	1
All aspects of the program are equally satisfying.	2

TABLE 7

AREAS OF PROGRAM STAFF WOULD
LIKE TO CHANGE

I. *Administrative Structural Changes*		(9)
Better Organization	3	
Decentralization of Authority	3	
Less Division Between Supervisors and Supervisees	2	
Differentiation of Staff Roles	1	
II. *Changes in Training Structure*		(5)
Better Developed Training Process	3	
Better Orientation of Staff	2	
III. *Changes in Services to Children*		(5)
Broaden Services to Admit Wider Range of Children	1	
More Interest in the Community	1	
Treatment for the Whole Child	1	
Better Admission Procedure	1	
Individual Rooms for Child Care Workers	1	
No Opinion		(5)

that their previous experience was not recognized. In contrast, two reported that the experience had "turned out better than I had anticipated," because they hadn't anticipated being allowed to work in all aspects of the program.

A further dimension of the evaluation of the experience was elicited in responses relative to aspects of the program that they would like to change. These responses are presented in Table 7.

The most commonly reported aspects that staff would have liked to change were structural factors, particularly in the area of program administration. Apparently staff members experienced difficulties in becoming part of this program because of the lack of guidance available to them.

In summary, staff had poorly defined criteria as to the characteristics of the patients with whom they were to deal and the procedure to be followed in therapy with the patients once they were admitted to the setting. The confusion reflected in the responses given by staff lends credence to the proposition that, although the stated goal of the program was to provide services to emotionally disturbed children, the actual goal was survival in the larger organizational milieu. Although staff attempted to delineate factors that would provide structure to their work, they implicitly acknowledged by their non-specific and confusing answers that decision making, for example, was not governed by criteria manifested by the patient but rather by political considerations involving those higher in the hierarchy. Within this framework, the work that they participated in was meaningless and irrelevant and they perceived themselves as pawns in a political game, the nature of which was not entirely clear to them. Staff, particularly, those employed less than four months, expressed considerable dissatisfaction while those employed longer periods of time and involved in direct work with children had compensated by obtaining satisfaction not in the program per se but in their work with children.

Characteristics of Children Accepted
or Rejected by the Program

A third indication of the form which the program assumed is derived from an analysis of characteristics of the clients accepted or rejected by the program. Information regarding clients contacting the program in search of help was obtained from two sources: (1) a review of all written materials on all cases on file at the end of the first year and (2) a review of the content of diagnostic seminars conducted in the last six months of the year.

Review of Written Materials

A child might be ruled "inappropriate" for the program at three different points: (1) at the initial telephone intake call, (2) at the first screening interview, and (3) in the diagnostic process. The analysis of all cases on file* at the end of the first year revealed the following numbers of cases processed through these three stages.

TABLE 8

NUMBERS OF CASES PROCESSED THROUGH INTAKE-SCREENING-DIAGNOSTIC PHASES

Intake	Screening	Diagnostic
77	51	24

Approximately two-thirds of all clients who called requesting services were filtered out between the initial telephone intake call and the diagnostic stage. This phase of the work was completely carried out by the social workers and untrained staff in the process of receiving training in "intake" without any psychiatric consultation. It may be hypothesized that intake staff ruled out certain cases on the basis of their understanding of the "desired" characteristics of the patients admitted to the program. Since staff involved in this activity were at the lower level of the status hierarchy and were also involved in a training process in which their work was reviewed by senior staff, a guage of their competence, in their minds, was the accuracy of their decisions as to what constituted an "appropriate" case to carry beyond the Intake level.

Table 9 illustrates the range of descriptive labels attached to cases that did not proceed beyond the telephone intake stage.

These problems, defined at the Initial Telephone Intake level and subsequently ruled out, are grouped in Table 10 which reflects the type of behavior emphasized in the decision that the child was "inappropriate" for the program.

Over one-half of the children ruled out at the Telephone Intake Level were considered to be "inappropriate" for this program on the basis of aggressive behavior directed toward others. Intake workers obviously perceived that "aggressive" children were not to be accepted into the program.

*All Intake calls were to be recorded on an Intake record sheet and placed in the file. However, it is likely that a worker might decide that a particular call did not warrant completion of the form, and therefore this would probably be a conservative estimate of the total number of calls received.

TABLE 9

DESCRIPTIVE LABELS APPLIED TO CASES
DROPPED AT TELEPHONE INTAKE LEVEL

1. Attacks other children
2. Acting-out child; aggressive
3. Threatened to stab teacher
4. Harms other children at school
5. Poor grades in school
6. Disturbed, hyperactive, impulsive
7. Withdrawn, negativistic, no speech
8. Disturbed, retarded, aggressive
9. Hyperactive, discipline problem
10. Childhood schizophrenia
11. Acting out
12. Depressed and suicidal
13. Hyperactive, hard to manage
14. Referred by court for testing
15. Presently on LSD and STP
16. Runs away, steals, temper tantrums
17. Disobeys, daydreams, ADC family, father beats child
18. Fights, steals, disobeys, homicidal
19. Functional disability, possibly schizophrenia
20. Autistic child—age 14
21. School problems
22. Retarded—mother deserts child
23. Extremely disturbed, homicidal and possibly suicidal
24. Tantrums, hits other children

Two cases were on file where no complaint was recorded

TABLE 10

CHILDREN FALLING WITHIN BEHAVIORAL
CATEGORIES RULED OUT AT THE
TELEPHONE INTAKE LEVEL

Behavioral Categories	Number
Aggressive Behavior	14
Withdrawn Behavior	5
School Problems	3
Miscellaneous	4

The second level of which cases could be ruled out was at the screening interview level. Decisions about which cases should be carried beyond the screening interview level were primarily made by Mrs. Carroll in collaboration with the senior social worker staff. A total of twenty-seven cases were dropped at this point. Table 11 shows the descriptive labels attached to children dropped at this stage.

TABLE 11

DESCRIPTIVE LABELS ATTACHED TO CASES
DROPPED AT THE SCREENING
INTERVIEW LEVEL

1. Acting out
2. Child out of touch
3. Tantrums, hits children
4. Hears voices
5. Steals—school problem
6. Retarded
7. Hyperactive and destructive
8. Hyperactive, soils and wets
9. Disturbed child—dangerous to himself and others
10. Parents over protective—child not the problem
11. Firesetter
12. Difficult to manage at home
13. Firesetter, burglary, poor school adjustment
14. Hyperactive—discipline problem
15. Destructive—homicidal
16. School complains about behavior—parents see no problem
17. Mother paranoid schizophrenic
18. Angry, chronically irritated child
19. No particular emotional problem
20. Stubborn and ill-tempered—marital conflict between parents
21. Angry, destructive and aggressive
22. Hyperactive and impulsive—temper tantrums
23. Severely disturbed, hostile unmanageable
24. Fights with other children
25. Acting out child—aggressive

No record of complaint on two cases

These problems, defined in the screening interview process and ruled out at that level, are grouped in Table 12, which shows the number of cases falling within categories of behavior considered inappropriate for the program.

Again nearly two-thirds of the children ruled out at this level were catalogued primarily as being aggressive.

TABLE 12

CHILDREN FALLING WITHIN BEHAVIORAL CATEGORIES
RULED OUT AT THE SCREENING INTERVIEW LEVEL

Type of Behavior	Number
Aggressive Behavior	17
Withdrawn Behavior	2
Parental Problems	2
School Problems, Retardation	3
Miscellaneous	3

TABLE 13

DESCRIPTIVE LABELS ATTACHED TO CHILDREN
SEEN IN DIAGNOSTIC SEMINARS

1. High strung and nervous; psychosomatic complaints
2. Non-verbal
3. Perceptually handicapped and disturbed
4. Behavior problem-aggression in school
5. Borderline psychotic—aggressive, firesetter
6. Disturbed child, aggressive
7. Steals, lies and has death wishes
8. Childhood schizophrenia
9. Severely withdrawn, autistic child
10. Chronic brain syndrome; childhood schizophrenia
11. Angry, possibly suicidal youngster
12. School phobia—frightened and confused child
13. Problems of regression and separation
14. Withdrawn—cries
15. School behavior problem—aggressive
16. Runs away, firesetter, aggressive
17. Stubborn; childhood schizophrenia
18. Autistic, withdrawn
19. Temper tantrums, lack of speech, schizophrenic reaction, childhood type
20. Trainable retarded child
21. Childhood schizophrenia
22. Rebellious, lies, runs away, steals
23. Infantile, temper tantrums, babyish and clinging
24. Psychotic

Since the ruling out of a high percentage of children on the basis of aggressive tendencies may simply be a result of the larger number of these cases referred to the program, further differentiation may be made by a review of the characteristics of cases that were finally seen at the diagnostic conference. Table 13 lists the characteristics of children reviewed in the diagnostic seminars.

Grouping these cases into behavioral categories, Table 14 reflects the numbers of children displaying specific types of behavior that were reviewed in diagnostic seminars.

TABLE 14

BEHAVIORAL CHARACTERISTICS OF CHILDREN
SEEN IN DIAGNOSTIC SEMINARS

Behavior	Number
Aggressive Behavior	8
Withdrawn Behavior	14
Retardation and other Physical Problems	2

The number of children seen in diagnostic seminars whose primary problem consisted of some form of aggressive behavior was only eight out of the twenty-four cases. This stands in contrast to the larger percentages of children in the aggressive category ruled out at earlier stages of their contact with the program.

The likelihood of a child's being seen through all levels of the Intake-Screening-Diagnostic process was greatly enhanced if his behavior was described as withdrawn rather than aggressive. This predisposition to select the withdrawn child rather than the aggressive child was in contradiction to the frequently stated axiom that "if the patient is still fighting, he is more hopeful (as a treatment candidate) than if he has given in to his environment." In terms of treatability this child was not the preferred choice, but in terms of manageability the withdrawn child was to be desired.

A further dimension in analyzing the characteristics of children deemed "appropriate" for this program was obtained by further dividing the aggressive and withdrawn groups defined by the initial intake calls according to the geographic area from which they were drawn. Table 15 shows the distribution of aggressive and withdrawn children from the city as opposed to suburban areas.

The highest proportion of aggressive children were from the inner city, while the larger percentage of withdrawn children were from suburban areas. The child from the ghetto, relying upon aggressive behavior as a means of survival in his deprived surroundings, was denied "help" in this particular treatment program for merely manifesting behavior necessary for his survival.

TABLE 15

PERCENTAGE OF CHILDREN FROM CITY AND
SUBURBS DISPLAYING AGGRESSIVE OR
WITHDRAWN BEHAVIOR

	City	Suburb	Total
Aggression	47%	18%	65%
Withdrawal	13%	22%	35%
Total	60%	40%	100%

Diagnostic Seminar Case Material

A review of diagnostic seminars in which eighteen of the twenty-four cases that remained at the third level of the Intake-Screening-Diagnostic process were scrutinized for additional data shows that, of these eighteen cases, five were accepted and thirteen were rejected.

Table 16 provides a list of characteristics defined as undesirable, both for the parent and for the child, that served as a basis for ruling the child out as unsuitable for the program.

TABLE 16
UNDESIRED CHARACTERISTICS OF CHILDREN
AND PARENTS REJECTED FOR THE PROGRAM

Child	Parent
1. "He's a firesetter . . . has a low I.Q. . . . You've got a child who is severely disturbed and a hazard."	1. "The mother is over-burdened and sick. . . . The pattern is chronic . . . and the mother keeps herself in a chronic state of panic."
2. "More hyperactive than any we've talked about . . . talks back to teachers . . . refuses to do school work . . . evidence of a perceptual handicap.	2. "Father dead—when he was alive discipline was excessive and brutal . . . mother still has a lot of anger toward father which she is unable to work through."
3. "Over-active, destructive, and violent . . . destroys toys."	3. "Family has not followed through at other places . . . mother is afraid of getting involved . . . live too far away . . . questionable motivation of parents."
4. "Organic emotional and perceptual problems . . . traumatic early history."	4. "Parents haven't gotten involved anywhere previously."

5. "Stubborn and aggressive behavior . . . difficulties in school. Lies and steals . . . suicidal thoughts."
6. "Reacts when mother goes to work . . . soils . . . steals."

7. "Tried to choke a child in school . . . kicked a teacher . . . aggressiveness is against him."

8. "Weight problem, sleeplessness, doesn't make friends easily."

9. "Case of chronic pathology . . . lies, steals, runs away . . . doesn't relate to anyone at school."
10. "School complains child is hyperactive . . . child difficult to handle . . . great deal of masochism in the child."
11. "He's getting worse . . . is a firesetter . . . runs away . . . ties other children up . . . can't relate."
12. "Chronically irritable child . . . throws knives and heavy objects at sister . . . downward trend in I.Q."
13. "Organic mental retardation . . . doesn't relate to peers . . . object relationships faulty . . . school complaints . . . firesetting."

5. "Parents divorced . . . mother depressed . . . mother needs help first."
6. "Father left family . . . mother probably severe and harsh in toilet-training mother's separation problems greatest consideration."
7. "Mother very disturbed . . . father has been hospitalized for emotional problems . . . paranoid schizophrenic sister . . . connection between boy's acting out and mother's rage . . . mother untreatable."
8. "Rejected by stepfather . . . marriage about to break up . . . child extension of the mother . . . symbiotic ties."
9. "Some of the motivation in this case may be to dump the child."

10. "Father has had breakdown and is very rigid with children . . . mother is so guilt-ridden that she can't provide structure."
11. "Discrepancies in mother's story . . . child has not been perceived as an individual . . . marital conflicts."
12. "Child illegitimate . . . stepfather rejects him."

13. "Parents want to dump this child."

In all of the cases rejected for treatment one major factor governing the decision making was the instability of the parents and not solely the difficulties that the child was presenting. As for the children, nine of the thirteen were characterized as having aggressive tendencies, three cases were considered primarily to be the result of problems of the parents that in turn implicated the child, and one case reflected a multiplicity of organic, emotional and perceptual problems.

Table 17 presents a listing of the diagnostic labels applied to these cases and the recommendations that were made for treatment.

TABLE 17

DIAGNOSTIC LABELS AND RECOMMENDATIONS FOR TREATMENT MADE FOR CHILDREN REJECTED BY THE PROGRAM

Diagnostic Label	Recommendation
1. Severe ego defect	Residential treatment on a locked unit
2. No diagnosis	Out-patient treatment
3. Psychotic	Take mother into treatment—find day care program for child
4. Organic, emotional, and perceptual problems	Use special education facilities of the school
5. No diagnosis	Referral to a family agency
6. Separation problem	Referral to a family agency
7. No diagnosis	Residential treatment
8. No diagnosis	Mother needs treatment
9. Severe ego defect	Treat parents . . . involve school
10. Atypical, borderline child	May need in-patient treatment
11. Severe ego disorder	Residential treatment—locked ward
12. Severe ego disorder	Residential treatment
13. Severe ego defect	Long-term treatment

TABLE 18

DESIRABLE ATTRIBUTES OF CHILDREN AND PARENTS ACCEPTED INTO DAY TREATMENT PROGRAM

Child	Parent
1. "If this child is reaching out it is hopeful . . . she did develop speech . . . you see fluidity in this child."	1. "The aunt provides structure . . . . she's fortunate that she has this aunt rather than the mother . . . the aunt has a great deal of feeling . . . she wants to do all she can."
2. "Wherever the child has been he has always made progress." (The child had been involved with various agencies for the past 6 years.)	2. "Home accommodate to his psychosis . . . parents are interested . . . parents have intellectual training."
3. "It would be hopeful if he were able to form any kind of object relationship no matter how primitive."	3. "Marriage described as happy with both parents working . . . child handled at home primarily by father . . . the father has not given up on him."
4. "Has speech."	4. (Nothing identified as desirable other than that the father is a teacher.)
5. "In some ways responsive—there seems to be a fluid emotional problem."	5. (No desirable characteristics listed other than that the father has his own construction business.)

Five of the children diagnosed as having a "severe ego defect" were designated as too sick for the program; and for four of the five, recommendations were made that they be placed on a residential unit, preferably locked. All children for whom this recommendation was made came from the inner city and were black. For two other cases, with a non-definitive diagnosis, a similar recommendation for in-patient treatment was made. These two cases were white and from an outlying middle-class area of the city. The remaining six children either were not considered sick enough to warrant admission to the program and alternative treatment resources were suggested, or their parents were defined as the primary patients in need of treatment.

Further indication of trends within the program is evidenced by the characteristics of children accepted into the program. Table 18 lists characteristics of children and parents that were determining factors in the admission of these children into the program.

All of the children accepted for treatment in the diagnostic seminars were defined as being "extremely sick." The first three cases, all black, were accepted primarily on the basis of the parents' motivations coupled with "interesting diagnostic problems" presented by the children. All three families were middle class and upwardly mobile, in contrast to the fragmented family structure of black children rejected for treatment. The last two cases had little that was considered desirable for the program other than the fact that their behavior was not considered aggressive. The parents in both instances were perceived as being uncooperative and were considered to have "severe emotional problems" of their own. In both cases there was a compounding of psychological and organic problems. Both children were from middle-class white suburbia, and had been seen in a number of agencies with one of the two having been seen for almost the entire twelve years of his life in a variety of agencies. Perhaps the most significant factor governing admission of the last two cases was that they were presented to the diagnostic seminar at a time when there was need for children, and they were not considered to present too difficult managerial problems.

Table 19 lists the diagnostic labels applied to these children and the recommendations that were made.

TABLE 19

DIAGNOSTIC LABELS AND TREATMENT RECOMMENDATIONS
FOR CHILDREN ACCEPTED INTO DAY-
TREATMENT PROGRAM

Diagnostic Label	Recommendation
1. Psychotic-infantile psychosis with separation problems	She needs adults as an auxiliary ego —take her to see what can be done
2. Psychotic	Good case to take on a diagnostic basis
3. **Autistic**	Good diagnostic case
4. Organic problem and psychosis	If you can get the parents motivated see if this boy can respond in any way
5. Borderline category psychotic at times	Take him on a diagnostic basis

All children accepted, in this sample of diagnostic seminars, were diagnosed as psychotic and were accepted on the promise of doing a more extensive diagnostic work-up. All were considered withdrawn rather than displaying the aggressive tendencies so predominant in those rejected.

In summary, of a total of seventy-seven cases on file as having contacted the program in search of help for a disturbed child, five were accepted into the program during the course of this study. The children predominately screened out at each level were those displaying aggressive tendencies from disrupted home environments. Children accepted into the program were predominately psychotic, manifested some form of withdrawn behavior, were from middle-class backgrounds with intact families and were taken for the purpose of "making a definitive diagnosis" rather than for treatment. These data support an earlier formulation that the prime factor controlling the decision-making process on admissions was the perceived manageability of both the parent and the child. Staff at all levels of the organization either consciously or unconsciously used this measure as a decision-making criterion.

In summary, written reports indicated that the program was actually providing services to a wide range of children. There was little consensus among staff as to specific criteria governing their work. A review of the actual cases processed through the program demonstrates a pattern of winnowing out troublesome children. The written reports of what the program was discrepant with the actual functioning of the organization. Staff caught between these discrepancies were dissatisfied and confused.

CHAPTER XII

Summary and Conclusions

While considerable theory exists on the care and treatment of the socially and emotionally maladjusted child, there is a paucity of research on the organization and development of institutions designed to address this problem. Therefore, this study had undertaken the task of tracing the evolution of a psychiatric treatment program for emotionally disturbed children within the context of a large-scale bureaucratic organization.

In analyzing the nature of the program that developed through this process, it been demonstrated that the children who were actually admitted for treatment and the type of treatment offered them represent an extension of more traditional, conservative treatment programs for children rather than the more innovative progressive psychiatric service envisioned at the inception of this program. This change of direction occurred in response to the political field in which this program developed, coupled with the ambiguity surrounding the functions of any psychiatric treatment institution. A psychiatric treatment program supposedly exists for the treatment of the mentally ill, but other societal institutions often exert a contradictory demand: that of controlling troublemakers.

Factors within the external organization effecting this course of development were considered to be: (1) the program was initiated at a time when external organizational pressures demanded that there be some visible evidence that children were being treated in this particular Mental Health Center, (2) the initial program proposal represented an attempt to translate the philosophy of the community mental health movement into an operational plan for processing children rapidly in and out of the program with no developed treatment methodology to effect these goals, (3) changes within the administrative organization necessitated a revision in strategy in that it was never entirely clear to the program director what was envisioned as an appropriate treatment program for children, (4) a conflict situation between the Regional Director and the Program Director was generated, and (5) this conflict situation stimulated the development of the program in such a way that the primary goal became that of survival within the political field of the larger bureaucratic organization with the treatment of children but one part of this overall consideration.

The development of the program, within this external environmental context was contingent also upon the types of individuals recruited into the program. It was hypothesized that two options were initially open: (1) that of recruiting highly trained professionals who as a concomitant of their credentials would bring prestige and recognition to the program or (2) that of hiring professionally untrained workers and establishing a system of training within the boundaries of the program. The second option was initially chosen. This is evidenced first by the progressive filtering out of those within the program possessing a high level of professional training and secondly by the emphasis upon recruitment of untrained staff and a group of select consultants to conduct training programs for this staff.

These arrangements facilitated the development of the program in conformity to external political stimuli rather than in conformity to any internally established goals or philosophy. Had the first option of hiring highly trained professionals been chosen, it is quite possible the program would have developed in a manner different from that outlined in this study in that the regulating of individuals would have been extremely difficult. Professionals, indoctrinated with a set of values and commitments unique to their profession, having an idea of themselves as competent and self-directed, would have been more apt to create a situation which included a set of internal programmatic goals.

Specific factors contributing to the recruitment and retainment of the participants within the program were considered to be: (1) the relatively low professional status of the program director, a social worker as opposed to higher ranking psychiatric professionals which necessitated the hiring of a staff less qualified than herself, which would be a threat to her authority, (2) the availability of a professionally untrained, college-educated, young staff drawn by the appeal of a job which offered them the opportunity to do what is defined as "professional work" without the education usually required. The opportunity to learn "professional" skills on the job that would be functional in their total life plans, either in pursuit of professional careers or in their personal careers as wives and mothers, served as incentives, (3) the recruitment of consultants to conduct training programs for the staff which contributed to the amount of control exercised by the program director. Incentives afforded the consultants served to bind the loyalty of the consultants to the program director. In addition to the supplemental income, consultants had much to gain through this work. First, being a consultant in any professional group is considered to be recognition of a high degree of competence in that field. Private practitioner psychiatrists repeatedly encountered children that needed services beyond those they could offer within the confines of their office practice. They, therefore, had a vested interest in the creation of a particular type of treatment program which could serve as an adjunct to their private practices. Social work consultants, employed in other agencies, sensing the precarious nature of their current full-time employment, used this consultation experience as a stepping stone to full-time employment within the program once their other programs were terminated. These incentives, plus contact with the organization under the control of the program director, served to cement their bonds of loyalty to the program director, and (4) the interlocking system of program director, staff and consultants which created a situation rendering the program director in full control of her staff. In this way the flow of information on external organizational factors, as well as the internal training of staff was monitored thus creating a situation in which the internal development of the program could be adjusted to meet the demands of the fluid external organization.

The flow of information was primarily controlled by the program director. Goal setting for the program was contingent upon the input of information about the external world; as the external organization changed so did the goals of the program. The organizational flux provided rationalizations for delays in the opening of the program and additional time for the collection of information about potential treatment alliances with other agencies as well as a more comprehensive knowledge of the nature of potential clients.

The availability of other treatment resources, particularly the alliance with a state-hospital program, provided the option of being selective in choosing clients for the program. As an increased knowledge of the potential client population was gained through contacts with those requesting services, decisions could be made as to which children would be considered "appropriate" for this program and which should be shunted elsewhere, namely, to the state hospital. Information about the external world was used in determining what courses of action the program could take that would increase their chance of survival given the political arena surrounding the program.

Given this input of information about the external world, the next consideration was the development of managerial ploys within the program to control the behavior of the participants as well as to manage relationships between the program and the larger organization.

The first managerial problem tackled by the program concerned the structuring of relationships between the participants to promote in-group solidarity and thereby diminish the probability of participants establishing relationships with others outside the confines of the program. Structuring of interpersonal relationships occurred through informal processes where communication between program participants was fostered by such means as providing a lounge for social purposes and arranging that all staff eat together. Formal structuring consisted of allocation of roles, first by the Program Director's designating the roles participants were to play; and, secondly, by the individuals' own innovative bargaining for unique positions within the organization. As the program developed, certain organizational roles proved acceptable while others were not. In particular, investment in a professional role or commitment to a divergent psychiatric ideology in conflict with dominant trends developing within the program resulted in staff members' being shunted into diversionary activities and out of the "in-group" within the program.

As the size of the program increased, need for more formalized managerial techniques arose. Rule setting occurred in response to immediate situations rather than through any formal, comprehensive process. The function of rules was to prevent disturbances that might bring the attention of the larger organization to bear on internal program problems and thus to preclude outside intervention. In addition to rule setting based on the "here and now" situation, a large proportion of meeting time was spent in anticipating potential future situations and predetermining how staff should respond in these instances. The focus upon these phases of management took precedence over any discussion of the types of treatment that would be offered children or the type of work that would actually be done in the setting. The primary emphasis was placed first upon control of the staff with provision of services to the children being of secondary importance.

In addition to maintaining control of the staff within the program boundaries, concomitant concerns were the monitoring of input into the program and the projecting of "impression management" across the boundaries of the program as demonstrated by the discussions centering on transportation as a means of regulating the inflow of clients into the program and on record-keeping and the issuance of official documents as a means of projecting a positive image to the outside world. The predominant emphasis upon the form and function of records, vis-à-vis the outside world, took precedence over considerations of the content and purpose of such procedures in providing services to patients.

Emphasis on management and control is further exemplified in two specific activities of the program: (1) the training process and (2) the diagnostic procedures. The training process functioned to provide untrained staff with a system for making judgments about parents and children from information elicited through Intake and Screening Interviews. The result of this type of training was that staff, in order to appear competent in these activities, needed to draw rapid conclusions as to the nature of the problem the patient was presenting. Once having drawn this conclusion, the interviewer then made a number of causal inferences in his mind, and focused the remainder of the interview on substantiating this view of the situation. Appraisal, then, was often not based on the information elicited from the parent but was rather a reflection of the interviewer's construction of the problem.

The training process was closely associated with diagnosis, in that, as the program developed, an increased emphasis was placed upon rapidly making decisions as to which children presented in Intake and Screening contacts would be suitable candidates for presentation in the diagnostic case conferences. In this manner, training was specifically designed to teach staff to do a specific type of work within the organization. This stands in contrast to educational philosophy which is theoretically designed to increase the individuals repertoire of knowledge and provide a basis for rational decision making. The result of such an indoctrination process was that staff focused upon getting the prescribed information by following the defined steps without indulging in any personal involvement in the clients' problems except if the problem seemed "appropriate" for consideration by the program. Excluding children from the interview situation helped the staff to maintain the desired distance from the reality of the problem.

The managerial problem to which both the training process and the diagnostic procedures addressed themselves was keeping the dilemmas presented by parents and children from interfering with the primary goal of survival of the program in the political realm of the larger organization.

Further validation of this premise was derived from an analysis of the content of diagnostic case conferences. While initially staff had discussed potential treatability as one criterion that should govern the decision-making process as to which children should be admitted, ultimately the criterion of the manageability of the problem presented by the child took precedence. While staff behavior could be controlled by the techniques described throughout this study, children presented a different type of problem. First, it was essential that children be admitted to the program at some point in time if support for the continued employment of staff within Children's Services was to be justified. But, on the other hand, children potentially had the power to upset the precarious balance existing between the program and the larger organization. They could destroy property or interfere with the work of other employees. The parents could divulge some of the secrets contained within the confines of the program. Thus, decisions about which children were to be admitted were crucial.

Since the dominating characteristic of children who would seek help from this type of program would be anti-social, hostile, and present the problem of control, the bulk of them were excluded from the beginning and the primary criterion for admittance into the program became that the child not be aggressive but withdrawn. Furthermore, although the withdrawn, schizophrenic, or autistic child represented the poorest candidate for treatment, this too, furthered the managerial goals of the program in that (1) these children were obviously in need of help, (2) they would not cause trouble by being aggressive or destructive, (3) their parents had searched long and desperately for a place where their child could be helped and would be unlikely to cause any repercussions, and (4) the prognosis of these children as untreatable further served to decrease the expectations of the external organization, it could not be expected that these children be cured.

An analysis of the structure evolved at the end of the first year of the program's development revealed an increased sophistication of the program in the political realm as evidenced by the documents produced with an accompanying decrease of emphasis on the nature of the treatment provided or the population of children to be served.

An analysis of the children for whom help was sought revealed that the large majority of them displayed some form of aggressive behavior and were ruled out at each step of the Intake-Screening-Diagnostic process. The small minority of withdrawn children were those selected for admission to the program.

Staff responses to a questionnaire designed to elicit their perceptions of factors governing the decision-making process indicate that although all staff members were involved in making these types of decisions, they either were unaware of the "real" criteria governing the process or perceived an unspoken agreement to deny the basis on which such decisions were made.

Conclusions

The development of this psychiatric program illustrates a process wherein what was the initial stated goal of the program—treatment of emotionally disturbed children—became but a means to achieving another end—maintenance of the program within the larger organization. In such a process both the children served by the program and the participants within the organization became pawns in a larger political game. Instead of the larger bureaucratic structure providing resources and support to assure the success of such a program it became perceived as an obstacle around which the program had to manipulate.

Despite the obvious problems outlined in this study, it should be pointed out that this particular program was the only one within the entire Mental Health Center that was initiated in any planful way. The traditional pattern in the opening of other program areas has been that public pressure dictated when units would open. A precipitous decision would be made that on a specific date patients would be admitted, staff would be taken away from other areas of the center, and patients would be admitted in a hodge podge manner. The Children's Program, in contrast, avoided this type of phenomenon through its successful political maneuvering. But, in so doing, the initial goals of treating "poor" children were subverted, and the accomplishments of the program became open to question.

Throughout the time span of this study, nine months elapsed between the hiring of the Program Director and the admission of the first children to the Day Treatment Program. Throughout this period staff ranging from an initial group of five members to a total of twenty-five at the time children were admitted were employed. Within the first year of operation five children were provided services in day treatment for a period of three months by this number of employees. The remainder of staff time was spent either in "planning," in the Intake-Screening-Diagnostic process, or in pursuit of personal goals and interests.

Not only were there a large number of employees with a minimal work load during this time period, but there was also an expensive, elaborate physical plant that was virtually unused for three years prior to the rendering of services to any children. This is in sharp contrast to the frequently voiced concern for the problems of the large numbers of emotionally disturbed children in our society.

Placing this within the broader context of the State Department of Mental Health and contrasting this program with one for children in the state-hospital that was paired with this Mental Health Center clarifies the problem. Relatively speaking, the entire staff employed within the state hospital program to provide care for approximately one hundred and fifty children and adolescents with all types of problems was not appreciably larger than the twenty-five employed to provide three months of care to five children in the Mental Health Center program. While the initial philosophy behind building the Mental Health Centers was to diminish the flow of patients into the state hospital, it may be questioned if the Mental Health Center hasn't become instead, a recruiting place for additional children for the State Hospitals.

Paradoxically, by investing millions of dollars in the new Mental Health Centers and creating beautiful architectural settings, a new problem was inadvertently created in that there was an underlying fear that if "poor people" are admitted to these settings they would destroy the buildings. Also, since the Mental Health Centers in this particular state had been pointed to as indicative of the progressive community mental health movement, staff recruited into these settings were more numerous, more highly qualified, and consequently more expensive than those employed within the state hospitals. Needed money and competent staff are siphoned off from the already seriously deprived state hospitals and these resources are shunted into the Mental Health Centers. These practices have simultaneously created a "class system" for mental patients in which the poor go to the state hospitals and the middle class go to the Mental Health Centers.

Viewing this particular program from a broader societal perspective, it is problematic if we, as a society, can afford the continued loss of human resources represented in the population of children designated "emotionally disturbed" who are brought to the attention of this program. Restricting admission of children to this defined population of withdrawn children who are, for all practical purposes, untreatable while simultaneously excluding aggressive children who represent greater treatment potential will accomplish nothing in terms of the overall societal problem.

What are the significant factors that contribute to this pattern? Using the data of this study it is possible to delineate three significant dimensions of the problem: (1) the organizational context surrounding such psychiatric treatment prorgams, (2) the current status of psychiatric treatment methodologies and the role of the psychiatric "professionals", and (3) the societal problem of the definition of mental illness.

The first question that bears consideration is the limitations imposed upon a psychiatric treatment program by a large scale, state-operated, bureaucratic organization. Such an agency, dependent upon the support of the taxpayers must, to some measure, be responsive to the dictates of the public. The state legislature, concerned with many divergent problems, views the operation of such an agency as the Department of Mental Health primarily in economic terms with little understanding of the complexities of psychiatric treatment. From the viewpoint of the legislators, primary concerns are with the cost per day of maintaining patients within mental institutions rather than in what happens to those confined in such institutions. To maintain an image of concern of the "mentally ill" the legislator is more sympathetic to plans for building new hospitals, such as the Mental Health Centers, than he is concerned with what transpires within the confines of these buildings. And, once these buildings are built, he is more concerned that the windows not be broken than he is with whether or not anyone receives positive treatment in this type of setting. The legislator, measuring success or failure in economic terms and looking at the general picture of the entire Department of Mental Health in the here and now situation is ill-equipped to consider alternatives, such as the prevention of hospitalization, as worthy of his support in that these alternatives are not measurable within this frame of reference. The state legislature must become aware of the complexity of the problems of maladjusted children and their special needs. Assistance must take more than just financial form.

Converseley, the psychiatric treatment program can rationalize its ineffectiveness on the basis of the large bureaucracy. This particular program could delay offering services to children for nine months through a series of rationalizations such as: the inability to hire staff, the lack of funds to offer salaries which could compete with other agencies, the nebulous character of the geographic boundaries. In actuality, none of these rationalizations were valid, but the bureaucratic structure provided a convenient justification for children. This interlocking of the state bureaucracy and a psychiatric treatment program provides a mutually convenient arrangement in which concerns for the form of the program predominate to the exclusion of any concern for the substantive nature of psychiatric treatment.

The lack of articulation of the substantive nature of treatment for emotionally disturbed children is compounded by the current status of psychiatric treatment methodology and the accompanying role of psychiatric "professionals" in providing this treatment. It is questionable whether current treatment methodologies are appropriate to the nature of the "disease". Preoccupation with the psychoanalytic formulation of the nature of emotional problems has eventuated in an emphasis upon diagnosis and causality with but limited formulations relevant to the nature of psychiatric treatment. The predominant existent treatment methodology, psychoanalysis, is appropriate for only a minimal number of those with emotional problems, and the form of treatment, the one-to-one relationship between client and therapist, is inadequate for the scope of the emotional problems identified in our society. Lacking any appropriate treatment methodology to bridge the gap between the private patient in the psychoanalysis office and the bulk of the mentally ill in the state hospital settings, there are few concrete guidelines to govern the delivery of psychiatric services.

This problem is further compounded by the role of psychiatric "professionals" who are trained in educational systems that emphasize theory to the exclusion of practice. These professionals, lacking any experience in working with patients other than on a very limited basis, are employed in psychiatric settings and are placed in positions where they are supervisors or trainers of those who must deal with the reality problems on a day-to-day basis as they work directly with patients in the hospital setting. Even where, as in this case, the majority of the staff were professionally untrained, the accent was placed upon turning them into quasi-professionals. The emphasis was not upon the impact of the relationships with the staff member upon the child so much as a concern that staff "have a disciplined, professional approach" to children. Indeed, a frequently expressed concern in psychiatric settings is that staff not respond to patients on the basis of concern for them as individuals and the natural empathy based on this concern but rather that they be trained to do professional work, devoid of any feeling. Yet, in terms of results it cannot be demonstrated that following any set procedure in relating to patients is successful, while it is apparent to those who have participated in therapy, that a genuine concern and compassion for patients, coupled with warm and sympathetic handling have yielded therapeutic gains in patients. The predominant emphasis of much training conducted by professionals in such settings is to relate to patients on a more objective basis than through natural understanding and compassion and to turn them into duplicates of the professional. In this manner, extensive periods of time are devoted to training processes that serve to defeat the one characteristic that staff might have to offer patients—consistent acceptance and the correlated therapy. In this case, training emphasized the shaping of staff into diagnosticians rather than into therapists.

Finally, the question of society's perception and definition of mental illness must be raised. In the case of the children defined as "mentally ill" this label was attached to them in a number of different ways. Primarily, if a child created problems, either within the home, the school, or a similar social setting, he was labelled mentally ill. But if one were to consider the context in which the behavior occurred, it may be argued that this behavior was a healthy sign of attempting to cope with an impossible situation. The child, living in deprived surroundings, with overburdened parents unable to find any dignity or self-respect in their daily existences, in attempting to break out of this environment through the use of aggressive maneuvers was perhaps more healthy than the child who, at an early age, had already yielded to his surroundings. Yet these children were labelled too seriously disturbed to be handled in this setting: they needed to be locked up. "Treatment" for them meant suppressing their aggressive tendencies. Instead of investing in these children to channel their aggressive tendencies into acceptable forms of activity, these children were "written off" by this program and in so doing a large number of potentially productive citizens were ruled out. By defining mental illness according to the criteria of how much trouble an individual causes others leads to a system in which the "trouble maker" is bounced from one institution to another, from home, to school, to mental institution, to reformatory. Each institution is primarily concerned with ridding itself of a problem rather than seeing that the child receive help. At each succeeding step the child is pushed farther and farther along the route of seeing himself as unworthy and incompetent, and the likelihood of his developing into a productive citizen is increasingly diminished.

Implications

The findings of this study pose some troublesome questions. First, can we continue to assume that because the legislature appropriates vast sums of money for the care of the "mentally ill," it is absolved of all further responsibility for the returns of this money? Are funds buying adequate psychiatric care facilities or are they being used instead to perpetuate institutions that function primarily to meet the needs of those employed within these organizations? Designs may be created and programs instituted, but unless the consequences are meeting the needs of disturbed children, the legislature and the programs have failed. Secondly, can we allow psychiatric programs developed within large scale governmental bureaucracies to continue rationalizing their lack of effectiveness on the basis of "insufficient funds" or "inadequate staffs" and therefore preclude treatment for the mentally ill?

The nature and scope of the problem of the vast numbers of those defined as "mentally ill" who are referred to large scale, governmentally sponsored treatment organizations justify the need for the development of more appropriate treatment methodologies that are relevant to the nature of the problem presented by the clients. Currently, it appears that much of the emphasis in psychiatric programs is on attempting to force the problems of clients into the psychiatric mold and make the disease fit a diagnostic category rather than engaging in reconstructive efforts based on the personality configurations of each disturbed child.

Furthermore at what point should the work of psychiatric professionals be evaluated? The psychiatric professions have created an aura in which only a few are admitted to the inner cult of the psychiatric practitioner; the selectivity of the process and the mystique surrounding their practice protects them from any challenge to the effectiveness of their work. The mystique is further perpetuated since it is these professionals who undertake the training of non-professionals, with the purpose of directing their natural compassion and empathy for people into a "disciplined" approach. Is it sufficient for those employed within the psychiatric professions to maintain that much of what is defined as "mental illness" is untreatable without assuming some responsibility for developing alternate approaches to the problem of treatment?

And can we as a society afford to exclude large numbers of potentially productive citizens from society merely because they pose problems or because they do not fit within the rigid norms of behavior outlined in various social groups? At what point should this ricocheting process of shifting atypical, troublesome individuals from one social group to another be interrupted? Instead of attaching a label such as "acting out" to a child and shipping him from one agency to another, doesn't the problem cry out for more appropriate methods of dealing with such problems within social agencies such as the home or the special school?

This study has raised questions that extend far beyond its initial scope, but in so doing confronts another problem relevant to sociological research. In studying such organizations as psychiatric hospitals, a study designed to focus on only internal organizational problems has a distorted perspective in that they are viewing a picture of only one piece of a much larger puzzle, and from this limited perspective the applicability of some of the findings in these works maybe questioned. The research dilemma posed by this study, however, is that of studying linkages between organizations and investigating ways in which these external linkages affect the internal structuring process while at the same time maintaining scientific controls. The entire chain and sequence that enters into the self-perpetuation of psychiatric institutions and ideologies needs to be more fully identified before any one facet of the problem can be dealt with adequately.

BIBLIOGRAPHY

Books

Argyris, Chris, *Understanding Organizational Behavior,* (Homewood, Ill.: The Dorsey Press, Inc.), 1960.

Becker, Howard S., *Sociological Work,* (Chicago: Aldine Press), 1970.

Becker, Howard S., Blanche Geer, David Reisman, and Robert S. Weiss (editors), *Institutions and the Person,* (Chicago: Aldine Press), 1968.

Becker, Howard S., *Outsiders: Studies in the Sociology of Deviance,* (New York: The Free Press of Glencoe), 1963.

Berkowitz, Leonard (editor), *Advances in Experimental Social Psychology,* Vol. 2, (New York: The Academic Press), 1965.

Bettelheim, Bruno, *The Empty Fortress,* (New York: The Free Press), 1967.

Blau, Peter, *Exchange and Power in Social Life,* (New York: John Wiley & Sons), 1964.

Blau, Peter and W. Richard Scott, *Formal Organizations,* (San Francisco: Chandler Publishing Co.), 1962.

Boszormenyi-Nagy, Ivan and James L. Framo (editors), *Intensive Family Therapy,* (New York: Harper & Row), 1965.

Bowers, Raymond (editor), *Studies on Behavior in Organizations,* (Athens, Ga.: University of Georgia Press), 1966.

Brim, Orville G. and Stanton Wheeler, *Socialization After Childhood,* (New York: John Wiley & Sons), 1965.

Brown, Roger, *Social Psychology,* (New York: The Free Press), 1965.

Buckley, Walter (editor), *Modern Systems Research for the Behavioral Scientist,* (Chicago: Aldine Press), 1968.

Buckley, Walter, *Sociology and Modern Systems Theory,* (Englewood Cliffs, New Jersey: Prentice Hall), 1967.

Caplan, Gerald, *Principles of Preventive Psychiatry,* (New York: Basic Books), 1964.

Cicourel, Aaron, *Method and Measurement in Sociology,* (New York: The Free Press of Glencoe), 1964.

Dahrendorf, Rolf, *Essays on the Theory of Society,* (Stanford, Calif.: Stanford University Press), 1967.

Despert, Louise J., *Schizophrenia in Children,* (New York: Robert Brunner, Inc.), 1968.

Douglas, Jack, *Understanding Everyday Life,* (Chicago: Aldine Press), 1970.

Etzioni, Amitai, *Complex Organizations,* (New York: Holt, Rinehart & Winston), 1961.

Faris, Robert (editor), *Handbook of Modern Sociology,* (Chicago: Rand McNally & Co.), 1964.

Gerth, H. H. and C. Wright Mills, *From Max Weber,* (New York: Galaxy Books), 1968.

Glaser, Barney (editor), *Organizational Careers: A Sourcebook for Theory,* (Chicago: Aldine Press), 1968.

Goffman, Erving, *Interaction Ritual,* (New York: Doubleday & Co.), 1967.

Goffman, Erving, *Asylums,* (New York: Doubleday Anchor), 1961.

Greer, Scott, *Social Organization,* (New York: Random House), 1955.

Haire, Mason (editor), *Modern Organization Theory,* (New York: John Wiley & Sons), 1959.

Homans, George, *The Human Group,* (New York: Harcourt, Brace & World, Inc.), 1950.

Jacobs, Glenn (editor), *Participant Observation,* (New York: George Braziller), 1970.

Joint Commission on Mental Health for Children, *Crisis in Child Mental Health: Challenge for the 70's,* (New York: Harper & Row), 1970.

Katz, Daniel and Robert Kahn, *The Social Psychology of Organizations,* (New York: John Wiley & Sons), 1966.

Manis, Jerome G. and Bernard Meltzer (editors), *Symbolic Interaction: A Reader in Social Psychology,* (Boston: Allyn & Bacon), 1967.

March, James G. (editor), *Handbook of Organizations,* (Chicago: Rand McNally, Inc.), 1965.

March, James G. and Herbert Simon, *Organizations,* (New York: Holt, Rinehart & Winston), 1961.

Mills, C. Wright, *The Power Elite,* (New York: Oxford University Press), 1969.

Park, Robert E., *On Social Control and Collective Behavior,* (Chicago, University of Chicago Press), 1967.

Parsons, Talcott, *The Social System,* (New York: The Free Press), 1951.

Presthus, Robert, *The Organizational Society,* (New York: Random House), 1962.

Rubenstein, Albert and Chadwick Haberstroh, *Some Theories of Organizations,* (Homewood, Ill.: Dorsey Press), 1960.

Scheff, Thomas (editor), *Mental Illness and Social Processes,* (New York: Harper & Row), 1967.

Scheff, Thomas, *Being Mentally Ill: A Sociological Theory,* (Chicago: Aldine Press), 1966.

Slooum, Walter, *Occupational Careers,* (Chicago: Aldine Press), 1966.

Strauss, Anselm, (editor), *George Herbert Mead on Social Psychology,* (Chicago: University of Chicago Press), 1965.

Strauss, Anselm, Leonard Schatzman, Rue Bucher, Danuta Ehrlich, and Melvin Sabshin, *Psychiatric Institutions and Ideologies,* (New York: The Free Press of Glencoe), 1964.

Street, David, Robert D. Vinter and Charles Perrow, *Organizations for Treatment,* (New York: The Free Press), 1966.

Thomas, W. I., *On Social Organization and Social Personality,* (Chicago: University of Chicago Press), 1966.

Thompson, James D. (editor), *Approaches to Organizational Design,* (Pittsburgh: University of Pittsburgh Press), 1966.

Ullman, Leonard P., *Institutions and Outcome,* (New York: Pergamon Press), 1967.

Weinberg, S. Kirson (editor), *The Sociology of Mental Disorders,* (Chicago: Aldine Press), 1967.

Zald, Mayer, *Power in Organizations,* (Nashville, Tenn.: Vanderbilt University Press), 1970.

Articles

Appleby, J., N. C. Ellis, G. W. Rogers and W. A. Zimmerman, "A Psychological Contribution to the Study of Hospital Social Structure," *Journal of Clinical Psychology,* Vol. 17, 1961, pp. 390–393.

Bazanz, C. N., "Psychiatric Aspects of Hospital Administration," *American Journal of Psychiatry,* Vol. 108, pp. 277–279.

Becker, Howard S., Notes on the Concept of Commitment," *American Journal of Sociology,* Vol. 16, No. 1, July 1, 1960, pp. 32–40.

Blau, Peter, "Patterns of Choice in Interpersonal Relations," *American Sociological Review,* Vol. 27, February 1967, No. 1, pp. 41–55.

Bucher, Rue and Joan Stelling, "Characteristics of Professional Organizations," *Journal of Health and Social Behavior,* Vol. 10, No. 1, March 1969, pp. 3–15.

Bucher, Rue and Anselm Strauss, "Professions in Process," *American Journal of Sociology,* Vol. 66, No. 4, January 1961, pp. 325–334.

Caudill, W., F. C. Redlich, H. R. Gilmore and E. P. Brody, "Social Structure and Interaction Processes on a Psychiatric Ward," *American Journal of Orthopsychiatry,* Vol. 22, 1952, pp. 314–334.

Coser, Ross L., "Authority and Decision Making in a Hospital? A Comparative Analysis," *American Sociological Review,* Vol. 23, 1958, pp. 56–63.

Cumming, Elaine and John Cumming, "The Locus of Power in a Large Mental Hospital," *Psychiatry,* Vol. 19, 1956, pp. 361–370.

Etzioni, Amitai, "Duel Leadership in Complex Organizations," *American Sociological Review,* Vol. 30, No. 5, October 1965, pp. 688–698.

Etzioni, Amitai, "Interpersonal and Structural Factors in the Study of the Mental Hospital," *Psychiatry,* Vol. 23, 1960, pp. 13–22.

Fidler, Jay W., "Hygiene Versus Therapy in Private Practice", *Psychiatry,* Vol. 25, November 1962, pp. 363–369.

Henry, Jules, "The Culture of Interpersonal Relations in a Therapeutic Institution for Emotionally Disturbed Children," *American Journal of Orthopsychiatry,* Vol. 27, 1957, pp. 725–734.

Henry, Jules, "Types of Institutional Structure," *Psychiatry,* Vol. 20, 1957, pp. 47–60.

Henry, Jules, "The Formal Social Structure of a Psychiatric Hospital," *Psychiatry,* Vol. 17, 1952, pp. 139–157.

Hersch, Charles, "Mental Health Services and the Poor," *Psychiatry,* Vol. 29, No. 3, August 1966, pp. 236–245.

Katin, Joel and Myron R. Sharaf, "Intrastaff Controversy at a State Mental Hospital: An Analysis of Ideological Issues," *Psychiatry,* Vol. 30, No. 1, February 1967, pp. 16–29.

Katz, Daniel, "The Motivation Basis of Organizational Behavior," *Behavioral Science,* Vol. 9, April 1964, pp. 131-146.

Lefton, M., S. Rettig, S. Dinitz, B. Pasamanick, "Status Perceptions of Psychiatric Social Workers and Their Implications for Work Satisfaction," *American Journal of Orthopsychiatry,* Vol. 31, 1961, pp. 102–110.

Lefton, M., S. Dinitz and B. Pasamanick, "Mental Hospital Organization and Staff Evaluation of Patients," *Archieves of General Psychiatry,* Vol. 2, 1960, pp. 462–467.

Lefton, M., S. Dinitz and B. Pasamanick, "Decision Making in a Mental Hospital: Real, Perceived, and Ideal," *American Sociological Review,* Vol. 24, 1959, pp. 822–829.

Levinson, Daniel J. and Gerald Klerman, "The Clinician-Executive: Some Problematic Issues for the Psychiatrist in Mental Health Organizations," *Psychiatry,* Vol. 30, No. 1, February 1967, pp. 3–15.

Mishler, E. G. and A. Trapp, "Status and Interaction in a Psychiatric Hospital," *Human Relations,* Vol. 9, 1956, pp. 187–205.

Panzetta, Anthony, "Causal and Action Models in Social Psychiatry," *Archives of General Psychiatry,* Vol. 16, March 1967, pp. 291–296.

Pearlin, Leonard, "Alienation from Work: A Study of Nursing Personnel," *American Sociological Review,* Vol. 27, No. 2, June 1962, pp. 314–326.

Perrow-Charles, "The Analysis of Goals in Complex Organizations," *American Sociological Review,* Vol. 26, 1961, pp. 854–966.

Perry, S. E. and L. C. Wayne, "Role Conflict, Role Definition and Social Change in a Clinical Research Organization," *Social Forces,* Vol. 38, 1959, pp. 62–65.

Rosengren, William R., "The Hospital Careers of Lower and Middle Class Child Psychiatric Patients," *Psychiatry,* Vol. 25, No. 1, February 1962, pp. 16–22.

Rosengren, William R., "Status Stress and Role Contradictions Emergent Professionalization in Psychiatric Hospitals," *Mental Hygiene,* Vol. 45, 1961, pp. 28–39.

Schneiderman, Leonard, "Social Class, Diagnosis and Treatment," *American Journal of Orthopsychiatry,* 1965, Vol. 35, pp. 99–105.

Scott, Frances G., "Action Theory and Research in Social Organization," *American Journal of Sociology,* Vol. 64, 1959, pp. 386–395.

Szurek, S. A., "Dynamics of Staff Interaction in Hospital Psychiatric Treatment of Children," *American Journal of Orthopsychiatry,* Vol. 17, 1947, pp. 652–664.

Tabbot, Eugene and Stuart C. Miller, "The Struggle to Create a Sane Society in the Psychiatric Hospital," *Psychiatry,* Vol. 29, No. 2, May 1966.

Thompson, James and William McEwen, "Organizational Goals and Environment" "Goal Setting as an Interaction Process", *American Sociological Review,* Vol. 23, February 1958, pp. 23–31.

Weinstein, Eugene and Paul Deutschberger, "Tasks, Bargains and Identities in Social Interaction," *Social Forces,* Vol. 42, No. 4, May 1964, pp. 451–456.

Index